Halal Logistics and Supply Chain Management

This book provides a comprehensive overview of Halal in logistics, supply chain management and the future implications for the Halal industry. It discusses a wide range of Halal logistics practices and theories in Japan, Korea, Spain, Oman and Southeast Asian countries.

The book examines technology applications, regulatory and certification procedure, Halal management system and quality control, and sustainability, as well as challenges for the logistics and Halal supply chain in the pandemic context. The book also looks at how to navigate the complexity of Halal logistics to achieve business sustainability. It uses a multidisciplinary approach to provide insights on the Halal logistics and supply chain study.

This book hopes to fill an existing gap and enrich the literature on Halal logistics and supply chain management specifically in the West, Middle East and regions in Asia. This will be a useful reference to those who would like to learn more about this industry.

Nor Aida Abdul Rahman is Associate Professor at Universiti Kuala Lumpur, Malaysia and currently serves as a Head of Aviation Management at Universiti Kuala Lumpur, Malaysian Institute of Aviation Technology, in Subang, Selangor, Malaysia. She has worked as internal and external trainer in management, supply chain, Halal logistics and postgraduate research. Her research work has appeared in several reputable academic journals such as *Industrial Marketing Management*, *Journal of Islamic Marketing* and others. She has also published a number of book chapters and refereed conference proceedings, and been part of the editorial team for a book project with Routledge. She is on the working group panel of the MS2400 Halal Supply Chain standard and TC10 for Halal Supply Chain Standard (SMIIC). She earned a PhD in Management (Supply Chain Management) from Brunel University, London, UK. She is also an academic advisor in college, a chartered member for the Chartered Institute of Logistics and Transport Malaysia (CILTM), an HRDF Certified Trainer, chairman (Academic Committee) for the Malaysian Association of Transportation, Logistics and Supply Chain Schools (MyATLAS), vice president (research journal) for the Institute for Research in Management and Engineering UK (INRME), JAKIM Halal Certified Trainer, UniKL Halal Professional Board and a member of Academy of Marketing, UK.

Azizul Hassan is a member of the Tourism Consultants Network of the UK Tourism Society. Dr Hassan has been working for the tourism industry as a consultant, academic and researcher for over 20 years. His research interest areas are technology-supported marketing for tourism and hospitality, immersive technology applications in the tourism and hospitality industry, and technology-influenced marketing suggestions for sustainable tourism and hospitality industry in developing countries. Dr Hassan has authored more than 150 articles and book chapters in leading tourism outlets. He is also part of the editorial team of 25 book projects, and is a regular reviewer of a number of international journals.

Hajjah Zawiah Abdul Majid is a senior lecturer at University Kuala Lumpur and served as Head of Teknoputra, International, Industrial & Institutional Partnerships (3IP) UniKL Business School. She has 20 years' experience teaching various courses such as Logistics, Entrepreneurship and Innovation Management. Currently, she is a Fellow at the Chartered Institute of Logistics and Transport (CILT), Woman in Logistics and Transport (WiLAT), Global Vice Chairperson (GVC) Southeast Asia and founder of WiLAT Malaysia. She has more than 30 years' experience in logistics industry and is currently pursuing her doctorate in Halal Supply Chain. She is on the working group panel of MS2400 Halal Supply Chain for DSM and TC10 for SMIIC, Istanbul, Turkey. She is also chairman of National Competency Standard (NCS) for Halal Logistics under MOHR, HDC and JPK, and a certified Halal Professional Board trainer endorsed by JAKIM.

Routledge Advances in Management and Business Studies

Competition, Strategy, and Innovation
The Impact of Trends in Business and the Consumer World
Edited by Rafał Śliwiński and Łukasz Puślecki

Critical Perspectives on Innovation Management
The Bright and Dark Sides of Innovative Firms
Edited by Patryk Dziurski

Operations Management in Japan
The Efficiency of Japanese Manufacturing
Hiromichi Shibata

Stakeholder Management and Social Responsibility
Concepts, Approaches and Tools in the Covid Context
Ovidiu Nicolescu and Ciprian Nicolescu

Japanese Business Operations in an Uncertain World
Edited by Anshuman Khare, Nobutaka Odake and Hiroki Ishiruka

Entrepreneurship and Culture
The New Social Paradigm
Alf H. Walle

Hospitality and Tourism Education in China
Development, Issues, and Challenges
Edited by Jigang Bao and Songshan (Sam) Huang

Halal Logistics and Supply Chain Management
Recent Trends and Issues
Edited by Nor Aida Abdul Rahman, Azizul Hassan and Hajjah Zawiah Abdul Majid

For more information about this series, please visit: www.routledge.com/
Routledge-Advances-in-Management-and-Business-Studies/book-series/SE0305

Halal Logistics and Supply Chain Management

Recent Trends and Issues

Edited by
Nor Aida Abdul Rahman,
Azizul Hassan and
Hajjah Zawiah Abdul Majid

LONDON AND NEW YORK

First published 2022
by Routledge
4 Park Square, Milton Park, Abingdon, Oxon OX14 4RN

and by Routledge
605 Third Avenue, New York, NY 10158

Routledge is an imprint of the Taylor & Francis Group, an informa business

© 2022 selection and editorial matter, Nor Aida Abdul Rahman, Azizul Hassan and Hajjah Zawiah Abdul Majid; individual chapters, the contributors

The right of Nor Aida Abdul Rahman, Azizul Hassan and Hajjah Zawiah Abdul Majid to be identified as the authors of the editorial material, and of the authors for their individual chapters, has been asserted in accordance with sections 77 and 78 of the Copyright, Designs and Patents Act 1988.

All rights reserved. No part of this book may be reprinted or reproduced or utilised in any form or by any electronic, mechanical, or other means, now known or hereafter invented, including photocopying and recording, or in any information storage or retrieval system, without permission in writing from the publishers.

Trademark notice: Product or corporate names may be trademarks or registered trademarks, and are used only for identification and explanation without intent to infringe.

British Library Cataloguing-in-Publication Data
A catalogue record for this book is available from the British Library

Library of Congress Cataloging-in-Publication Data
Names: Abdul Rahman, Nor Aida, editor. | Hassan, Azizul, editor. | Majid, Hajjah Zawiah Abdul, editor.
Title: Halal logistics and supply chain management: recent trends and issues / edited by Nor Aida Abdul Rahman, Azizul Hassan and Zawiah Majid.
Description: Abingdon, Oxon; New York, NY: Routledge, 2022. | Series: Routledge advances in management and business studies | Includes bibliographical references and index.
Identifiers: LCCN 2021042992 | ISBN 9781032122373 (hardback) | ISBN 9781032122397 (paperback) | ISBN 9781003223719 (ebook)
Subjects: LCSH: Business logistics–Islamic countries. | Business logistics–Asia. | Halal food–Transportation. | Halal food industry.
Classification: LCC HD38.5.H347 2022 | DDC 658.7–dc23
LC record available at https://lccn.loc.gov/2021042992

ISBN: 978-1-03-212237-3 (hbk)
ISBN: 978-1-03-212239-7 (pbk)
ISBN: 978-1-00-322371-9 (ebk)

DOI: 10.4324/9781003223719

Typeset in Galliard
by Newgen Publishing UK

Contents

List of figures x
List of tables xii
Notes on contributors xiii

Introduction 1
NOR AIDA ABDUL RAHMAN, AZIZUL HASSAN AND
HAJJAH ZAWIAH ABDUL MAJID

PART I
Context and theories 5

1 Halal logistics and supply chain management in Asia, the West and the Middle East: recent issues, developments and trends 7
ABDELSALAM ADAM HAMID AND
NOORUL SHAIFUL FITRI ABDUL RAHMAN

2 The new age of Halal logistics and supply chain standards in Asia, the Middle East and the West: IHIAS, SMIIC and MS 17
NOR AIDA ABDUL RAHMAN, KAMRAN MAHROOF,
AZIZUL HASSAN AND NARISSARA SUJCHAPHONG

3 Theories in Halal logistics and supply chain management research 32
MOHAMED SYAZWAN AB TALIB, ABDUL HAFAZ NGAH AND
DWI AGUSTINA KURNIAWATI

4 Theories used in Halal logistics studies: a literature review 45
AU YONG HUI NEE AND ZAM ZURIYATI MOHAMAD

PART II
Technology applications and sustainability — 65

5 Traceability technology in Halal logistics and supply chain: critical success factors — 67
ZUHRA JUNAIDA BINTI IR MOHAMAD HUSNY HAMID AND
MOHD ISKANDAR BIN ILLYAS TAN

6 Technology and traceability in Halal logistics: critical success factors — 78
MOHD FARID SHAMSUDIN AND HAJJAH ZAWIAH ABDUL MAJID

7 Halal logistics sustainability: a conceptual framework — 89
HALIZA MOHD ZAHARI, RUZAIDIN MOHAMMED ZAIN AND
NUR HIDAYAH BINTI AZHAR

PART III
Halal meat cartel, transportation, port management and pandemic challenges — 109

8 Exploring the Islamic work ethics and Halal meat supply chain: an insight — 111
EMI NORMALINA BINTI OMAR, NOR BAKHRIAH SARBANI,
ISMAH OSMAN, HEIZAL HEZRY OMAR AND
HARLINA SUZANA JAAFAR

9 Exploring the Halal meat cartel case: a legal framework and insight from the regulator — 122
FARADINA BINTI AHMAD, MUHAMMAD ZALY SHAH AND
ZUHRA JUNAIDA BINTI IR MOHAMAD HUSNY HAMID

10 Halal integrity in the supply chain: the impacts of the fake Halal meat cartel scandal towards Halal integrity — 132
ANIS NAJIHA AHMAD, SITI BALQIS ZULFIGAR,
BAIDURI ZAIYYANNA MOHD FARUDZ AND
NUR NAJIHAH BINTI ZULKIFLI

11 Halal transportation adoption among SMEs in Malaysia — 151
ABDUL HAFAZ NGAH, SERGE GABARRE AND RAMAYAH THURASAMY

12 Halal port development: issues and challenges — 165
MUNA NORKHAIRUNNISAK USTADI AND SHARINA OSMAN

PART IV
Halal logistics review, certification and regulatory frameworks · 173

13 Halal logistics, supply chain and quality control in Malaysia · 175
MUNA NORKHAIRUNNISAK USTADI, SHARINA OSMAN AND
RAJA ZURAIDAH RAJA MOHD RASI

14 Development of the Halal industry in South Korea:
pilot project of Halal logistics · 186
JAMES (JANG SUH) NOH

15 Halal logistics certification and regulations in Japan · 196
NURUL FAEZAWATY JAMALUDIN AND KOSEI SUGAWARA

16 Halal market opportunities and logistics in Spain · 211
FERNANDO MAYOR-VITORIA

17 Halal logistics certification: a Middle East perspective · 222
NOR AIDA ABDUL RAHMAN AND ZAINAB AL BALUSHI

18 Halal logistics and supply chain management research:
recent COVID-19 effects and future development · 230
MUHAMMAD MUNZIR KHAIRUDDIN, FATHIEN AZUIEN YUSRIZA,
NOR AIDA ABDUL RAHMAN, ABDUL MANAN DOS MOHAMED,
SUZARI ABDUL RAHIM AND MD FAUZI AHMAD

Index · 236

Figures

1.1	Halal supplier selection iceberg	12
2.1	The Halal principles in Halal application and research	19
2.2	The Halal ecosystem	21
2.3	The role of Halal logistics service providers (HLSPs) in supply chain activity	23
3.1	Three-step review process	34
3.2	HLSCM articles published in JIMA (N=32)	36
4.1	Frequency of Halal logistics articles in Scopus database	48
4.2	Number of Halal logistics articles in top ten journals	50
4.3	Number of Halal logistics publication by country	51
4.4	Frequency of Halal supply chain articles in Scopus database	54
4.5	Number of Halal supply chain articles in top ten journals	55
4.6	Number of Halal supply chain publications by country	56
7.1	Halal pharmaceutical framework	96
7.2	Halal food SC framework	97
7.3	Factors influencing the integrity of the Halal food SC	98
7.4	Halal logistics sustainability conceptual framework	99
8.1	Halal meat import clearance process in the seaport environment	113
9.1	Halal meat stakeholders	124
9.2	Legal process framework for Halal violation	126
10.1	Malaysian beef supply chain	134
10.2	Process flow of imported meat to Malaysia	142
11.1	Framework of the research	155
11.2	Measurement model	158
12.1	Malaysia's export destinations for Halal products in 2018 (RM billion)	167
13.1	The flows of a conventional supply chain	177
13.2	Conceptual model of Halal supply chain management	179
13.3	Application of Halal standards	181
14.1	Overall outline of Sejung Shipping's Halal logistics pilot project	192
15.1	The circular economy in the logistics landscape	198
15.2	Forwarder facilities emerging around the airport (40 firms in 42 locations)	201

15.3	Airport South Industrial Park	202
15.4	Asia Pacific Halal logistics market size by component	202
15.5	Halal supply chain ecosystem	206
15.6	Nippon Express Halal logistics system	208
17.1	Example of global key players in the Halal market	224
17.2	Key benefits of having Halal certification for Halal goods and service providers	225
17.3	Halal logistics certification in Malaysia	226
17.4	Halal and Made in Oman logos	227

Tables

2.1	A number of standards developed by the SMIIC	25
2.2	MS2400 Halal Supply Chain Management System	26
2.3	Halal standards for Halal ecosystem members' references	27
2.4	Halal references Middle Eastern countries	28
2.5	Halal certification centres or authorities in the West	28
2.6	Halal certification centres or authorities in the Asia region excluding Malaysia	29
3.1	Theories used in HLSCM research	35
3.2	Methodologies use within theories in HLSCM research	41
4.1	Selected Halal certification/logistics/supply chain studies overseas	46
4.2	Theories applied in Halal logistics research	51
4.3	Theories applied in Halal supply chain research	57
5.1	The CSFs selected by respondents	74
9.1	List of news articles about the Halal meat scandal	124
10.1	Chronology of the event	135
11.1	Convergent validity	157
11.2	Discriminant validity	158
11.3	Hypothesis testing	159
11.4	PLS-predict	160
13.1	Definition of Halal	176
13.2	Differences between conventional and Halal supply chains	178
13.3	Definitions of Halal logistics	180
13.4	The MS2400 series on Halal supply chains	182
14.1	Table of contents – research report to KFRI	190
16.1	SWOT analysis	213
18.1	Various industries affected by the COVID-19 pandemic	231

Contributors

Faradina binti Ahmad is a lecturer at the Malaysian Institute of Industrial Technology, Universiti Kuala Lumpur. Her area of expertise is legal and logistics. She pursued her Bachelor's degree in law at Universiti Teknologi MARA, Shah Alam, Selangor and continued her studies in Master's in Law at Tulane University, US, in 2005. Currently, she is furthering her studies at the PhD level in the field of Transportation Planning at Universiti Teknologi Malaysia. The chapter of the book that she has contributed is part of the results of her PhD research.

Md Fauzi Ahmad is on the academic staff at Universiti Tun Hussein Onn Malaysia. He started his career as a quality engineer and has been assigned to various areas, such as product quality assurance, quality control, product planning and sales departments. He has contributed to establishing company strategy for improving customer satisfaction and other major improvement projects.

Anis Najiha Ahmad attended Universiti Sains Malaysia from 2005 to 2008 and graduated with a BSc in Food Technology. In 2012, she obtained her MSc in Food Technology from the same university. Her Master's thesis focused on the development of method for routine ethanol quantification, and determination of alcohol limits in Halal certification. For her doctorate study, she decided to move in the opposite direction from the hard-analytical detection to managerial approach to address challenges to ensure the wholesome state of Halal food production. Her PhD thesis focused on the development of an instrument that assess the effectiveness of the Halal food management system in SMEs. She is currently an assistant professor in the International Institute for Halal Research and Training, International Islamic University Malaysia. Her research interests include (1) Halal, quality and food safety management, (2) countermeasures for food fraud as well as three core competencies in Halal industry.

Zainab Al-Balushi PhD, MSc, MCom, BSc, is assistant professor of Operations Management at the College of Economics and Political Science, Sultan Qaboos University. Currently she is the head of Quality Assurance and the Academic

Accreditation Unit. She is also a Faculty Fellow in the Center of Excellence in Teaching and Learning. She is a founding member of the Oman Logistics Association and a member in formulating the Sultanate of Oman Logistics Strategy 2040 and chairperson for Women in Transport and Logistics. She is a reviewer for various journals and has published in international journals such as *Supply Chain Management: An International Journal* and *International Journal of Physical Distribution & Logistics Management*. Her research interests include regional supply chains, supply chain uncertainty and risk management, competitiveness, CSR and sustainability, 4IR and logistics digitalization, and logistics education.

Nur Hidayah Binti Azhar is a graduate research assistant at the National Defense University of Malaysia (NDUM), where she is pursuing a Master's in Resources Management. She holds a Bachelor's degree in Security and Defense Management with first class honours from the NDUM. She is very interested in the research areas of logistics and transportation and supply chain management. Currently, she is a team member in the Fundamental Research Grant Scheme (FRGS) on Eliminating Old Vehicle Impacts Towards B40 Well-Being Research.

Baiduri Zaiyyanna Mohd Farudz is currently undertaking her final degree semester in Bachelor of Tourism Planning and Hospitality Management (Hons), Kulliyyah of Languages and Management, International Islamic University Malaysia (IIUM). She is now an internship student at International Institute for Halal Research and Training, IIUM in which she is involved in the development of the Halal Micro-credential. She was an active member of the Committee of Tourism Department at the KLM Students Society. She took part in an innovation and research programme in Penang International Invention Innovation and Design (2019) where she managed to bring back a Silver Medal with the project title "TourMouve Application: Interactive Navigation and Mobile Application in Creating Efficient Tourist Movement in Muar, Johor". As a tourism student, she has learned many skills and gained knowledge from multiple assessments and workshops. She hopes to contribute these skills and knowledge to the betterment of the national tourism.

Serge Gabarre is currently an assistant professor at the College of Arts and Sciences, University of Nizwa. He received his PhD from the Faculty of Education at the National University of Malaysia. His research interests are foreign language acquisition, mobile-assisted language learning, qualitative data analysis and research methodology. He can be contacted at sergegabarre@unizwa.edu.om

Abdelsalam Adam Hamid obtained his PhD from the College of Business Studies, Sudan University of Science and Technology, in Supply Chain. He is an Assistant Professor of Supply Chain at the International Maritime College of Oman. He worked as Assistant Professor and Head of the Business Administration Department at Sudan University of Science and Technology.

Abdelsalam has published in a variety of journals; his research interests lie in the field of supply chain practices, logistics operations and management and industrial business and marketing. He is a reviewer for many journals.

Azizul Hassan is a member of the Tourism Consultants Network of the UK Tourism Society. Dr Hassan has been working for the tourism industry as a consultant, academic and researcher for over 20 years. His research interest areas are technology-supported marketing for tourism and hospitality, immersive technology applications in the tourism and hospitality industry, and technology-influenced marketing suggestions for sustainable tourism and hospitality industry in developing countries. Dr Hassan has authored more than 150 articles and book chapters in leading tourism outlets. He is also part of the editorial team of 25 book projects, and is a regular reviewer of a number of international journals.

Zuhra Junaida Binti Ir Mohamad Husny Hamid is a senior lecturer at Faculty of Built Environmental and Surveying under the Department of Urban and Regional Planning. She also holds the position of Deputy Director of the Centre for Innovative Planning and Development in Universiti Teknologi Malaysia. She holds a Doctor of Philosophy Degree in Transportation Planning from the Faculty of Built Environmental and Surveying. Her PhD research focused on Halal Logistics Services. She is also a chartered member of the Chartered Institute of Logistics and Transport (CILT) Malaysia. She has more than 15 years of industry experience and ten years of teaching experience in the field of logistics and transportation planning, and currently teaches at Universiti Teknologi Malaysia. She is also a certified trainer by PSMB and JAKIM. She co-founded of HOLISTICS Lab Sdn Bhd, a spinoff company of UTM that provides technology and training solutions.

Harlina Suzana Jaafar graduated with a PhD in Logistics from Loughborough University, UK, in 2006, and a Masters in Transport from Cardiff University, UK, in 1993. She was actively involved in the development of the Halal supply chain standard for Malaysia and OIC countries, and she is now the chairman of the Technical Committee 10 Halal Supply Chain under the Standard Metrology Institute for Islamic Countries based in Istanbul and Islamic Standard Committee member at Standards Malaysia. She is also participating in several taskforces under the Ministry of Transport and has been appointed as trainer for the Certified Professional Halal Executive Programme by the Department of Islamic Development of Malaysia (JAKIM). She has also published more than 100 journal articles, proceedings, book chapters, technical reports, professional reports and policy papers in the area of third-party logistics, Halal supply chain, trade logistics, green logistics and smart mobility cities.

Nurul Faezawaty Jamaludin is a senior lecturer at Universiti Kuala Lumpur, Malaysia, in Bioengineering Technology with Process and Food Engineering qualification. She was formerly appointed as Special Operation Officer at Asia

Food Validation Centre to carry out GMP, HACCP and Halal-related matters. She has experience in engaging with industries locally and internationally.

Muhammad Munzir Khairuddin is currently a researcher and lecturer at Universiti Kuala Lumpur, Malaysian Institutes of Aviation Technology in Selangor, Malaysia. He has a background of aviation industry education from his Bachelor's degree and some industry experience from his training at a well-known air freight operator company in Malaysia. He earned his Master's degree in management from Universiti Kuala Lumpur, Business School. His Master's research titled "An Investigation Towards the Factors Impeding the Success of Halal Compliance in Air Cargo Warehouse in Malaysia" investigates the Halal compliance factors for a Malaysian air cargo warehouse operator which led them to success in operating a Halal warehouse. Currently, he is doing his PhD in Aerospace, in which his research is also related to the Halal industry. He has published a few papers on his serendipity research finding to and encourage warehouse operators to become Halal status warehouses.

Dwi Agustina Kurniawati is an assistant professor in the Industrial Engineering Department, Faculty of Science and Technology, Universitas Islam Negeri Sunan Kalijaga, Yogyakarta, Indonesia. She received her Bachelor's degree in 2003 in Industrial Engineering from Institut Teknologi Bandung, Indonesia. After that, in 2006, she received her Master of Engineering degree from Universiti Teknologi Malaysia. Finally, in 2016, she received her PhD degree in Systems and Engineering Management from Nanyang Technological University, Singapore. She has published many papers in the industrial engineering research area, both in international and national journals. Her research interests are mathematical modelling, operation research, Halal-related issues, supply chain management, cross-docking warehouse, optimization, scheduling and metaheuristics method.

Kamran Mahroof is a lecturer in Supply Chain Analytics and programme leader for BSc (Hons) Management and Business Analytics in the Faculty of Management, Law and Social Sciences at the University of Bradford. He has extensive practical experience, having worked in various positions for leading companies, most recently for Morrisons PLC, where he led business improvement initiatives in Logistics and Supply Chain. He received the Dean's Award for Innovation and Impact for his doctoral research in which he explored the increasing role of data analytics within the UK's healthcare sector. He is an experienced lecturer and continues to hold a strong connection in both public and private sectors through his ongoing research. His industrial experience has helped shape his research interests, through which he is actively researching in the areas of technology adoption, industry 4.0 technologies, circular economy and applied artificial intelligence.

Hajjah Zawiah Abdul Majid is a senior lecturer at Universiti Kuala Lumpur and served as Head of Teknoputra, International, Industrial & Institutional Partnerships (3IP) UniKL Business School. She has 20 years' experience teaching various courses such as Logistics, Entrepreneurship and Innovation Management. Currently, she is a Fellow at the Chartered Institute of Logistics and Transport (CILT), Woman in Logistics and Transport (WiLAT), Global Vice Chairperson (GVC) Southeast Asia and founder of WiLAT Malaysia. She has more than 30 years' experience in logistics industry and is currently pursuing her doctorate in Halal Supply Chain. She is on the working group panel of MS2400 Halal Supply Chain for DSM and TC10 for SMIIC, Istanbul, Turkey. She is also chairman of National Competency Standard (NCS) for Halal Logistics under MOHR, HDC and JPK, and a certified Halal Professional Board trainer endorsed by JAKIM.

Fernando Mayor-Vitoria is an industrial engineer with a PhD in Economics from the Universitat Politecnica de Valencia; he also holds a MBA and a Master's in Textile Engineering. He has more than 20 years of international business experience in different sectors such as textile, footwear and lighting. He is professor at the Universitat Politècnica de València in the areas of Economics and Business Administration. He has published papers related to the fields of logistics, big data and decision science as well as books and chapters about operational management and business strategy.

Zam Zuriyati Mohamad is an assistant professor at Universiti Tunku Abdul Rahman and a chartered accountant belonging to the Malaysian Institute of Accountants. After 14 years of experience in the corporate sector, in 2011 she decided to change her career and become an academic. She is currently an assistant professor at Universiti Tunku Abdul Rahman, teaching Business Accounting, Corporate Reporting Current Issues, Advanced Financial Accounting, Financial Information for Management and serves as head of department for Commerce and Accountancy in year 2018. Her recent publications include "Embedding eco-friendly and smart technology features in affordable housing for community happiness in Malaysia" (*GeoJournal*) and "Comprehensive board diversity and quality of corporate social responsibility disclosure: evidence from an emerging market" (*Journal of Business Ethics*). Her current research interests include digital technology, digital accounting, housing affordability and sustainable development goals.

Abdul Manan Dos Mohamed is an associate professor at UniKL MICET. He is the head of the Special Task Force Halal Entrepreneurship Committee, certified trainer under the Halal Professional Board, JAKIM, and responsible to lead Halal activities in UniKL and related organizations, locally and abroad. He has 30 years' experience working in education and research activities that include being a lecturer at Universiti Sains Malaysia (USM); senior research fellow and head of Downstream Technology Section at Craun Research Sdn Bhd, Sarawak; editor at *CRAUN Sago Research Journal*; head of Food Technology Section at Universiti Kuala Lumpur MICET; dean/head of campus at Universiti Kuala Lumpur MICET; general manager at Inkubator Teknologi Makanan (MARA INTEM), Kepong. He is certified trainer for the Food Handler's Course (MOH), MeSTI programme (MOH), Halal lead auditor (IHI Alliance), lead auditor for HACCP (SIRIM) and HALAL JAKIM (Halal Professional Board, JAKIM). He has completed 18 research projects and has published more than 100 refereed papers and 30 proceedings. He completed supervising six PhD and 14 Master's students. He has patented a starch extraction process and flavour technology invention.

Au Yong Hui Nee is an associate professor and the dean of the Faculty of Business and Finance, University Tunku Abdul Rahman, Malaysia. She received her BSc (Hons) in Resource Economics from Universiti Pertanian Malaysia, MA in Economics from the University of Tsukuba, Japan, and PhD from Universiti Sains Malaysia. She was a Japanese Government MEXT (Monbukagakusho) Scholar. Prior to joining academia, she held management positions in Fortune/Forbes multinational corporations and the public sector. She has extensive experience managing supply chain and logistics and compliance risk management. She has received research grants to the amount of RM600,000 in the past six years, and also provided consulting projects for clients in Japan and Malaysia. She has published more than 30 scientific papers in Scopus/Web of Science-indexed journals and proceedings. She serves as a member of editorial board of five international referred journals and reviewer for 15 SSCI/SCIE-indexed journals. She is a recipient of the Malaysian Institute of Management Tun Razak Youth Leadership Award.

Abdul Hafaz Ngah received his PhD from the Universiti Malaysia Pahang and is currently a senior lecturer in the Faculty of Business, Economy and Social Development, Universiti Malaysia Terengganu. His research interests include Halal supply chain, tourism management, technology adoption and employability skills. He has published in several international journals. He has been appointed as a reviewer for several international journals and conferences of repute.

James (Jang Suh) Noh is president of the Korea Institute of Halal Industry and chairman of the Korea Halal Export Association. He has led major research projects commissioned by the Korean government, including the "In-Depth Halal Logistics Industry Survey" published in 2017. His institution has been providing international-level education for the Korean Halal industry through partnerships with Malaysian educational institutions.

Emi Normalina Binti Omar obtained her degree in Professional Studies from the Chartered Institute of Logistics and Transport at Universiti Teknologi MARA (UiTM), Malaysia. Previously, she was attached to the logistics industry and after that she pursued her Master's study in MSc International Logistics at the University of Plymouth (UK). After that, she did her PhD in transport and logistics at the Malaysia Institute of Transport (MITRANS). Her PhD thesis is specifically in the area of Halal supply chain management. Currently, she is a senior lecturer at the Centre for Technology and Supply Chain Management Studies, Faculty of Business and Management. She is also involved in various programmes and courses related to Halal, logistics and supply chain with the

Islamic Development Department of Malaysia (JAKIM), MITRANS, UiTM and IHALALMAS, UiTM, Malaysia. She has published various papers in the area of the Halal supply chain, poultry supply chain, green supply chain, transport and logistics in journals and proceedings papers. She was also one of the invited speakers for the World Halal Summit for 2018 and 2020 in Istanbul, Turkey.

Heizal Hezry Omar has more than 20 years of experience as a lecturer in the Department of Economics and Financial Studies, Faculty of Business and Management, Universiti Teknologi Mara (UiTM) Puncak Alam. He graduated with a degree in Islamic Studies (Hons) from Ibnu Tofail University, Kingdom of Morocco (1997) as well as an MBA from UiTM (2000). He also holds a Diploma in Investment Analysis from RIIAM-RMIT, a certificate in Islamic Studies and a certificate in Contemporary Shariah Studies, both from Universiti Kebangsaan Malaysia, as well as a certificate in Shariah Studies from the University of Malaya. He has been teaching Islamic banking-related subjects such as Islamic Legal Maxims, Introduction to Fiqh Muamalat, Advanced Fiqh Muamalat, Islamic Jurisprudence and also Islamic Theology since 2000. He is the recipient of UiTM's 2019 Academic Award for teaching (Business and Management cohort) and has also written a book entitled *Tafsir Ayat-Ayat Ramadan* (PTS Publication, 2012).

Ismah Osman obtained a PhD in Islamic Banking and Finance from the International Islamic University (2011), an MBA from the University of Keele, UK (1997) and a Human Sciences Degree Programme from the International Islamic University (1994). She joined UiTM in 2000. She has been a lecturer at UiTM for 21 years, and her research interests are Halal management and marketing, Islamic economics and entrepreneurship. She is currently an assistant editor for the *Journal of Islamic Marketing*, an executive editor for the *Malaysian Journal of Consumer and Family Economics*, as well as an Exco member of the Malaysian Consumer and Family Economics Association. She holds a professional certificate of Islamic Financial Planning and an Associate Qualification in Islamic Finance from IBFIM. She is also an HRDF Certified Trainer and a Halal Trainer (certified by HDC). She is an MQA panel member for programme accreditation.

Sharina Osman is a senior lecturer and the Head of Tourism at the Universiti Kuala Lumpur Business School. She earned her PhD in Management at the University of Exeter, UK, and Masters of Human Resource Management and BBA (Marketing) Honours from Universiti Utara Malaysia, Malaysia. Her research interests include identity, image and reputation, organizational culture, human resource development, gastronomic tourism, tourism destination identity and branding, participative tourism development and e-tourism. Dr Osman carries with her an array of experience which ranges from human resources to marketing (image and branding) and tourism. She is also on the Editorial Advisory Board for several journals and has been invited as keynote or guest speaker for local and international seminars and conferences. Being in an academic and a research environment, coupled with vast hands-on experience in the industry, she helps organizations in competency and capacity-building through training and consultations. She believes in interacting and experiential learning and has conducted many workshops in different sectors, including government and private.

Suzari Abdul Rahim is a senior lecturer in the Graduate School of Business, Universiti Sains Malaysia. He received his PhD in Supply Chain Management from Brunel University of London, UK. His current research interests include Halal logistics and supply chain management, and investigating improvements for the Halal industry and community.

Nor Aida Abdul Rahman is Associate Professor at Universiti Kuala Lumpur, Malaysia and currently serves as a Head of Aviation Management at Universiti Kuala Lumpur, Malaysian Institute of Aviation Technology, in Subang, Selangor, Malaysia. She has worked as internal and external trainer in management, supply chain, Halal logistics and postgraduate research. Her research work has appeared in several reputable academic journals such as *Industrial Marketing Management*, *Journal of Islamic Marketing* and others. She has also published a number of book chapters and refereed conference proceedings, and been part of the editorial team for a book project with Routledge. She is on the working group panel of MS2400 Halal Supply Chain standard and TC10 for Halal Supply Chain Standard (SMIIC). She earned a PhD in Management (Supply Chain Management) from Brunel University, London, UK. She is also an academic advisor in college, a chartered member for the Chartered Institute of Logistics and Transport Malaysia (CILTM), an HRDF Certified Trainer, chairman (Academic Committee) for the Malaysian Association of Transportation, Logistics and Supply Chain Schools (MyATLAS), vice president (research journal) for the Institute for Research in Management and Engineering UK (INRME), JAKIM Halal Certified Trainer, UniKL Halal Professional Board and a member of Academy of Marketing, UK.

Noorul Shaiful Fitri Abdul Rahman is an associate professor in Maritime Logistics Operations and Transport at the International Maritime College of Oman. He is now the Head of the Department Logistics Management. He received his Master's in Transport and Maritime Management from ITMMA, University of Antwerp, Belgium, in 2009; his PhD in Maritime Logistics Operations from Liverpool John Moores University, UK, in 2012; and his post-doctorate in Maritime Logistics Operations from the University of Liverpool in 2015. He has published about 52 refereed journal articles and 41 conference papers under his research interests of logistics management, warehousing operations, supply chain studies, logistics 4.0, maritime operations, shipping and port management, container terminal, and risk assessment management by using various multiple criteria decision-making approaches (e.g., Bayesian Networks, Analytical Hierarchy Process, Fuzzy Logic, Rule-based

Reasoning, TOPSIS, Risk Matrix, Broda Method, Bowtie, Critical Path Analysis, Evidential Reasoning, Fault Tree Analysis, Event Tree Analysis, Cause and Effect Analysis, SWOT/TOWS Analysis, etc.).

Raja Zuraidah Raja Mohd Rasi is an associate professor of Supply Chain and Operations Management at Universiti Tun Hussein Onn Malaysia. She received her Bachelor of Technology Management, majoring in Manufacturing from the Universiti Teknologi Malaysia; and holds a PhD in Industrial Sciences from Swinburne University of Technology, Melbourne, Australia. Her research interests include sustainable supply chains, sustainability and operations performance.

Nor Bakhriah Sarbani is a lecturer at PICOMS International University College, Kuala Lumpur. She has passed her Doctoral Philosophy viva in Transport Logistics at Malaysia Institute of Transport recently. She obtained her MSc in Transport and Logistics (2014) from Universiti Teknologi MARA, and her Bachelor of Business Administration Transport (Hons) in 2004 from University Teknologi MARA, Shah Alam. Her doctoral thesis combines several research perspectives from logistics and supply chain point of view particularly cross border logistics, trade facilitation, logistics operational strategy, Halal logistics and supply chain and trade logistics. In 2014, during her PhD, she was selected as an exchange student to represent Universiti Teknologi MARA to Turku School of Economics, Turku University, Finland under the North South-South programme.

Muhammad Zaly Shah obtained a BSc in industrial engineering from Bradley University, Peoria, Illinois, US, and an MSc and PhD in Transportation Planning from Universiti Teknologi Malaysia, Skudai Johor, Malaysia. He worked with a major Japanese manufacturing firm and an international airline before joining academia in 2002. Currently, he is a professor in the field of Transportation Planning at the Faculty of Built Environment and Surveying, Universiti Teknologi Malaysia. He has published extensively, and his articles have appeared in *Safety Science*, *Transport Review*, *Land Use Policy* and *Traffic Injury Prevention*, among others. His current research interests include pedestrian modelling and traffic safety. Muhammad Zaly Shah is a Chartered Fellow of the Chartered Institute of Logistics and Transport. He was the recipient of an Outstanding Teaching Award in 2007 and Outstanding Service Award in 2015. He also sits on the Board of Directors for Johor Public Transport Corporation – a government-linked corporation that regulates public transportation services in the state of Johor, Malaysia.

Mohd Farid Shamsudin is an associate professor of Universiti Kuala Lumpur specializing in marketing research. He has 22 years of experience working in the banking and telecommunication industries. Prior to joining UniKL he was a senior product manager at a large telecommunication company and actively participated in writing and attending conferences.

Notes on contributors

Kosei Sugawara is a coordinator and special officer of a Japanese non-governmental organization (NGO), coordinating many types of collaboration between Malaysia universities and companies. He is currently in Take Co. Ltd, as a director, operating subsidiary company business in Malaysia (Takexco Malaysia Sdn Bhd) to control Halal-certified products and its sales in Malaysia and other ASEAN countries.

Narissara Sujchaphong is a lecturer at Mahasarakham Business School, Mahasarakham University, Thailand. She obtained a PhD in Management from Brunel University, and an MA in Marketing from London Metropolitan University, UK. She has published in internationally refereed journals. She has contributed to several books such as *Asia Branding* and *Branding in Higher Education*. Her research interests span areas of internal branding, university branding, B2B branding and brand-related leadership.

Mohamed Syazwan Ab Talib is an assistant professor of Logistics Management at the UBD School of Business and Economics, Universiti Brunei Darussalam. He holds a PhD in Management from Universiti Teknologi Malaysia, an MBA from Universiti Selangor, and a BBA from Universiti Teknologi MARA. He was a senior lecturer in Marketing at Azman Hashim International Business School, Universiti Teknologi Malaysia and formerly a lecturer in Logistics Management at the Faculty of Business and Information Science, UCSI University. His research and teaching focus primarily on logistics and supply chain management, specializing in Halal principles, distribution and standards.

Mohd Iskandar bin Illyas Tan is a senior lecturer at Azman Hashim International Business School (AHIBS). He holds a Doctor of Philosophy Degree in Information Science from the Faculty of Computing, Universiti Teknologi Malaysia. Due to his interest in entrepreneurship and frequent involvement in such activities, he co-founded a company called HOLISTICS Lab Sdn Bhd that commercialized QuikHalal, the cloud-based mobile Halal auditing application. HOLISTICS Lab is also a training provider recognized by JAKIM Halal Professional Board. He received various awards including the 2015 Halal Hi-Tech Challenge and received grants from UTM and PlatCOM Venture. In addition, he has been recognized by various agencies in Malaysia and has received support from the Halal Hub Division, JAKIM, Penang Islamic Affairs Department, Penang International Halal Hub, Malaysian Global Innovation and Creativity Center (MaGIC), Malaysian Industry-Government Group for High Technology (MiGHT) and the Ministry of Higher Education, Malaysia to further develop QuikHalal.

Ramayah Thurasamy is currently a professor of Technology Management at University Sains Malaysia, a visiting professor at King Saud University, Kingdom of Saudi Arabia, Universiti Malaysia Sarawak, (UNIMAS) and Universiti Teknologi Malaysia (UTM), and an adjunct professor at Sunway University, Multimedia University (MMU) and Universiti Tenaga Nasional (UNITEN), Malaysia. He graduated with a Master's of Business administration from Universiti Sains Malaysia, Penag, Malaysia. His research interest is in technology management.

Fathien Azuien Yusriza graduated from the Malaysian Institute of Aviation Technology (UniKL MIAT), Subang, Malaysia with a Bachelor's Degree in Aviation Management. She is also a Master's candidate at UniKL MIAT, where she is furthering her research study on the effectiveness of aviation's supply chain management operation. Her interest in research relating to aviation's procurement supply chain began from the day she completed her undergraduate thesis on the effectiveness of inventory management in airline operation. She will complete her Master's by the end of 2022 and aspires to serve and bring meaningful conversations to the table that will benefit the aviation industry as a whole.

Haliza Mohd Zahari is a senior lecturer at the Faculty of Defence Studies and Management, National Defence University of Malaysia (NDUM). Prior to her NDUM secondment in 2018, she served the Royal Malaysian Navy for 25 years as a naval officers. Haliza Zahari holds a PhD in Technology, Operation and Logistics from Universiti Utara Malaysia. Her research interests are defence logistics, humanitarian logistics, supply chain management and logistics and transportation. She has been teaching Logistics and Supply Chain Management courses for undergraduate and Procurement Management for Master's in Business Administration. Currently she is working on three Ministry of Education grants: Team Leader for Transdisciplinary Research Grant Scheme (TRGS) on Humanitarian Logistics Support Research, Team Leader for Fundamental Research Grant Scheme (FRGS) on Eliminating Old Vehicle Impacts Towards B40 Well-Being Research and as a Team Members in FRGS research on Depression, Anxiety, Stress, Work Life Balance and Emotional Intelligence in Malaysian Armed Forces. She is an active member of the Chartered International of Logistics and Transportation.

Ruzaidin Mohammed Zain is a graduate research assistant at the National Defense University of Malaysia (NDUM) where he is pursuing a doctorate in Humanitarian Logistics. Prior to his appointment in NDUM, he served for 13 years as a Naval Officer in the Royal Malaysian Navy. Graduating with a Master's degree in Project Management from the University of Malaya, he is very interested in the research areas of defence logistics, humanitarian supply chain management and project management. His current research projects are on logistics support coordination in humanitarian aid and disaster relief, as well as studying the impact of old vehicle elimination towards low-income population well-being. He is actively involved in both projects as a research team member.

Siti Balqis Zulfigar is a senior lecturer at Bioprocess Technology Industry at the School of Industrial Technology, Universiti Sains Malaysia. As a strong advocate of green technologies, her research interest focuses especially on biocatalysis, enzymatic hydrolysis and unearthing bioactive peptides from natural resources. She is currently teaching the undergraduate subjects of Enzyme Technology, Safety and Quality of Bioprocess Products and Practical of Downstream Processing at Universiti Sains Malaysia.

Nur Najihah binti Zulkifli was born in Jitra, Kedah and had her secondary education at Maahad Muhammadi Perempuan, Kota Bharu. She currently is in her final year pursuing Bachelor of Science with Honours (Food Biotechnology), in Universiti Sains Islam Malaysia (USIM). She is one of the committee members in the Halal Istihlak (Consumerism) Seminar, Exhibition and Competition (HISEC 2018) organized by Institute of Halal Research and Management, USIM. She also involved with the Activities Committee in the Halal Food Seminar (HAFOS 2019), organized by USIM. She enjoys travelling and has participated in voluntary works internationally through Global Islamic Society Outreach (GISO) to Yogyakarta, Indonesia as a vice-president. Enthusiastic in learning foreign languages, she enrolled in multiple elective classes for Mandarin, Japanese and French language during her study years in USIM. She currently is an intern student at International Institute for Halal Research and Training. Najihah hopes to complete her degree and works as a competent food biotechnologist in the Halal industry or related fields.

Introduction

Nor Aida Abdul Rahman, Azizul Hassan and Hajjah Zawiah Abdul Majid

The Halal industry is seen as a key vehicle for economic growth for many countries, including non-Muslim countries. It stimulates the economy through import-export activities, tourism and travel, and value-added trade, as well as industry and academic research. The Halal industry has expanded from Halal food and beverage to Halal banking, Halal hotels, Halal tourism, Halal retailing, Halal auditing, Halal clothing, Halal cleaning and Halal logistics. Halal logistics is an innovation in the logistics industry where it refers to the Halal management system in maintaining Halal integrity of the Halal product throughout the supply chain, especially focusing on transporting and warehousing activities. The aim of Halal logistics is to maintain the integrity of Halal status products from the point of origin to the point of consumption. It ensures the activities and equipment used in handling Halal products throughout transport and warehouse activities are in accordance with Islamic law or known Shariah principles.

This book is unique in providing a composite overview of Halal in the logistics and supply chain areas by groundbreaking research, application, theoretical, review, conceptual model and experience by practitioners as well as academicians. Expert contributors from research and practice provide relevant discussion on Halal logistics and supply chain issues across the globe. This book is very special as it gathers its contributors from three regions, namely Asia, the Middle East and the West. The contributors are from Spain, the United Kingdom, South Korea, Japan, Oman, Thailand, Brunei and Malaysia.

This not only opens up new areas for future research in the wider context of Asia, the West and the Middle East, but also allows readers to access information regarding Halal logistics and supply chains, current issues and development, future trends, international issues, international trends and the theory and practice of Halal in the logistics sector. This book will be beneficial to those in logistics, supply chain management, the Halal industry, marketing, transportation and warehouses.

This book will be a valuable resource for readers as it provides basic and advanced material that informs the reader about Halal logistics and supply chain management from a wide context, covering the Middle East, Asia and Western countries. This book is a contribution towards the very limited knowledge of Halal logistics and supply chain management in the wider region. The book aims

DOI: 10.4324/9781003223719-1

to accommodate recent developments in the Halal logistics industry, as well as highlighting recent developments and issues including technology application, updates on regulatory and certification procedure, management systems and quality control, as well as challenges caused by the COVID-19 pandemic and the controversial issue of Halal logistics meat cartels. This book carefully addresses and unifies the issues in the Halal logistics industry.

Chapter 1 addresses recent issues and trends of Halal logistics and supply chain management in context of Asia, the West and the Middle East. In this chapter, Hamid and Rahman aim to build a solid background of Halal logistics and supply chain research in these three regions. A number of future research recommendations are also provided.

In Chapter 2, Rahman, Mahroof, Hassan and Sujchaphong provide a brief history of standard development at the local and international level, providing the International Halal Logistics Standard (IHIAS), the Standards and Metrology Institute for Islamic Countries (SMIIC) and the Malaysia Standard (MS) as principal references. The authors also provide a future agenda for researchers in the context of Halal standards.

In Chapter 3, Talib, Ngah and Kurniawati systematically review and discuss their findings on Halal theories used in Halal logistics and supply chain management (HLSCM) research. Theories used in HLSCM research are then categorized into relevant theory groups.

Chapter 4 is a literature review discussion on various theories applied in Halal logistics and supply chain research. This research project by Nee and Mohamad conducts a systematic analysis to assess published Halal logistics and supply chain academic literature in the past decade. This chapter also elaborates on theoretical aspects of future research recommendation.

In Chapter 5, Hamid and Tan determine critical success factors of traceability technology in Halal logistics and supply chain. The goal of this system is to implement a Halal control system by tracking and tracing all product handling and delivery operations. This also enables entire corporate visibility, resulting in improved profits, lower costs and fewer human errors while maintaining the Halal product's purity from point of origin to point of consumption.

Shamsudin and Majid in Chapter 6 provide an explanation on the critical success factor for traceability in Halal logistics. Integration of technology and traceability in the Halal industry helps the Halal stakeholders evaluate the effectiveness of using specific information technology systems in logistics.

Zahari, Zain and Azhar in Chapter 7 develop a conceptual framework for Halal logistics sustainability. A Halal logistics sustainability framework was developed by adopting technology as monitoring tools for Halal compliance. This framework is crucial and will be used as a guideline by the researchers and the industry in Halal logistics management for effective implementation.

Omar, Sarbani, Osman, Omar and Jaafar in Chapter 8 highlight the Islamic work ethics and controversial issue of the Halal meat cartel case in the Halal meat supply chain. They emphasize that the recent scandal of the meat cartel needs to be further evaluated, specifically on its issues and challenges, including its impact on the local producers and consumers at large.

Ahmad, Shah and Hamid in Chapter 9 also discuss the Halal meat cartel case, but from a legal perspective. This study provides the Halal legal framework from the regulators' perspective. Additionally, findings suggest that individual officers must gain relevant knowledge by taking the relevant legal training and education in relation to the investigation and prosecution of any issue related to this Halal logistics controversy.

In Chapter 10, Ahmad, Zulfigar, Farudz and Zulkifli discuss Halal integrity in the supply chain and the Halal integrity effects of the fake Halal meat cartel scandal. This interesting topic highlights the chronology of the event and discusses the multiple implications of this scandal for direct and indirect stakeholders.

In Chapter 11, Ngah, Gabarre and Thurasamy discuss Halal transportation adoption by small and medium-sized enterprises (SMEs) in Malaysia, utilizing a Partial Least Square (PLS) structural equation modelling approach. Their findings show that complexity, cost, and supplier availability are obstacles, while competitive pressure and organizational readiness are facilitators to the acceptance of Halal transportation by Malaysian Halal SMEs.

In Chapter 12, Ustadi and Osman discover interesting challenges in Halal port development. This chapter addresses the question of how port authorities tackle the challenges in this dynamic market environment in terms of the industrial complex, value-added logistics hub and transport hub.

In Chapter 13, Ustadi, Osman and Rasi provide information on Halal logistics and supply chain quality control, using Malaysia as a case study. This chapter highlights a few simple ways of implementing Halal logistics, supply chains and quality control that could enhance the total implementation concept at the least cost to create benefit to all society. The chapter also deals with a few possible implementations and practice aspects to facilitate the Halal logistics approach in daily operations in Malaysian practices.

In Chapter 14, Noh explores the developments of the Halal industry in South Korea, focusing on the pilot project of Halal logistics. This chapter records the key results of major projects for each year in chronological order, including an in-depth survey of the Halal logistics industry in 2017, a survey on Halal product production, distribution and Halal logistics demand in 2018, and the implementation of a Halal logistics pilot project in 2019.

In Chapter 15, Jamaludin and Sugawara explain Halal logistics certification in Japan. Also discussed are the seven Foreign Halal Certification Bodies (FHCBs) certified by JAKIM, with its own Halal Certificates and Halal Logo.

Mayor-Vitoria in Chapter 16 provides information regarding Halal market opportunities and logistics in Spain. The chapter provides an initial overview of the current state of Halal certification in Spain and highlights the opportunities that can be generated in the near future in the logistics field.

In Chapter 17, Rahman and Balushi discuss the developments of Halal certification and opportunities of Halal logistics certification in the Middle East. This study also highlights a dearth of past studies focusing on the Halal logistics issue in the Middle East region.

Chapter 18 by Khairuddin, Yusriza, Rahman, Mohamed, Rahim and Ahmad highlights the effects of the COVID-19 pandemic on Halal logistics and supply chain management research. The chapter discusses the major challenges and possible solutions to sustainability in the Halal industry in the future.

Part I
Context and theories

1 Halal logistics and supply chain management in Asia, the West and the Middle East

Recent issues, developments and trends

Abdelsalam Adam Hamid and
Noorul Shaiful Fitri Abdul Rahman

Introduction

Halal is a concept linked to Islamic jurisprudence and Islamic Shariah, as Islam is concerned with the extent of Shariah and ethical commercial practices in all its aspects. The perspective of Islamic jurisprudence on commercial transactions is based on confirmation and compatibility with the discipline of the spirit of the law (Shariah) and the principles of transactions in Islamic law through jurisprudential conditioning of contracts of trade, sale, purchase, offer and acceptance. In Islam, trade is considered permissible as long as it is based on trade in what is legitimate and clear and is based on the acceptance and consent of both parties.

Halal logistics is referred to as a basic principle of Halal in logistics to ensure segregation of Halal cargo from non-Halal cargo, to avoid cross-contamination and to ensure that the Halal logistics system is aligned to the expectations of Muslim consumers. Halal logistics is regarded as a new application of Shariah law to logistics activities in a way that will eventually protect Halal integrity along the whole supply chain and follow requirements as stated by Shariah law (Tarmizi et al., 2014; Jaafar et al., 2011; Tieman, 2011).

Most of the literature reviewed focused on a single dimension of Halal practices, such as Halal food, as discussed by Zulfakar et al. (2012). Halal product, Halal consumerism and the issues associated with Halal products dominated the field of Halal studies, while other activities have been neglected (Aziz and Zailani, 2016; Jaafar et al., 2011).

Previous studies on Halal logistics and supply chain are growing significantly as a result of the growth in demand in the Halal market as well as expanding the understanding of Halal from the narrow scope of the Halal product idea to the broader scope of Halal (Talib et al., 2014; Tieman et al., 2012). With the broadening of the scope of the Halal supply chain as a practice, the requirements of the Halal supply chain have increased in terms of the independence of the Halal chain and the activities associated with it, which requires a reconceptualization of the Halal supply chain and its scope, as well as a restructuring of its activities and practices.

DOI: 10.4324/9781003223719-3

In addition, the traditional supply chain environment, with all its components of equipment, facilities, equipment and systems, is not suitable for the Halal supply chain in order to avoid any interaction or confusion between the Halal products and the non-Halal products (Zailani et al., 2017). Compliance with the doctrines of Islamic Shariah goes beyond the stage of confirming the systems and procedures to constructing a system that is built from the ground up as a Halal supply chain system and not just a system that seeks to obtain recognition as a Halal supply chain from Halal bodies. The issue of permissibility is a matter of principle in Islam, given that this is a way of living in Islam, which obliges Muslims to follow everything that is permissible (Halal) and to avoid everything that is forbidden (Haram) because God punishes the forbidden (Talib et al., 2014).

This chapter sheds light on the practices of the supply chain and Halal logistics, as the study tries to cover all Halal logistical practices since previous studies were studying and covering Halal logistics practices separately or according to the purposes of those studies, in addition to reviewing some challenges and some missed practices in the Halal supply chain and logistics. This chapter seeks to achieve theoretical contributions related to Halal practices as contained in the literature on the supply chain and Halal logistics and the rules of the Islamic Shariah that govern Halal practices in business logistics activities. In addition, the study seeks to look at Halal logistical practices holistically in terms of comprehensiveness and conceptual framing. This chapter is structured as follows: discussion of Halal phenomena, theoretical demonstration of Halal literature and Halal logistics practices, presenting the Halal practices in detail, and some concluding thoughts.

Halal literatures

The development of the Halal industry has led to limited growth in the Halal supply chain literature. According to Karia (2019), Halal supply chain and logistics research is still far behind the other areas of research, therefore more studies, research and proof is needed for expanding and supporting the existing theory in the Halal area of research. However, the principles that shape the Halal supply chain remain unclear. Several authors have different interpretations of what makes the supply chain Halal. For example, Tieman et al. (2012) and Tieman and Ghazali (2013) argue that the critical points in the Halal supply chain are during transportation, storage and plant operation. Jaafar et al. (2011) identified Halal supply chains as including purchasing and preparing authentic Halal ingredients to manufacture and deliver the finished product to customer shelves. This includes separating Halal ingredients or non-Halal end products, such as alcoholic products or pork-related products, across the entire chain. Others recommend that similar measures should be taken (Ahmad et al., 2015; Alam and Sayuti, 2011; Ahmad and Shariff, 2016; Tieman, 2011).

Halal can be defined as permissible, legitimate, permitted for consumption, and as a symbol of purity and safety. The opposite of the Halal is Haram, which is the prohibition on eating. As a primary reference for Muslim behaviour, the

Holy Quran orders Muslims to consume only Halal products. Not only food, this also includes products such as medicine, cosmetics and many others (Ngah et al., 2015).

The concept of Halal and Toyyiban as "beneficial" as stipulated in Islam includes nutrition, quality, hygiene and safety for all and is not intended only for the Islamic community that can be practised in food production. For example, the Halal certification of food products must cover the source of raw materials for consumers. All the activities along the supply chain (e.g., handling, warehousing and distribution) must be Shariah-compliant as the Toyyiban Halal concept can be applied. No Halal products can be mixed with Haram products, they must be separated from each other (Jaafar et al., 2011).

Halal supply chain practices

Halal supply chain and logistics is a chain that operates in a Shariah-compliant manner from the source of inputs (upstream) in the supply chain, through processing and manufacturing processes, then to (downstream) warehousing, distribution, wholesalers, retailers and delivery to end customers (Hamid and Ibrahim, 2013). This can be summarized in the necessity for all elements in the supply chain to comply with Islamic law (Halal and forbidden) (Fakhruzzaman et al., 2019).

The Halal market, including various products and services other than Halal products, has become a fundamental influence on the industry in the world due to the spread of this market from South and East Asia to the Middle East, Africa, Australia, and some growth in Europe due to the growth of Muslim communities on the continent (Jaafar et al., 2016).

The practice of the Halal supply chain is not an easy process due to the difficulties related to the process of separating the Halal chain operations from the conventional chains because the structure of the Halal supply chain is not built separately, but rather the Halal supply chain is practised in the same traditional facilities (Zailani et al., 2017).

Despite the difficulties of implementing and adopting the Halal supply chain, companies realize that the Halal supply chain leads to achieving many competitive advantages by dealing with the Halal market, which is characterized by specificity that gives advantages to companies serving this extra market (Lestari et al., 2018).

As long as the Halal supply chains include all activities and operations, from the planning process, purchase and preparation of Halal specifications to the transportation, handling, processing, transportation and delivery of Halal value, all these actions and decisions need to be adopted across the Halal supply chain (Milestad et al., 2010).

Karia and Asaari (2016) confirmed that the practices of the Halal supply chain include six basic practices that are in line with the rules of Islamic law, that should be consistent with the practices or products under Halal or forbidden rules in Islamic Shariah, and these practices are Halal procurement, Halal storage,

Halal transportation, processing requests, handling and packing (Fakhruzzaman et al., 2019).

Halal upstream

Many researchers in the field of the Halal supply chain have proved that the Halal chain begins with the logistical companies ensuring that the conditions and requirements of Halal (compliance with Shariah) are met, starting from upstream (the original source) until the delivery to the end customer (Karia and Asaari, 2016). Most studies have confirmed that Halal practices are associated with the upstream activities, such as Halal transportation and warehousing. Zailani et al. (2017) and others have indicated that they also include all systems, information and certificates that flow across the supply chain in accordance with the rules of Islamic Shariah doctrines, and the principle of Halal and Haram.

Halal supply chain management must be based on awareness and belief of management on practising the Halal supply chain so that the company can develop plans and information systems, and follow procedures and certification systems of Halal in a transparent manner, as transparency is an important factor in the Halal supply chain because the whole process is based on trust of the declared information by logistical companies, especially regarding the issue of separating Halal products and processes from non-Halal.

The discussion on Halal supply chain practices can be summarized as a process that starts from the original source until the final delivery, which includes the purchase, storage, transportation, information and Halal recognition certificates (Ahmad and Shariff, 2016). Therefore, the following sections will discuss these practices.

Halal market

The Muslim world is one of the fastest growing markets in comparison with other consumer markets (Akram, 2020). All the international and multinational companies seek to gain more market shares in Muslim markets or countries with a large Muslim population, and most of these markets are concentrated in South and East Asia, in countries such as Indonesia, India, Pakistan and Bangladesh (Africa Islamic Economic Foundation, 2019).

Although the Halal market includes approximately 1.6 billion consumers and contains further potential for a wide variety of customers segments, products and commercial activities, research and studies are still dealing with the Halal market as a dark area in terms of the amount of data, reports and explanations associated with this market.

The legitimacy of a trade in Islam defines the frameworks regulating business activity in the market and society, and the Prophet Muhammad emphasized and encouraged business and commerce. The Prophet Muhammad prayed that God bless the market for the people of Medina (Ahmed, 2017).

The market in Islam is permissible to bring benefits to the people and satisfy the desires of needy people. The market has specific conditions in Islam according to the Quran or Sunnah, and these conditions are: (1) freedom of market entry, (2) honesty, (3) prevention of monopoly and (4) prevention of fraud. These four conditions make the market a competitive and fair place where everyone is allowed to work honestly. Monopoly and fraud are considered commercial practices that are harmful to customers and society.

Halal sourcing (purchasing)

Sourcing is the task of material acquisition, set within an overall sourcing system that includes activities such as vendor certification and vendor contracting (Harrison and Van Hoek, 2008). Purchasing is one of the main supply chain pillars for securing and obtaining Halal inputs, including all production elements (raw material, Halal packing materials and Halal transportation and storage). It is hard to find any experimental and theoretical research examining the Halal purchasing implementation in the literature. Whereas the subject of the studies was on Halal foods and the focus was on establishing proof that the product was Halal and ensuring that all ingredients were Halal (Wilson and Liu, 2011), just Halal materials or Halal ingredients of the product is not enough, the purchasing process requires more Halal practices, starting from planning, policy development, implementation, control and Halal monitoring. According to the evolution of the concept and Halal execution, Halal practice has a direct impact on sourcing/purchasing and supply beyond just dealing with Halal ingredients, and here the need for an integrated model for Halal purchasing appears alongside guidelines and regulations for the Halal purchasing process (Wilson, 2018; Tieman, 2011). Halal procurement can be applied by developing Halal value chain, Halal compliance and Halal supply chain (Weele, 2002).

Determine the specifications

Determine the specifications that must be available in the Halal product or the Halal inputs: Halal products usually require certificates that prove that primary inputs are Halal (including other materials, such as packaging materials), but in the case of services, they must comply with the requirements of Islamic law (Tieman and Ghazali, 2013). In addition to other accompanying logistical activities such as transportation, storage, and handling, they must be in line with the standards of Halal products as the International Standard for Halal Logistics (IHIA, 2010).

Supplier selection

The purchase of Halal products is not only limited to ensuring that the ingredients are Halal, but the supplier must also be in compliance with the principles and

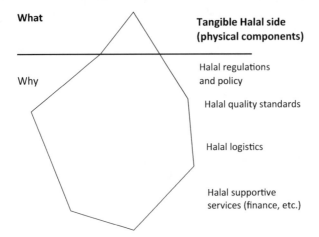

Figure 1.1 Halal supplier selection iceberg.
Source: Tieman and Ghazali (2013).

systems of Halal products that are determined by the rules of Islamic law in buying and selling, including the absence of deception, fraud and other things that are not permissible according to Islamic law (Al-Saudi, 2014; Al-Qaradawi, 2007). Figure 1.1 illustrates the process of Halal section.

Contract

A contract is a commitment that can only be made by two or more parties, and it is dependent on the offer and acceptance. It is issued by the individual willingly, and that leads to results and rights. Contracts in Islamic law are originally permissible, except for what would result in harm or not be decided by the Shariah (Ahmed, 2011). In the Islamic Shariah of the contract, there are elements without which there are no such things as the parties to the contract, the form of the contract and the goods or product.

Order

When fulfilling orders or responding to them, it is important to ensure that the Halal requirements are met, represented in providing Halal product information, signs and symbols indicating whether the product is Halal, and this information and symbols must be available all along the supply chain so that all parties (customs authorities, calibration and measurement authorities, and others) in the chain can deal with the product in accordance with Islamic Shariah standards and the regulations of international and national Halal bodies (IHIA, 2010). The evaluation is one of the matters that requires checking to ensure that the shipments conform to the codes and documents attached to the Halal goods, in addition to the Halal certificates issued by recognized bodies. All transactions and activities in trade and supply chains are subject to the objectives of Islamic Sharia and the legislation based on it (Ahmed, 2011).

Halal transportation

Transportation is one of the critical elements in any supply chain and a key element in the Halal supply chain (Ngah et al., 2014). Ensuring that all activities and stages of logistical work and the supply chain comply with Halal requirements guarantees the delivery of the required Halal value to customers. Without Halal transportation, a Halal product cannot be delivered. Halal transportation is based on separating Halal products from non-Halal products, whereby Halal products are transported in separate containers from non-Halal products (Ngah et al., 2019). At present, Halal transportation providers are certified by JAKIM based on the MS 2400-1:2010, Halalan Toyyiban Assurance Pipeline Management System Requirements for Transportation of Goods and/or Cargo Chain Services.

Halal warehousing

Each part of the Halal cycle is related to the other, as it is impossible to partially fulfil the Halal conditions without completing all the other parts of the cycle. Halal warehousing is the degree to which areas are allocated for Halal products (Karia, 2019). Halal warehousing can be defined as a commitment to separate Halal products from other non-Halal products in area of storage (allocating a special zone for Halal products). As well as the warehousing facilities, having the appropriate temperatures may also make the product Halal, as some products may interact at extreme temperatures to produce or become alcoholic to the extent that makes it impermissible according to the rules of Islamic Shariah (Rahman et al., 2018). Halal facilities include equipment and systems (e.g., pallets, boxes, pumping and water systems, cleaning and disposal systems, etc.). Segregating Halal warehousing facilities may lead to an increase in cost or spatial requirements (Zailani et al., 2017).

Halal supply chain information sharing

The business activity is characterized by reliance on technological tools in general and the supply chain, in particular, requires extensive technological use to achieve a complete Halal supply chain (Bahrudin et al., 2011; Tan et al., 2012). The main purpose of using technology in the Halal supply chain is to ensure the integrity of the Halal value from any legal barriers (according to Islamic law). Therefore, reliance on information systems increases for transportation, monitoring and control of Halal shipments by sharing information between the parties of the Halal chain and providing the highest level of transparency (Nasir et al., 2011). The technological applications and information systems previously used in the conventional supply chain can be adopted and applied in Halal chains. This achieves many advantages, such as radio frequency identification (RFID) for traceability and instant text messaging systems (Lina and Ho, 2009). However, until now, there are no dedicated technologies for Halal supply chains to achieve higher quality and reliability in the Halal supply chain (Bahrudin et al., 2011).

Conclusion

This study reviewed the previous literature related to the Halal supply chain to identify the key dimensions and practices applied to have a complete Halal supply chain. The study operationalized the Halal supply chain from the perspective of upstream and downstream and found that there are different practices due to the different definition of the Halal supply chain, as well as the difficulties of separating the Halal supply chain from the conventional supply chain, as the Halal chain was based on the conventional chain structure that served all customers, not just Halal customers. Besides, the perception and awareness of logistical practitioners and logistical companies of Halal requirements and procedures may not be widespread throughout the chain, which may be a global chain that passes through a large number of parties. Through the literature, it has also been concluded that the Halal theory also needs more effort and investigation to turn into a pure academic theory that can be tested and criticized, away from its reliance on the texts of the Quran and Sunnah. This chapter operationalizes Halal supply chain practices as upstream and downstream Halal supply chain practices that includes all activities, such as procurement, supplier qualification, and even Halal certification, information sharing, commitment and the interrelationship of each aspect of the Halal supply chain. This chapter also provided other researchers with a review of the current issues related to the Halal supply chain, which still needs more research efforts to analyse and identify the Halal practices and activities in the chain. Future studies should investigate the theoretical depth of Halal supply chain concepts and define clear meanings and precise definitions of Halal practices.

References

Africa Islamic Economic Foundation (2019). *The Global Halal Industry: An Overview.* Ghana: Africa Islamic Economic Foundation.

Ahmad, N. and Shariff, S. M. (2016). Supply chain management: Sertu cleansing for Halal logistics integrity. *Procedia Economics and Finance*, 37, pp. 418–425.

Ahmad, A. N., Rahman, A. A. and Ab Rahman, S. (2015). Assessing knowledge and religiosity on consumer behavior towards Halal Food and cosmetic products. *International Journal of Social Science and Humanity*, 5, pp. 10–14.

Ahmed, A. (2017). *E-commerce from an Islamic Jurisprudence Perspective.* Master's thesis. Batna: University of Hadj Lakhdar.

Ahmed, H. (2011). Maqasid al-Shari'ah and Islamic financial products: a framework for assessment. *ISRA International Journal of Islamic Finance*, 3(1), pp. 149–160.

Akram, H. W. (2020). Assessment of global Halal market: challenges and opportunities. *African Journal of Business & Economic Research*, 15(4), pp. 15–23.

Alam, S. S. and Sayuti, N. M. (2011). Applying the Theory of Planned Behaviour (TPB) in Halal food purchasing. *International Journal of Commerce and Management*, 21(1), pp. 8–20.

Al-Qaradawi, Y. (2007). *The Lawful and the Prohibited in Islam*. Kuala Lumpur: Islamic Book Trust.

Al-Saudi, A. W. M. M. (2014). Legal rulings on uncertainty in contracts of donations: a comparative study of Islamic jurisprudence. *Islāmiyyāt*, 36(2), pp. 103–116.

Aziz, A. A. and Zailani, S. (2016). Halal logistics: the role of ports, issues and challenges. In D. S. Mutum, M. M. Butt and M. Rashid (Eds.), *Advances in Islamic Finance, Marketing, and Management*. Bingley: Emerald Group Publishing Limited, pp. 309–321.

Bahrudin, S. S. M., Illyas, M. I. and Desa, M. I. (2011). Tracking and tracing technology for Halal product integrity over the supply chain. *Proceedings of the 2011 International Conference on Electrical Engineering and Informatics*, 2011, pp. 1–7. doi: 10.1109/ICEEI.2011.6021678

Fakhruzzaman, M. N. N., Abidin, N. Z., Aziz, Z. A., Lim, W. F., Richard, J. J., Noorliza, M. N., Hani, M. H., Norhayati, R., Zamzurina, A. B., Zuraina, M. Y. F., Hisyam, M. J., Teh, L. K., Norazmi, M. N. and Zaki, M. S. (2019). Diversified lineages and drug-resistance profiles of clinical isolates of Mycobacterium tuberculosis complex in Malaysia. *International Journal of Mycobacteriology*, 8(4), 320.

Hamid, A. A. and Ibrahim, S. B. (2013). Investigation into the relationship between supply chain management practices and supply chain performance efficiency. *Sudan Journal of Science and Technology*, 16(1), pp. 49–67.

Harrison, A. and Van Hoek, R. I. (2008). *Logistics Management and Strategy: Competing through the Supply Chain*. London: Pearson Education.

IHIA (2010). *ICCI-IHI Alliance Halal Standard – Logistics – IHIAS 0100:2010*. Kuala Lumpur: International Halal Integrity Alliance Ltd.

Jaafar, H. S., Endut, I. R., Faisol, N. and Omar, E. N. (2011). Innovation in logistics services: Halal logistics. *The 16th International Symposium on Logistics (ISL)* 10–13 July. Berlin: Springer, pp. 844–851.

Jaafar, H. S., Faisol, N., Rahman, F. A., & Muhammad, A. (2016). Halal logistics versus Halal supply chain: a preliminary insight. In S. K. Ab Manan, F. Abd Rahman and M. Sahri (Eds.), *Contemporary Issues and Development in the Global Halal Industry: Selected Papers from the International Halal Conference 2014*. Springer, Singapore, pp. 579–588.

Karia, N. (2019). Halal logistics: practices, integration and performance of logistics service providers. *Journal of Islamic Marketing*. https://doi.org/10.1108/JIMA-08-2018-0132

Karia, N. and Asaari, M. H. A. H. (2016). Halal value creation: its role in adding value and enabling logistics service. *Production Planning & Control*, 27(9), pp. 677–685.

Lestari, Y. D., Susanto, J. M., Simatupang, T. M. and Yudoko, G. (2018). Intention towards Halal logistics: a case study of Indonesian consumers. *Journal of Global Business Advancement*, 11(1), pp. 22–40.

Lina, M. and Ho, H. (2009). *Essentials of Supply Chain Management*. Hoboken, NJ: John Wiley & Sons, Inc.

Milestad, R., Bartel-Kratochvil, R., Leitner, H. and Axmann, P. (2010). Being close: the quality of social relationships in a local organic cereal and bread network in lower Austria. *Journal of Rural Studies*, 26(3), pp. 228–240.

Nasir, M., Norman, A., Fauzi, S. and Azmi, M. (2011). An RFID-based validation system for Halal food. *The International Arab Journal of Information Technology*, 8(2), pp. 204–211.

Ngah, A. H., Zainuddin, Y. and Ramayah, T. (2014). Adoption of Halal supply chain among Malaysian Halal manufacturers: an exploratory study. *Procedia – Social and Behavioral Sciences*, 129, pp. 388–395.

Ngah, A. H., Zainuddin, Y. and Thurasamy, R. (2015). Barriers and enablers in adopting of Halal warehousing. *Journal of Islamic Marketing*, 6(3), pp. 354–376.

Ngah, A. H., Ramayah, T., Ali, M. H. and Khan, M. I. (2019). Halal transportation adoption among pharmaceuticals and cosmetics manufacturers. *Journal of Islamic Marketing*. https://doi.org/10.1108/JIMA-10-2018-0193

Rahman, N. A. A., Mohammad, M. F., Rahim, S. A. and Noh, H. M. (2018). Implementing air cargo Halal warehouse: insight from Malaysia. *Journal of Islamic Marketing*, 9(3), pp. 462–483.

Talib, M. S. A., Hamid, A. B. A., Zulfakar, M. H. and Jeeva, A. S. (2014). Halal logistics PEST analysis: the Malaysia perspectives. *Asian Social Science*, 10(14), pp. 119–131.

Tan, M. I. I., Razali, R. N. and Desa, M. I. (2012). Factors influencing ICT adoption in halal transportations: a case study of Malaysian Halal logistics service providers. *International Journal of Computer Science*, 9(2), pp. 62–71.

Tarmizi, H. A., Kamarulzaman, N. H., Latiff, I. A. and Rahman, A. A. (2014). Factors influencing readiness towards Halal logistics among food-based logistics players in Malaysia. *UMK Procedia*, 1, pp. 42–49.

Tieman, M. (2011). The application of Halal in supply chain management: in-depth interviews. *Journal of Islamic Marketing*, 2(2), pp. 186–195.

Tieman, M. and Ghazali, M. C. (2013). Principles in Halal purchasing. *Journal of Islamic Marketing*, 4(3), pp. 281–293.

Tieman, M., Van der Vorst, J. G. A. J. and Ghazali, M. C. (2012). Principles in Halal supply chain management. *Journal of Islamic Marketing*, 3(3), pp. 217–243.

Weele, J. (2002). *Purchasing and Supply Chain Management: Analysis, Planning and Practice*. London: Thomson.

Wilson, J. A. J. (2018). *Halal Branding*. Swansea: Claritas Books.

Wilson, J. A. J. and Liu, J. (2011). The challenges of Islamic branding: navigating emotions and Halal. *Journal of Islamic Marketing*, 2(1), pp. 28–42.

Zailani, S., Iranmanesh, M., Aziz, A. A. and Kanapathy, K. (2017). Halal logistics opportunities and challenges. *Journal of Islamic Marketing*, 8(1), pp. 127–139.

Zulfakar, M. Jie, F. and Chan, C. (2012). Halal food supply chain integrity: from literature to a conceptual framework. *The 10th ANZAM Operations, Supply Chain and Service Management Symposium*, Melbourne, 14–15 June.

2 The new age of Halal logistics and supply chain standards in Asia, the Middle East and the West
IHIAS, SMIIC and MS

Nor Aida Abdul Rahman, Kamran Mahroof, Azizul Hassan and Narissara Sujchaphong

Introduction

Are Halal business, Halal logistics and supply chain significant?

The growth in Halal business has been seen as a major breakthrough activity for many industries, including logistics. From the report by Statistica (2021), the Muslim market worldwide has reached USD 2.11 billion and is expected to grow to USD 3 billion by 2023. Specifically, the global Halal food market is forecasted to grow to USD 2.04 billion by 2027 (Shahbandeh, 2019). Malaysia is one of the major Muslim countries which supplies Halal products, and has the potential to expand globally due to the growing Halal market. The purchasing power of Muslim buyers is also increasing globally and has made Halal logistics crucial to ensure the Halal status of the Halal product is maintained throughout its supply chain.

The Muslim population globally has shown significant growth in recent years, a trend which is expected to continue in the foreseeable future. Currently, the total Muslim population worldwide has reached two billion, making Islam the second largest religion in the world. As listed in World Population Review (2021), Indonesia is recognized as the largest Muslim country in the world with estimation of 229 million Muslims, followed by Pakistan, India, Bangladesh and Nigeria.

The growing societies around the world increase the connection between buying and consumption behaviour in line with their religious beliefs We have learned over the past several decades that the impact of religion plays a significant role in choosing foods and products used by Muslims. Religion plays a significant role in shaping the lifestyle of its followers. As highlighted in Sack (2001, p. 218), "most religions forbid certain foods (e.g., pork and not ritually slaughtered meat in Judaism and Islam, pork and beef in Hinduism and Buddhism), with the notable exception of Christianity, which has no food taboos". Fundamentally, there are two notable religious products in the world, known as Halal and Kosher.

DOI: 10.4324/9781003223719-4

Halal is for Muslim while Kosher is for Jews. Each of these two religious products has its own fundamental references.

Additionally, it is acknowledged that Thaurat is the main reference to Kosher while Holy Quran, Hadith, Ijmak and Ijtihak are the main reference for Halal. Even though these two religions may impose strict dietary laws, the numbers of people following them may vary considerably. It is expected that by the year 2060, Muslims will surpass Christians as the world largest population. This demonstrates that the demand for Halal products will most certainly be increased globally.

In the Halal industry, Malaysia is known as a pioneer or leading country for Halal market with more than 40 years of experience. Malaysia was the first country that came out with Halal standards and guidelines. In Malaysia, the infrastructure is ready to support the development of the Halal industry with the development of the Halal Industrial Master Plan 2008 to 2020, as well as Halal Industry Master Plan 2030. The key strategic thrust from this master plan is making Halal a consumer lifestyle, for business, for government as a key reference body and propagating new talents for Halal industry (Halal Industry Development Corporation, 2021). Essentially, there are six driving forces of Halal industry demand locally and globally. First, it is about the sizeable and growing Muslim population (Pew Research Centre, 2021; Statistica, 2021). Second, it is about the growing economic development in Muslim countries. The other factors are emergence of world Halal players, indirect marketing and promotion, Muslim lifestyle, tourism and cuisine, as well as the growth of the Halal ecosystem. As published in the Malaysia Halal Industrial Master Plan 2030, it is expected the Halal market will grow to USD 5 trillion and USD 113.2 billion for domestic growth. This shows a significant need to focus on Halal logistics and supply chain handling management systems in order to uphold the Halal integrity of the Halal product. Rigorous standards, accreditation and robust certification are needed to ensure the integrity of the Halal supply chain in supporting both Halal import export activities.

At present, the expansion of Halal practice and research has progressively grown within the industry, as well as in scholarship. We have learned much over the past year about the importance of Halal in many areas, such as Halal food, Halal banking, Halal restaurants, Halal cosmetics, Halal tourism, Halal cleaning and many more (Rahman et al., 2018a). The term Halal logistics refers to the movement of the Halal product from one location to another, and is not limited to Halal transport only, but encompasses g the storing activity of the Halal products, as well as at the retail stage. In fact, Halal logistics and supply chain has become a popular topic recently and received much attentions by scholars and practitioners.

Practically, with the expansion of Halal market worldwide, there is a strong need for the standards and guidelines to be further developed and established in ensuring the status of Halal product is secure throughout the supply chain. Having this as a background, this chapter aim to specifically highlight the establishment of standards and guidelines from Western, Asian and Middle Eastern perspectives. This chapter will discuss the Halal logistics standard and guidelines establishment from three viewpoints, namely the International Halal Logistics Standard (IHIAS), the Standards and Metrology Institute for Islamic Countries (SMIIC) and the Malaysia Standard (MS). IHIAS and SMIIC are Halal standards at the international level, while MS is a standard developed in Malaysia, a leading Halal country. These standards or guidelines focus on the Halal supply chain, including Halal transportation and Halal warehousing/storing, as well as Halal retailing. As one of the earliest in the Halal industry and a reference to other Muslim countries for Halal market and Halal standardization, this chapter also covers the key areas of importance in Halal logistics and supply chain. Before going further on standards and guidelines discussion, the next section will offer a brief definition and explanation of Halal, Halal logistics and the Halal ecosystem.

Halal background

The notion of Halal, Halal principles, Halal ecosystem, Halal logistics and Halal supply chain

Halal definition and Halal principles

Halal is a brand associated with Muslims and the religion of Islam (Wilson and Liu, 2011). Halal is an Arabic term that consist of two elements – permissible and Toyyiban (Khairuddin et al., 2018; Rahman et al., 2018a). Permissible here means the food is not Haram (prohibited) and it is lawful in traditional Islamic law. Toyyiban refers to cleanliness, healthiness, safety and quality. Fundamentally, being Halal permissible is linked to Shariah or Islamic law which means the product is safe (not harmful) to consume. Muslims are only allowed to consume Halal products; it is an order from Allah as stated in the Quran and Hadith.

Essentially, Halal can be viewed from three angles, namely the religious point of view, the business point of view and the scholars' point of view (see Figure 2.1). From the religious point of view, it is about the obligation that should be fulfilled by every Muslim. From the business point of view, it is about a business opportunity at a global or international level, as well as at a local level. While from the scholars' perspective, it is regarding the opportunity for potential research in many Halal areas of study. It is acknowledged that the life of every Muslim is to be guided by Shariah or Islamic law. Essentially, the Islamic law is based on four

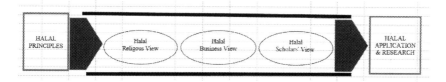

Figure 2.1 The Halal principles in Halal application and research.

creeds (principles) namely the Holy Quran, Hadith (saying of the Prophet), Ijma' (consensus of the scholars) and Qiyas (deriving ruling through analogy).

In principle, the objective of Islamic law can be divided to five main sections, namely preservation of faith, preservation of life, preservation of intellect, preservation of progeny and preservation of property (Saifuddeen et al., 2014). From the business point of view, Halal is referred to as the major breakthrough activity for many sectors. Halal has become an important aspect for many businesses to adopt in order to increase their sales, penetrate new markets and attract new customers. Many business organizations in many sectors – including banking, hotels, restaurants and many more – go for Halal business and get certified and carry logo certification to ensure their product is marketable and sellable. In fact, at present, Halal is not only consumed by Muslim customers, but it is acceptable to other users also. Halal products are recognized as being properly prepared, clean and safe to use or consume. Importantly, this image represents the Halal product and has created recognition for Halal product and services. With that, the establishment of Halal brand products and services is acknowledged.

El-Bassiouny (2016) posits that Muslim believers naturally expect that business conduct and marketing activity are impacted by the precepts of their faith. As recommended by Rahman et al. (2018b), and Khairuddin et al. (2018), Halal business players are responsible for ensuring that the Halal product status is maintained throughout the supply chain, from the point of origin to consumption.

Halal ecosystem

The increased Muslim population, as well as Muslim tourism has led to an increased the demand for Halal products. The greater number of Halal products and demand for services has made the Halal ecosystem grow faster and wider universally. The Halal ecosystem can be defined as a network that involved consumers, industry and other stakeholders. The delivery of Halal products contributes to the economy and creates a constant evolving relationship among Halal industry stakeholders towards sustainability. Historically, Halal product and services have expanded from food to the banking sector, hotels, pharmaceuticals, personal care and many other sectors including tourism (Rahman et al., 2018a). To recognize the Halal ecosystem, the living (people) and the system (Halal-related system) components should interact well in the Halal environment to ensure every party receives benefits and to better support understanding in balancing the Islamic requirement and the harmonization in the community.

Successful adoption of Halal branding in Malaysia has successfully increased the number of tourists to the country (Rahman et al., 2018a). Malaysia is known as a Halal country, with almost all of the restaurants serving Halal produce. Malaysia is a leading country that supports Halal tourism as it provides Halal spas, Halal saloons, Halal flight menus, Halal banking, Halal hotels and Halal logistics (including Halal transport, warehouse and packaging).

There are approximately 14 Halal-related systems that have been identified in supporting the ecosystem or Halal community. As shown in Figure 2.2, the 14

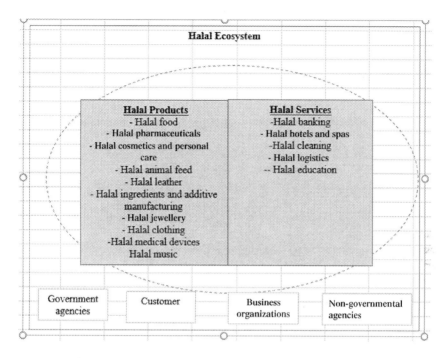

Figure 2.2 The Halal ecosystem.

Halal systems that support Halal ecosystem are derived from both Halal products and Halal services. There are Halal food, Halal animal feed, Halal banking, Halal hotels and spas, Halal clothing, Halal cleaning, Halal music, Halal jewellery, Halal medical devices, Halal education, Halal leather, Halal ingredients and additive manufacturing, Halal cosmetics and personal care, Halal pharmaceuticals and Halal logistics. From the 14 aspects of the Halal ecosystem highlighted in Figure 2.2, we could classify them as nine Halal products and five Halal services. As seen in Figure 2.2, the Halal ecosystem is a dynamic system that integrates many parties together in a social living network. This includes businesses institutions, government agencies, non-government agencies, as well as personal family members. In order to establish a Halal ecosystem, every person, including non-Muslims, should support and engage as a part of this system. For each aspect of this Halal provision, it is important to everyone note to maintain the integrity of the Halal product and services.

The development of Halal logistics and supply chain and Halal logistics standards

Halal logistics is an integral part of the Halal ecosystem as it supports Halal businesses in transporting and warehousing activities. Rahman et al. (2019)

and Rahman (2012) indicate that logistics is a key component in supply chain activity that links suppliers to manufacturers, wholesalers, retailers and customers. Logistics providers ensure products are delivered as scheduled and that quality is preserved (Rahman et al., 2014). Halal logistics, on the other hand, extends the role of the service provider or Halal logistics service provider (HLSP) to include requirements for Shariah compliance principles in logistics activities – transportation, packaging, warehousing and storing Rahman et al. (2018b). The HLSP's participation in networking is significant to maintain the Halal credentials of products throughout the supply chain.

The fundamental issue of Halal logistics is to ensure the physical segregation of Halal and non-Halal substances and products (Shariff and Ahmad, 2015). This is to avoid cross-contamination during channelling activities (Ngah et al., 2015, 2017). The cleanliness aspect of the services is also vital in making sure the Halal qualities of products are well-maintained (Rahim et al., 2016). As previously mentioned, Halal is not only about what is permissible but also what is Toyyiban (clean and wholesome). Figure 2.3 displays the role of HLSPs in both inbound and outbound, and direct and reverse logistics activities.

A recent study by Rahman et al. (2018b) explains that Halal logistics include the processes of transportation, packaging, warehousing and storing. At each stage of activity throughout the supply chain, it is vital to ensure that there is no possible chance for cross-contamination between Halal and non-Halal or Haram substances to occur. The cleanliness aspect of the process or services is also important, as is the security aspect, ensuring that the Halal product is well guarded (Rahim et al., 2016). As mentioned earlier, Halal is not only about what is permissible, but also what is clean and wholesome to be used or consumed. Hence, the participation of Halal logistics service providers (HLSPs) in each supply chain activity is critical to ensure that the status of the Halal products they carry throughout the supply chain is still Halal when they reach their final destination. The role of HLSP activity in the supply chain network is explained in Figure 2.3. Figure 2.3 shows the two main activities by HLSP namely transportation and warehousing. This activity is a key activity for HLSP for both inbound and outbound activity, as well as for both direct and reverse logistics activity.

Additionally, it is vital to ensure Halal product integrity throughout the chain directly and indirectly is secured. For instance, with a simple product of Halal bread, it is produced with a combination of products – such as butter from Australia, flour from Thailand and seeds from Iran – which makes the supply chain of one Halal product complex and international. Therefore, it is very important to further understand the guidelines of carrying and handling Halal products throughout the supply chain to ensure the Halal status of the product is maintained from the point of origin to the point of consumption. It is the responsibility of every party throughout the supply chain to follow Halal standards and guidelines to avoid cross-contamination. The next section will discuss the three popular standards or guidelines for Halal logistics and supply chain, namely, IHIAS, SMIIC and MS.

The new age of Halal logistics 23

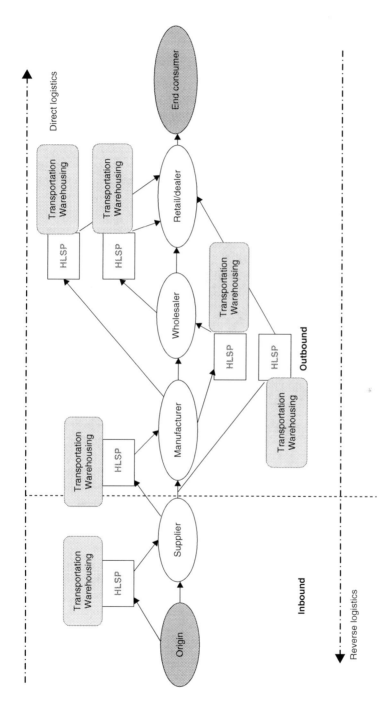

Figure 2.3 The role of Halal logistics service providers (HLSPs) in supply chain activity.
Source: Adapted from Rahman et al., 2018b.

International vs local Halal logistics and supply chain standards: a view on IHIAS, SMIIC and MS

IHIAS 0100:2010 logistics

Essentially, standards are important to be used as basic guideline to give direction to any Halal players to handle Halal products as well as to obtain any related Halal certification. The International Halal Logistics Standard (IHIAS) was launched a decade ago in year 2010. It was developed under the Islamic Chamber of Commerce and Industry and the International Halal Integrity Alliance. This standard is used by both local and international players including food manufacturers, restaurants, logistics service providers, retailers and many more.

In general, this standard provides guidelines for managing Halal products during transportation, at the warehouse and at the point of retail. For instance, it is vital to look at handling during storage or at the warehousing process, especially at the receiving point, put away, storage, cross-docking, shipping, order-picking and other occasions. In term of transportation, the handler need to ensure the handling equipment – such as container, pallet, rack, forklift or trolley or any other transportation vehicle – is in a good separation and segregated appropriately.

In terms of retail, it is also important to make sure that Halal products are not on the same rack or near Haram or non-Halal products. In fact, in certain supermarkets this has been performed, and they now follow Halal retail guidelines. Many supermarkets or hypermarkets such as Tesco in the UK and Carrefour in France are adding Halal value by having Halal shelves and racks to attract Muslim consumers in non-Muslim countries. At present, the demand for Halal products is not only coming from Muslim customers, but also from non-Muslim customers.

SMIIC

The Standards and Metrology Institute for Islamic Countries (SMIIC) is an organization that establishes standards and guidelines for Islamic countries in supporting import-export activities for their Organisation of Islamic Cooperation (OIC) member states. The SMIIC was established in August 2010 with the aim to support its member countries to set standards and review their standards regularly. It started with ten Islamic countries and its headquarters is located in Istanbul, Turkey. One-off policy advice is not sufficient since technology is changing, new issues always arise, new countries become involve with Halal and many more. The SMIIC was developed to harmonize the standards among the Islamic states. Among the standards developed by the SMIIC is the Halal supply chain standard. It is important for all standards or guidelines developed by the SMIIC to support the economy of their OIC country members. The aim of the SMIIC is to establish standards that support the business activities of the state members, as well as eliminate trade barriers and facilitate trade between them. As acknowledged by all, Islamic countries have own specific needs and issues,

Table 2.1 A number of standards developed by the SMIIC

No	Name of standards	Year
1	General Guidelines on Occupational Safety and Health (OSH) OIC/SMIIC 5: 2017	2017
2	Halal Cosmetics – General Requirements OIC/SMIIC 4: 2018	2018
3	General Requirements for Halal Food OIC/SMIIC 1: 2019	2019
4	Conformity Assessment – Requirement for Bodies Providing Halal Certification OIC/SMIIC 2: 2019	2019
5	Conformity Assessment – Requirements for Halal Accreditation Bodies Accrediting Halal Conformity Assessment Bodies OIC/SMIIC 3: 2019	2019
6	Halal Tourism Services – General Requirements OIC/SMIIC 9: 2019	2019
7	Halal Supply Chain Management System – Part 1: Transportation – General Requirements OIC/SMIIC 17-1: 2020	2020
8	Halal Supply Chain Management System – Part 2: Warehousing – General Requirements OIC/SMIIC 17-2: 2020	2020
9	Halal Supply Chain Management System – Part 3: Retailing – General Requirements OIC/SMIIC 17-3: 2020	2020

including Halal, a requirement to follow to Islamic rules. A common standardization framework is fundamental for the development of Halal, which consists of cleanliness elements, quality food, feed, cosmetics, Halal integrity, etc.

At the moment, there are 42 countries that have joined the SMIIC as member states, including Malaysia, Bangladesh, Pakistan, Cameroon, Egypt, Lebanon, Libya, Qatar, Saudi Arabia, Somalia, Sudan and many more. The first standard established by the SMIIC – General Guidelines on Occupational Safety and Health – was published in 2017, followed by Halal Cosmetics in 2018. In 2019, a number of standards and guidelines were also established and published, namely standards for Halal food, Halal certification and Halal accreditation bodies.

At the international level, the SMIIC has taken the lead in publishing new Halal logistics and supply chain standards. In 2020, the Halal Supply Chain Management System was published as three international standards related to Halal logistics and supply chain: Part 1 on Transportation, Part 2 on Warehousing and Part 3 on Retailing. See Table 2.1 for details of standards developed by SMIIC.

MS: Malaysia Standard as a key reference for many industries, countries and academic scholars

In the Malaysian context, in order to help the HLSPs to further understand their role and responsibilities in carrying and handling Halal products, the

Standards Department of Malaysia together with certification body Jabatan Agama Kemajuan Islam Malaysia (JAKIM) established Halal logistics standards. Since Halal logistics is a service, this document has been established to help the HLSPs to smoothly provide their services according to Shariah compliance. The Halal logistics standards developed by the Standards Department of Malaysia is known as MS2400 Halalan- Toyyiban Assurance Pipeline – Management System Requirements for Transportation of Goods and/or Cargo Chain Services, and is a main reference document for HLSPs. MS2400 is considered as a Halal management system that requires the HLSP to comply certain Shariah requirements in order to maintain the integrity of whatever classification of Halal product that they carry or store at the warehouse. In 2019, MS2400 was improved and is now known as MS2400 Halal Supply Chain Management System.

Table 2.2 shows the three critical aspects discussed in MS2400. This standard has been developed by Malaysia Standards Development, together with JAKIM. It is used in the industry as the main reference in getting Halal logistics certification and in handling Halal business activity. The standard provides explanation on scope, related Halal terms and definitions used in the documents, the requirement of each Halal process (in transportation, warehousing and retail), steps to enable risk management, operation of a Halal risk management plan, general requirements (on premise, infrastructure, facilities and personnel), assurance pipelines and many more key guidelines.

MS 2400 Halal Supply Chain Management System is widely used in auditing and certifying Halal logos in logistics. MS2400 is one of the 15 standards developed for the Halal ecosystem in Malaysia. All these 15 standards are the main guidelines for the industry, as well as for consumers to know about relevant laws and regulations in Malaysia. The other fourteen Halal standards that are used as key references for the Halal users and players in the Halal ecosystem in Malaysia are presented in Table 2.3.

Table 2.2 MS2400 Halal Supply Chain Management System

MS2400	Key description
MS2400-1: Halal Supply Chain Management System: Part 1 – Transportation	This MS prescribes management system requirements for pipeline assurance for products or cargo being handled or transported via various modes of transportation.
MS2400-1: Halal Supply Chain Management System: Part 2 – Warehousing	This MS prescribes pipeline management system requirements for assurance of the Halal integrity of goods/products/cargo at storage or at the warehouse.
MS2400-1: Halal Supply chain management system: Part 3 – Retailing	This MS prescribes pipeline management system requirements for assurance of the Halal integrity of any goods or products/cargo at the point of retail.

Source: Standards Department of Malaysia, www.jsm.gov.my/standards.

Table 2.3 Halal standards for Halal ecosystem members' references

Name of standards	Description
MS1500:2009	Halal food
MS1900:2014	Shariah-based quality management system
MS2610:2015	Muslim-friendly hospitality
MS2424:2012	Halal pharmaceuticals
MS2393:2013	Islamic and Halal principles
MS2627:2017	Detection of porcine DNA in food
MS2200-1:2008	Islamic Consumer Goods (ICG) – cosmetics and personal care
MS2565:2014	Halal packaging
MS2400-1:2010	Halal Toyyiban – transport
MS2200-1:2008	ICG – Usage of Animal Bone
MS2200-1:2008	ICG – Usage of Animal Bone
MS2400-2:2010	Halal Toyyiban – warehouse
MS2400-3:2010	Halal Toyyiban – retail
MS1900:2015	QMS – Islamic perspectives

New age of standards and guidelines

Considering the increasing amount of Halal import-export activity worldwide, there is a need to frequently review the quality and risk management system of the current Halal supply chain management standards to ensure any issue related to cross-contamination throughout the pipeline can be reduced and avoided. In fact, with the current development of technologies, complex import-export activity and situation where many countries are looking to enter into the Halal industry, it is vital to ensure that the integrity of the Halal product is secured by current standards and guidelines. Below Tables 2.4, 2.5 and 2.6 list the references for Halal centres and references in certain countries in Asia, the West and the Middle East region.

Middle East standard establishment and reference

The Middle East refers to a region that consists of 17 countries which are located between Europe and Asia. Generally, the countries that make up Middle East are varied in term of culture, language, people, climate and size. Among all these 17 countries in Middle East region, Bahrain is the smallest country in term of physical size, while Saudi Arabia is the largest. Among the prominent religions practised by Middle Eastern populations are Islam, Christian, Judaism and others. Table 2.4 shows the list of 17 countries under Middle East region and their centres for standards and guidelines references.

In this chapter we have documented the evolving definition of logistics service providers (LSPs), the role of these LSPs, as well as the new innovative area of research in logistics service provision, namely Halal logistics service providers (HLSPs). The contribution of this chapter is on the foundation of logistics service provision as discussed in literature, as well as the proposal for future research

Table 2.4 Halal references Middle Eastern countries

No	Country	Example of centre for reference or consultant for standard, certification and guidelines for Halal-related issue
1	Saudi Arabia	SFDA Saudi Halal Centre
2	Egypt	Egypt Halal certification body, Egyptian Organization for Standardization & Quality (EOS)
3	Iran	Iran standardization and Certification Body; Islamic Chamber Research and Information Centre (ICRIC)
4	Turkey	Halal Accreditation Agency
5	Iraq	IAS
6	Jordan	Jordan standards and metrology organization
7	Syria	Certvalue
8	Yemen	Yemen Standardization Meytrology and Quality Control Organization; TopCertifier
9	United Arab Emirates	The Ministry of Environment & Water of the United Arab Emirates
10	Oman	Quality Control Department, Ministry of Commerce and Industry
11	Lebanon	Certivatic
12	Palestine	Palestine Standards Institution
13	Israel	IAS (Integrated Assessment Services)
14	Bahrain	Certivatic
15	Cyprus	Certvalue
16	Kuwait	Ministry of Commerce and Industry, Public Authority of Industry Kuwait
17	Qatar	Qatar Supreme Council of Health, Department of Health Outlets and Food Control

Table 2.5 Halal certification centres or authorities in the West

No	Country	Example of centre for reference or consultant for standard, certification and guidelines for Halal-related issue
1	Ireland	Department of Halal Certification EU
2	Australia	Australian Halal Authority & Advisers (AHAA); Islamic Association of Geraldton
3	Argentina	Islamic Centre of the Argentine Republic
4	Brazil	Federation of Muslims Associations in Brazil
	Canada	Halal Montreal Certification Authority
5	France	Ritual Association of Lyon's Great Mosque
6	Italy	Halal International Authority (HIA)
7	Netherlands	Control Office of Halal Slaughtering and Quality Control
8	New Zealand	New Zealand Islamic Development Trust
9	Poland	The Muslim Religious Union in Poland
10	United Kingdom	The Muslim Food Board; Halal Food Authority
11	United States	Islamic Services of America (ISA); Islamic Food and Nutrition Council of America (IFANCA)

Table 2.6 Halal certification centres or authorities in the Asia region excluding Malaysia

No	Country	Example of centre for reference or consultant for standard, certification and guidelines for Halal-related issue
1	China	China Islamic Association, Shandong Islamic Association
2	India	Halal Committee-Jamiat-Ulama-E-E-Maharashta; Halal India PVT LTD
3	Indonesia	Indonesian Council of Ulama (MUI)
4	Japan	Japan Muslim Association; Japan Halal Association
5	Korea	Korean Muslim Federation
6	Philippines	National Commission on Muslim Filipinos
7	Sri Lanka	Halal Accreditation Council
8	Taiwan	Taiwan Halal Integrity Development Association (THIDA)
9	Thailand	The Central Islamic Committee of Thailand (CICOT)
10	Brunei	Lembaga Mengeluarkan Permit Import Halal, Kementerian Hal Ehwal Agama

from the LSP point of view. The salient features of the proposed future research are comprehensive and close the current gap on the logistics service provision issue as discussed in the literature. On the other hand, the main contribution of this paper to logistics and supply chain literature is twofold. First, the evolution of the LSP definition from the 1980s to 2019 provided in this study reflects the evolution of logistics activity in the industry. It addresses the key features of logistics activities development in the industry.

Conclusion and future research agenda

To conclude, this chapter highlights the three main Halal standards for local and international use by the practitioners, regulators, academicians and publics. The contribution of this chapter is from its analysis of the three Halal logistics standards namely MS, IHIAS and SMIIC. On the other hand, by looking at the opportunity of this area, future researchers or scholars are invited to focus and study Halal logistics certification. As for recommendations, it is vital to study the issue of challenges and barriers in implementing Halal logistics. The strength and weaknesses of each standard implementation could also be a focus for future scholars for further improvement. Through comprehensive analysis of the standard and guidelines used in any country, it would be beneficial for all involved parties to monitor the Halal logistics implementation performance.

References

El-Bassiouny, N. (2016). Where is "Islamic marketing" heading? A commentary on Jafari and Sandikci's (2015) "Islamic consumers", markets, and marketing. *Journal of Business Research*, 69(2), pp. 569–578.

Halal Industry Development Corporation (HDC) (2021). *Halal Industry Master Plan*. Retrieved from: www.hdcglobal.com/wp-content/uploads/2020/02/Halal-Industri-Master-Plan-2030.pdf (assessed 24 November 2021).

Khairuddin, M. M., Rahman, N. A. A., Mohamad, M. F., Majid, Z. A. and Fauzi, M. A. (2018). Regulator perspective on Halal air cargo warehouse compliance. *International Journal of Supply Chain Management*, 7(3), pp. 202–207.

Ngah, A. H., Zainuddin, Y. and Thurasamy, R. (2015). Obstacles and facilitators in adopting of Halal warehousing. *Journal of Islamic Marketing*, 6(3), pp. 354–376.

Ngah, A. H., Zainuddin, Y. and Thurasamy, R. (2017). Applying the TOE framework in the Halal warehouse adoption study. *Journal of Islamic Accounting and Business Research*, 8(2), pp. 161–181.

Pew Research Centre (2021). *World's Muslim Population More Widespread Than You Might Think*. Retrieved from: www.pewresearch.org/fact-tank/2017/01/31/worlds-muslim-population-more-widespread-than-you-might-think/ (assessed 24 November 2021).

Rahim, S. A., Mohammad, B. and Rahman, N. A. A. (2016). Influencing factors on Halal fourth-party logistics (4PL) in Malaysia. In S. K. A. Manan, F. A. Rahman and S. Mardhiyyah (Eds.), *Contemporary Issues and Development in the Global Halal Industry*. Singapore: Springer, pp. 543–556.

Rahman, N. A. A. (2012). *The Car Manufacturer (CM) and Third Party Logistics Provider (TPLP) Relationship in the Outbound Delivery Channel: A Qualitative Study of the Malaysian Automotive Industry*. PhD thesis. London: Brunel University.

Rahman, N. A. A., Melewar, T. C. and Sharif, A. M. (2014) The establishment of industrial branding through dyadic logistics partnership success (LPS): The case of the Malaysian automotive and logistics industry. *Industrial Marketing Management*, 43(1), pp. 67–76.

Rahman, N. A. A., Mohamad, M. F., Muda, J., Ahmad, M. F., Rahim, S. A. and Majid, Z. A. (2018a) Linking Halal requirements and branding: an examination of Halal flight kitchen provider in Malaysia. *International Journal of Supply Chain Management*, 7(3), pp. 208–215.

Rahman, N. A. A., Mohamad, M. F., Rahim, S. A. and Noh, H. M. (2018b). Implementing air cargo Halal warehouse: insight from Malaysia. *Journal of Islamic Marketing*, 9(3), pp. 462–483.

Rahman, N. A. A., Muda, J., Mohammad, M. F., Ahmad, M. F., Rahim, S. A. and Vitoria, F. M. (2019). Digitalization and leap frogging strategy among the supply chain member: facing GIG economy and why should logistics players care? *International Journal of Supply Chain Management*, 8(2), pp. 1042–1048.

Sack, D. (2001). *Whitebread Protestants: Food and Religion in American Culture*. New York, NY: Palgrave.

Saifuddeen, S. M., Rahman, N. N. A. I., Munirah, N. and Baharuddin, A. (2014). *Science and Engineering Ethics*, 20(2), pp, 317–327.

Shahbandeh, M. (2019). *Halal Food Market Revenue Worldwide 2018–2027*. Retrieved from: www.statista.com/statistics/785499/halal-food-market-revenue-global/ (assessed 24 November 2021).

Shariff, M. S. and Ahmad, N. (2015). Halal logistics operations in MS2400 Standards: a literature review. *Conference Proceedings of International Malaysia Halal Conference (IMHALAL) 2015*, KLCC Malaysia, 1–2 April.

Statista (2021). *Global Muslim Market Size in 2017 and 2023*. Retrieved from: www.statista.com/statistics/796103/global-muslim-market-size/ (assessed 24 November 2021).

Wilson, J. A. J. and Liu, J. (2011). The challenges of Islamic branding: navigating emotions and Halal. *Journal of Islamic Marketing*, 2(1), pp. 28–42.

World Population Review (2021). *Muslim Population by Country 2021*. Retrieved from: https://worldpopulationreview.com/country-rankings/muslim-population-by-country (assessed 25 August 2021).

3 Theories in Halal logistics and supply chain management research

Mohamed Syazwan Ab Talib, Abdul Hafaz Ngah and Dwi Agustina Kurniawati

Introduction

The logistics and supply chain management (LSCM) field has experienced remarkable innovations over the years. Revolutionary innovations from containerization, electronic data interchange (EDI) and radio frequency identification (RFID) to the more recent application of big data, blockchain technology and electric vehicles (Verhoeven et al., 2018; Juan et al., 2016; Wang et al., 2016; Grawe, 2009) have significantly transformed the way businesses operate. Moreover, the relentless push towards globalization (Kiessling et al., 2014), pressure for more environmentally sustainable operations (Björklund and Forslund, 2018) and overall service advancements (Busse and Wallenburg, 2011) have amplified innovative drives further. Besides, propelled by the currently matured and overly saturated logistics services (Kiessling et al., 2014; Bottani and Rizzi, 2006), scholars and practitioners are forced to establish viable LSCM services to rejuvenate the industry. Hence, these circumstances give rise to another innovation in LSCM, particularly in servicing the growing Halal food and consumer markets – Halal logistics and supply chain management (HLSCM).

The last decade has seen a surge in HLSCM research. According to Talib et al. (2020), despite being a relatively new branch in the LSCM domain, HLSCM research is gaining strong interest from academic scholars. Similarly, Haleem et al. (2020) demonstrate that HLSCM is among the prominent research clusters and has plenty of room for academicians and practitioners to explore and research. However, despite the progress, there is much to improve for the HLSCM field to remain a viable and significant section within the LSCM domain. For instance, Talib et al. (2020), argue that HLSCM research and literature lack theoretical application. Meanwhile, Karia (2019) critiques the glaring theoretical gap in the extant LSCM literature and urges more theory application and development.

The dearth of theory-based research in HLSCM is unsurprising. Even in the conventional and broader LSCM literature, the same issue persists. Scholars (Chen and Paulraj, 2004; Wallenburg and Weber, 2005; Halldorsson et al., 2007; Defee et al., 2010; Manuj and Pohlen, 2012) have long argued that LSCM research lacks theoretical building, development and structure, suggesting that more needs to be done. According to Defee et al. (2010, p. 420), researchers in

DOI: 10.4324/9781003223719-5

this domain should increase the use of theories because doing so would "remove the burden of interpretation from the reader, ease the understanding of the work and reinforce the standard of acceptable research". Additionally, even though much of the theories in LSCM research derives from other disciplines (Defee et al., 2010; Swanson et al., 2017), the field still lacks a socioeconomic theoretical basis (Halldorsson et al., 2007). Therefore, with regards to HLSCM, this corroborates Karia's (2019) view that more theory development, specifically one that is exclusive to HLSCM, should be established.

A focus on theory, not only in HLSCM or LSCM, is paramount (Defee et al., 2010). For the LSCM discipline to progress, theoretical applications must be practised – along with the integration with empirical evidence (van Donk and van der Vaart, 2005). Additionally, a theory is an essential component in research and crucial in explaining current phenomena or predicting future presage (Cooper and Schindler, 2014). Although the literature suggests more theory-driven studies (Chen and Paulraj, 2004; Wallenburg and Weber, 2005; Halldorsson et al., 2007; Defee et al., 2010; Manuj and Pohlen, 2012), past HLSCM research and scholars have yet to scrutinize the full extent of theory application in the field. Therefore, this chapter aims to provide a comprehensive review of the theories used in HLSCM. Two research questions are drawn to achieve the objective and steer the deliberation, specifically (1) What are the theories found in HLSCM research? (2) To what extent are theories applied in HLSCM research? These research questions are based on the work done by Defee et al. (2010).

Review methods

To address the research questions, the authors conducted a comprehensive literature review of HLSCM research published in the *Journal of Islamic Marketing* (JIMA). Research published in JIMA was sampled because it is the leading journal for the Halal business and management field – including HLSCM (Haleem et al., 2020; Talib et al., 2020). Additionally, JIMA is a pioneering outlet for cutting-edge Halal research and has reputable standing in the Halal research communities (Mubarrok et al., 2020; Alserhan, 2010). Following the approach of Mubarrok et al. (2020), other established journals, such as the *International Journal of Islamic Marketing and Branding*, are omitted from the review given that they are not indexed in Scopus – a definitive standard for high-quality research in the business and management domains in general (Levine-Clark and Gil, 2008).

To search for relevant HLSCM articles published in JIMA, the authors performed a three-step process. First, the authors referred to the source's table of contents, where the entire collection of volumes and issues were made available through an institutional subscription. The authors carefully inspected every volume and issue to ensure that all relevant HLSCM articles were included. The search also considered "EarlyCite" articles as this would ensure a more comprehensive review. There was no restriction on the year of publication. The authors argue that not limiting to a specific timeframe would generate ampler sample articles. A total of 33 HLSCM articles were identified and downloaded.

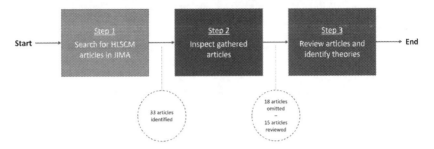

Figure 3.1 Three-step review process.

In the next step, the authors read each article to ensure relevancy with the research objective and questions. It is crucial to separate between theory-based and theoretical research. In this review, the term "theory" is a relevant, sound and systematic concept that would enable the explanation or the prediction of a subject in question (Cooper and Schindler, 2014). Meanwhile, as the name indicates, theoretical means a study that is not based on or concerned with theory – usually involving review or viewpoint pieces. A total of 18 articles were omitted from further consideration (see Figure 3.1). These sampled articles were removed from the review as they did not specify or use any theory.

Lastly, in the final step, the authors reviewed the remaining HLSCM articles. To ensure a degree of reliability and validity in the review process, all authors individually read the 15 articles and listed the theories using a word processing document. Once done, the lists were consolidated and cross-checked to ensure that each author uncovered a similar list of identified theories. Fourteen theories were identified from this process. A complete listing of the papers and their supporting theories are presented in Table 3.1. It should be noted that several articles applied more than one theory and therefore, explains the discrepancies between the number of sampled articles and applied theories.

Analysis and discussions

Publication trend

Between the year 2011 and April 2021, there were 33 HLSCM-relevant articles published in JIMA (Figure 3.2). It is apparent in Figure 3.2 that there is a reasonable upward trend in HLSCM research over the past decade. This means that HLSCM research is gaining interest in academic circles and signifies the growing importance of the distributional aspects of Halal supply chains. Additionally, findings from this review corroborate Haleem et al.'s (2020) bibliometric review that HLSCM is among the growing trends in the Halal business domain.

Furthermore, a closer look at the findings shown in Table 3.1, it appears that theoretical application did not emerge from the onset. Theory-based research

Table 3.1 Theories used in HLSCM research

Author (year)	Objective	Theory
Talib and Hamid (2014)	To identify the strengths, weaknesses, opportunities and threats of Halal logistics in Malaysia	SWOT
Shahijan et al. (2014)	To examine the causal relationship between normative belief, subjective norms, behavioural belief, attitude, behaviour intention, actual behaviour and retail performance	Theory of Reasoned Action and Theory of Planned Behaviour
Tieman (2015)	To propose a Halal cluster concept to better organize the production and trade of Halal food	Cluster Theory
Talib et al. (2015)	To uncover the factors that are critical in the Halal food supply chain	Critical Success Factors
Ngah et al. (2015)	To identify the Halal warehousing adoption factors	Technology–Organization–Environment Framework and Diffusion of Innovation Theory
Talib et al. (2016)	To establish the Halal certification–logistics performance relationship	Resource-Based View and Institutional Theory
Rahman and Zailani (2017)	To investigate the effectiveness and viability of the Muslim-friendly medical tourism supply chain practices in Malaysia	Theory of Relational View, Resource-Based View and Transaction Cost Theory
Zulfakar et al. (2018)	To investigate the role of institutional forces in shaping the operations of Halal meat supply chains in Australia	Institutional Theory
Selim et al. (2019)	To investigate Halal logistic services' impact on manufacturers' trust and satisfaction	Disconfirmation of Expectations Paradigm
Karia (2019)	To examine the Halal value creation in Halal logistics practices and Halal logistics integration	Resource-Based View
Noorliza (2020)	To examine the extent of emergent resource-capability, configuration and impacts on customer service innovation and cost advantages	Resource-Based View and Contingency Theory
Ngah et al. (2020a)	To identify factors influencing Halal transportation adoption	Technology–Organization–Environment Framework, Diffusion of Innovation Theory, Institutional Theory
Ngah et al. (2020b)	To identify the factors of willingness to pay for Halal transportation	Theory of Planned Behaviour
Talib (2020)	To identify Halal logistics constraints in Brunei	Theory of Constraints
Ali et al. (2021)	To explore the impacts of supply chain integration on Halal food supply chain integrity and, consequently, food quality	Resource-Based View

Figure 3.2 HLSCM articles published in JIMA (N=32).

only emerged in 2014 with Shahijan et al. (2014) on Halal meat supply chains and Talib and Hamid's (2014) Halal industry environmental analysis. This means that the initial and ground-breaking research by Professor Marco Tieman (2011, 2015; Tieman et al., 2012) do not report any theory application. Nevertheless, Tieman's approach is understandable considering his seminal works are the ontogenesis towards HLSCM.

Moreover, Table 3.1 also provides evidence that theories have been consistently used in HLSCM research since 2014. In general, this is an encouraging trend. However, despite the constancy, less than half of the sampled articles applied theories. It may seem that scholars have steadily applied various theories in HLSC, but a large section of HLSCM scholars have largely disregarded theoretical application in their research. This reflects that theory-based research is unpopular and that grounded theory, a form of theory development approach, is lacking in HSLCM. The review observation proves Karia's (2019) outlook, which expressed concerns on the need for more theory-driven research in HLSCM.

Theories used in HLSCM research

Table 3.1 presents a breakdown of theories used in HLSCM research. From this table, a majority of the sampled articles uses a single theory while few applied two or more theories. More specifically, Rahman and Zailani (2017) and Ngah et al. (2020a) use three theories, while Shahijan et al. (2014), Ngah et al. (2015), Talib et al. (2016), and Noorliza (2020) apply two theories. The combination of two or more theories in underpinning LSCM research is common (Defee et al., 2010) and it is good to see the same applies in HLSCM studies.

A further inspection of Table 3.1 shows that the review identified a total of 14 theories. Resource-Based View (RBV) is the most used theory with five papers (Talib et al., 2016; Rahman and Zailani, 2017; Karia, 2019; Noorliza, 2020; Ali et al., 2021). Subsequently, Institutional Theory is found in three papers (Talib et al., 2016; Zulfakar et al., 2018; Ngah et al., 2020a) while the Technology–Organization–Environment (TOE) Framework, the Diffusion of Innovation (DOI) and Theory of Planned Behaviour (TPB) (Ngah et al., 2015, 2020a, 2020b; Shahijan et al., 2014) are found in two papers. The remaining theories were used once within the 33 sampled articles. Overall, the 14 identified theories are a positive indication that there is a considerable breadth of theories used in HLSCM research. This also signals that efforts are being made to develop the HLSCM domain further and therefore, theory-based research is a necessary element for growth (Defee et al., 2010). For a more meaningful discussion, this chapter will deliberate further on the "popular" theories in HLSCM – the RBV, Institutional Theory, TPB and TOE Framework. Due to the similarity between DOI and TOE (Ngah et al., 2015), the subsequent discussions on TOE will jointly represent DOI.

Resource-Based View in HLSCM

It is not a surprise that RBV is frequently applied in HLSCM research. According to Talib et al. (2016), the Halal industry, as with any industry in the world, is highly dependent on tangible and intangible resources – crucial for the marketing and distribution of Halal goods and services. Moreover, the basis of Halal logistics operations of transportation, warehousing and terminals are the "key" resources, not only for service integration but for overall organizational performance (Karia, 2019). Additionally, aside from the "hard" physical resources, the "soft" strategic resources of internal and external supply chain integrations (Ali et al., 2021) are equally pertinent towards achieving good performance. Combining these notions, along with the constant realization and connection between Halal practices and business performance (Talib et al., 2016, 2017), the use of RBV is very much definitive in explaining the competitiveness (Defee et al., 2010) and the link between Halal strategic resources and business performance.

Institutional Theory in HLSCM

Institutional Theory is among the frequently used concepts in LSCM (Defee et al., 2010). The logistics industry and the supply chain of goods and services are heavily reliant on decrees and governance from the government (Talib et al., 2020). For instance, regulations and policies imposed by a government are necessary to coerce supply chain parties, particularly the upstream members of the Halal supply chain, to practice ethical, safe and uncompromised operations (Zulfakar et al., 2018). According to Zulfakar et al. (2018), although pressure from industry norms and inter-firm competition are generally notable, the institutional forces from the government are more prominent. Additionally, aside from regulatory support, financial assistance, manpower support and the drive towards legitimizing operation are among the factors that reinforce the role of government in Halal logistics and supply chains (Talib et al., 2016). Therefore, taken together, these explain the use of Institutional Theory in HLSCM research, in which the synergy between the government sector, private firms and consumers are paramount for uncompromised and comprehensive Halal supply chains.

Theory of Planned Behaviour in HLSCM

TPB, which originates from the psychology field, is also often applied in HLSCM. This review finding is consistent with Defee et al.'s (2010) study where social psychological theories are generally utilized in understanding the affinity between LSCM and marketing or purchasing topics. Based on this review and a broader scope, the conception remains given that TPB is popular in Halal research (Mubarrok et al., 2020). Hence, Shahijan et al.'s (2014) research on retailers' behaviour in Halal meat supply chains and Ngah et al.'s (2020a) on consumers' willingness to pay for Halal services were able to prove the relevancy of TPB in HLSCM research. Additionally, TPB in HLSCM research has been applied in different contexts, specifically firm-oriented and consumer-based research. The suitability of TPB in predicting and explaining multiple contexts within the HLSCM field is an indication that researchers are filling in the literature gaps given that much of Halal research is focused on Halal products and less on Halal services, in this case, HLSCM.

TOE Framework in HLSCM

The TOE framework is a widely accepted context or concept in the domain. The TOE framework is usually applied in the circumstance of adopting new practices, in this case, the HLSCM (Ngah et al., 2020b). As the Halal industry is generally susceptible to the surrounding environments (i.e., political, economic, social and technology), the feasibility of operationalizing Halal practices throughout the supply chains is crucial. Moreover, apart from the external environments and industrial context, the TOE framework can predict how organizations utilize the available resources in order to react and respond to a new industry phenomenon (Ngah et al., 2015), such as the HLSCM. Therefore, based on these assertions, the TOE framework is used in HLSCM research to justify the association and impact between the internal and external factors have towards Halal logistics adoption.

Non-LSCM Theories in HLSCM

Another observation worthy of mentioning is the theories used in HLSCM research that are "borrowed" or originate from non-LSCM disciplines. For example, Rahman and Zailani's (2017) use of Transaction Cost Theory originates from economics disciplines, while Shahijan et al. (2014) and Ngah et al. (2020b) applied Theory of Reasoned Action and TPB, both of which are derived from a social psychology background. These approaches are by no means wrong as scholars in LSCM have been doing so for decades (Swanson et al., 2017), but it augments the call from Defee et al. (2010) on the need for more internal theory development, specifically one that applies distinctively to LSCM. Besides, this review's observation substantiates Karia's (2019) observation on the absence of HLSCM's very own theory. Nevertheless, efforts towards a more conformant theory for HLSCM seem to move in the right direction. The research by Karia (2019) and Noorliza (2020) on the application of Resource-Based Halal Logistics (RBHL), is a commendable attempt. Even though RBHL is derived from the RBV, the Islamic-based dimensions, which are unique within the Halal business and management domain, that have never been used in HLSCM research should be further developed and tested.

Explicit use of theories in HLSCM

Further review of the HLSCM literature reveals that all sampled articles, except one by Selim et al. (2019), explicitly mentioned the use of theories. In other words, HLSCM scholars clearly identified the underpinning theories that ground their respective research. This review is similar to that of Defee et al. (2010)

who found that LSCM research commonly specifies the theories being applied and such an approach is encouraged and must be continued. The clear mention of what theories were used in HLSCM research perhaps is JIMA's requirement or possibly a generally good practice of acceptable research by the authors. Regardless, the manner of clear delineation of theories as the basis of research in HLSCM would improve readers' understanding and interpretation.

Methods used within theories

Following the approach by Defee et al. (2010), the review classifies the methodology used in each of the sampled articles (Table 3.2). In Table 3.2, the methods are classified into four categories, namely survey, concept, literature review and interview. In addition, the survey method is the most employed approach and is based on various theories. Survey methodology, in which questionnaires are often preferred, is a popular technique in LSCM research (Defee et al., 2010; Talib et al., 2020). Connecting the findings in Table 3.1 and 3.2, the RBV theory is used in five papers (Ali et al., 2021; Karia, 2019; Noorliza, 2020; Rahman and Zailani, 2017; Talib et al., 2016), of which four use survey method.

Additionally, Table 3.2 also shows that the conceptual approach appeared four times when RBV and Institutional Theory were used by Talib et al. (2016), the Theory of Constraints in Talib (2020) and Cluster Theory by Tieman (2015). Moreover, literature review techniques in conjunction with the concepts of critical success factors and SWOT analysis are used in identifying the internal and external factors that are important in HLSCM (Talib and Hamid, 2014). Cross-referencing review findings in Table 3.1 and 3.2 indicates that the SWOT concept and Institutional Theory are also applied in interviews done by Talib and Hamid (2014) and Zulfakar et al. (2018), respectively.

Collectively, the review reveals that HLSCM scholars are fonder of quantitative than qualitative research. The inclination towards quantitative research, in this instance survey methodology, could be because much of extant HLSCM studies are based on borrowed theories from various disciplines where concepts have matured and been tested repeatedly. As opposed to qualitative theory, scholars have yet to apply a grounded theory or inductive reasoning approach in generating a theory, especially one in developing HLSCM-unique theory.

Conclusions, implications and limitation

In this chapter, the first aim was to ascertain theories found in HLSCM research. Understanding theories used in HLSCM research would enable the field to mature and progress. The review of 33 extant literature published in JIMA has revealed that 14 different theories from 15 articles have been applied in HLSCM over the past decade. Among the prominent theories were the RBV, TPB, Institutional Theory, TOE Framework and DOI. In general, the theories were derived from non-HLSCM origins and were mainly from the economic, psychology and marketing disciplines. Additionally, the second aim of this chapter was

Table 3.2 Methodologies use within theories in HLSCM research

Theory Method	RBV	IT	TPB	TOE	DOI	TRA	DEP	CT	TRV	TCT	TOC	CLU	CSF	SW
Survey	✓	✓	✓	✓	✓	✓	✓	✓	✓	✓				
Concept	✓	✓										✓		
Literature Review													✓	✓
Interview		✓												

Note: RBV (Resource-Based View); IT (Institutional Theory); TPB (Theory of Planned Behaviour); TOE (Technology-Organization-Environment Framework); DEP (Disconfirmation of Expectations Paradigm); TRA (Theory of Reasoned Action); DOI (Diffusion of Innovation Theory); CT (Contingency Theory); TRV (Theory of Relational Value); TCT (Transactional Cost Theory); TOC (Theory of Constraints); CLU (Cluster Theory); CSF (Critical Success Factors); SW (SWOT).

Source: Developed by the authors, 2021.

to review the extent of theories applied in HLSCM research. Specifically, the review revealed that many HLSCM scholars explicitly delineate the underpinning theories in their research. This allows for better understanding and interpretation for readers. Moreover, findings from the review also indicate that theories are mainly utilized for survey methods, thus are appropriate for quantitative survey research, common in LSCM studies, of testing the theories' premises. Taken together, the review indicates that, although the use of theories in HLSCM research is gaining pace, scholars should intensify theoretical application in their studies. Besides, underpinning theories that are of LSCM origin or that depict are unique to HLSCM is indeed desired.

Implications of this chapter are of pertinence to academics. For scholars, as no formal research in the past has ever attempted to examine the theories used in HLSCM research, insights of this chapter could be useful to instigate a greater internal theory development. Consequently, the information contained in this chapter would be helpful for scholars to devise agendas for future research, especially in inductive or grounded theory research. Furthermore, aside from academic scholars, journal editors or reviewers would equally benefit from this chapter. For instance, given that more than half of the identified articles did not report any use of theories, perhaps it is befitting for editors and reviewers to demand more theoretical application in HLSCM research. Such an approach is not only an indication of good research undertakings but it also would enhance and develop the HLSCM domain further. Hopefully, the push from the journal editors or reviewers would encourage researchers to either apply relevant theories or advances internal theoretical development.

Despite the constructive review and suggestions for relevant communities and the future, this chapter has several limitations. Being limited to studies published in JIMA, the review disregard papers published in other journals and hence might overlook theories that were used in other outlets. Perhaps future research of similar objectives should expand the publication source or retrieve more information from established databases such as Google Scholar or Scopus. This approach might garner more results for a thorough in-depth review. Additionally, the narrative and simplistic review in this chapter might not fully unearth intricate search results or analytics. Rather, the review is more on a "face value" and therefore might not paint a complete picture of theories in HLSCM research. A more systematic approach and using an advanced application, such as VOSviewer, should be considered for future research because such methods would generate more sophisticated bibliometric, clustering and scientometric analyses. Nevertheless, despite the confined and subjective nature of this chapter, it does shed light on the need for more theory use in HLSCM research.

References

Ali, M. H., Iranmanesh, M., Tan, K. H., Zailani, S. and Omar, N. A. (2021). Impact of supply chain integration on Halal food supply chain integrity and food quality performance. *Journal of Islamic Marketing*. doi: 10.1108/JIMA-08-2020-0250

Alserhan, B. A. (2010). Islamic marketing: the birth of a new social science. *Journal of Islamic Marketing*, 1(1). doi: 10.1108/jima.2010.43201aaa.001

Björklund, M. and Forslund, H. (2018). Exploring the sustainable logistics innovation process. *Industrial Management and Data Systems*, 118(1), pp. 204–217.

Bottani, E. and Rizzi, A. (2006). A fuzzy TOPSIS methodology to support outsourcing of logistics services. *Supply Chain Management: An International Journal*, 11(4), pp. 294–308.

Busse, C. and Wallenburg, C. M. (2011). Innovation management of logistics service providers. *International Journal of Physical Distribution and Logistics Management*, 41(2), pp. 187–218.

Chen, I. J. and Paulraj, A. (2004). Towards a theory of supply chain management: the constructs and measurements. *Journal of Operations Management*, 22(2), pp. 119–150.

Cooper, D. R. and Schindler, P. S. (2014). *Business Research Methods* (12th edn). Singapore: Mcgraw-Hill Education.

Defee, C. C., Williams, B., Randall, W. S. and Thomas, R. (2010). An inventory of theory in logistics and SCM research. *The International Journal of Logistics Management*, 21(3), pp. 404–489.

Grawe, S. J. (2009). Logistics innovation: a literature-based conceptual framework. *The International Journal of Logistics Management*, 20(3), pp. 360–377.

Haleem, A., Khan, M. I., Khan, S. and Jami, A. R. (2020). Research status in Halal: a review and bibliometric analysis. *Modern Supply Chain Research and Applications*, 2(1), pp. 23–41.

Halldorsson, A., Kotzab, H., Mikkola, J. H. and Skjøtt-Larsen, T. (2007). Complementary theories to supply chain management. *Supply Chain Management: An International Journal*, 12(4), pp. 284–296.

Juan, A. A., Mendez, C. A., Faulin, J., De Armas, J. and Grasman, S. E. (2016). Electric vehicles in logistics and transportation: a survey on emerging environmental, strategic and operational challenges. *Energies*, 9(2), pp. 1–21.

Karia, N. (2019). Halal logistics: practices, integration and performance of logistics service providers. *Journal of Islamic Marketing*. doi: 10.1108/JIMA-08-2018-0132

Kiessling, T., Harvey, M. and Akdeniz, L. (2014). The evolving role of supply chain managers in global channels of distribution and logistics systems. *International Journal of Physical Distribution and Logistics Management*, 44(8/9), pp. 671–688.

Levine-Clark, M. and Gil, E. L. (2008). A comparative citation analysis of Web of Science, Scopus and Google Scholar. *Journal of Business and Finance Librarianship*, 14(1), pp. 32–46.

Manuj, I. and Pohlen, T. L. (2012). A reviewer's guide to the grounded theory methodology in logistics and supply chain management research. *International Journal of Physical Distribution and Logistics Management*, 42(8), pp. 784–803.

Mubarrok, U. S., Ulfi, I., Sukmana, R. and Sukoco, B. M. (2020). A bibliometric analysis of Islamic marketing studies in the *Journal of Islamic Marketing*. *Journal of Islamic Marketing*. doi: 10.1108/JIMA-05-2020-0158

Ngah, A. H., Zainuddin, Y. and Thurasamy, R. (2015). Barriers and enablers in adopting of Halal warehousing. *Journal of Islamic Marketing*, 6(3), pp. 354–376.

Ngah, A. H., Ramayah, T., Ali, M. H. and Khan, M. I. (2020a). Halal transportation adoption among pharmaceuticals and comestics manufacturers. *Journal of Islamic Marketing*, 11(6), pp. 1619–1639.

Ngah, A. H., Gabarre, S., Eneizan, B. and Asri, N. (2020b). Mediated and moderated model of the willingness to pay for halal transportation. *Journal of Islamic Marketing*. doi: 10.1108/JIMA-10-2019-0199

Noorliza, K. (2020). Resource-capability of Halal logistics services, its extent and impact on performance. *Journal of Islamic Marketing*. doi: 10.1108/JIMA-12-2019-0255

Rahman, M. K. and Zailani, S. (2017). The effectiveness and outcomes of the Muslim-friendly medical tourism supply chain. *Journal of Islamic Marketing*, 8(4), pp. 732–752.

Selim, N. I. I. B., Zailani, S., Aziz, A. A. and Rahman, M. K. (2019). Halal logistic services, trust and satisfaction amongst Malaysian 3PL service providers. *Journal of Islamic Marketing*. doi: 10.1108/JIMA-05-2018-0088

Shahijan, M. K., Preece, C. N., Rezaei, S. and Ismail, W. K. W. (2014). Examining retailers' behaviour in managing critical points in Halal meat handling: a PLS analysis. *Journal of Islamic Marketing*, 5(3), pp. 446–472.

Swanson, D., Goel, L., Francisco, K. and Stock, J. (2017). Applying theories from other disciplines to logistics and supply chain management: a systematic literature review. *Transportation Journal*, 56(3), pp. 299–356.

Talib, M. S. A. (2020). Identifying Halal logistics constraints in Brunei Darussalam. *Journal of Islamic Marketing*. doi: 10.1108/JIMA-09-2019-0189

Talib, M. S. A. and Hamid, A. B. A. (2014). Halal logistics in Malaysia: a SWOT analysis. *Journal of Islamic Marketing*, 5(3), pp. 322–343.

Talib, M. S. A., Hamid, A. B. A. and Zulfakar, M. H. (2015). Halal supply chain critical success factors: a literature review. *Journal of Islamic Marketing*, 6(1), pp. 44–71.

Talib, M. S. A., Hamid, A. B. A. and Chin, T. A. (2016). Can Halal certification influence logistics performance? *Journal of Islamic Marketing*, 7(4), pp. 461–475.

Talib, M. S. A., Ai Chin, T. and Fischer, J. (2017). Linking Halal food certification and business performance. *British Food Journal*, 119(7), pp. 1606–1618.

Talib, M. S. A., Pang, L. L. and Ngah, A. H. (2020). The role of government in promoting Halal logistics: a systematic literature review. *Journal of Islamic Marketing*. doi: 10.1108/JIMA-05-2020-0124

Tieman, M. (2011). The application of Halal in supply chain management: in-depth interviews. *Journal of Islamic Marketing*, 2(2), 186–195.

Tieman, M. (2015). Halal clusters. *Journal of Islamic Marketing*, 6(1), pp. 2–21.

Tieman, M., van der Vorst, J. G. A. J. and Che Ghazali, M. (2012). Principles in Halal supply chain management. *Journal of Islamic Marketing*, 3(3), pp. 217–243.

van Donk, D. P. and van der Vaart, T. (2005). A critical discussion on the theoretical and methodological advancements in supply chain integration research. In H. Kotzab, S. Seuring, M. Müller and G. Reiner (eds.), *Research Methodologies in Supply Chain Management*. Cham: Springer, pp. 31–46.

Verhoeven, P., Sinn, F. and Herden, T. (2018). Examples from blockchain implementations in logistics and supply chain management: exploring the mindful use of a new technology. *Logistics*, 2(3), 20.

Wallenburg, C. M. and Weber, J. (2005). Structural equation modeling as a basis for theory development within logistics and supply chain management research. In H. Kotzab, S. Seuring, M. Müller and G. Reiner (Eds.), *Research Methodologies in Supply Chain Managemen*. Heidelberg: Physica-Verlag Heidelberg, pp. 171–186.

Wang, G., Gunasekaran, A., Ngai, E. W. T. and Papadopoulos, T. (2016). Big data analytics in logistics and supply chain management: certain investigations for research and applications. *International Journal of Production Economics*, 176, pp. 98–110.

Zulfakar, M. H., Chan, C. and Jie, F. (2018). Institutional forces on Australian Halal meat supply chain (AHMSC) operations. *Journal of Islamic Marketing*, 9(1), pp. 80–98.

4 Theories used in Halal logistics studies

A literature review

Au Yong Hui Nee and Zam Zuriyati Mohamad

Introduction

The global Muslim population is anticipated to increase from 1.8 billion in 2015 to nearly three billion by 2060 according to the Pew Research Centre (2019). It is estimated that Muslims are expected to make up 26.4% of the global population by 2030 as compared to 19.9% in 1990. Consequently, the Muslim consumer expenditure across Halal food and lifestyle in 2015 was reported to be worth USD 1.9 trillion which is anticipated to grow to USD 3.0 trillion by 2021 (Zawya, 2016), displaying possible development for Halal food products and services of the industry. The Muslim priority in searching and consuming Halal products has increased due to the growing awareness to comply with Shariah law. Having considered that Halal products not only involve Halal material or end products, Muslims seek other interrelated dimensions of Halal products, including logistics and supply chain.

Halal logistics and supply chain literature review

According to Indarti et al. (2020), Halal supply chain (HSC) research is in its initial development. With the ever-growing Halal market, more researchers are becoming involving in Halal-related research. Within ten years, the HSC publications have increases significantly, mostly in non-indexed and low citation rate journals (Indarti et al., 2020). According to Radzman et al. (2016), Malaysia as a leading country in the Halal industry has a good infrastructure to provide Halal players with Halal knowledge and Halal practice guidance related to the Halal supply chain. The main Halal food research originates from Asia and emerging countries in other continents, and considers Halal food and sustainability, innovation and technology (Shahbaz et al., 2018).

In the current study, the focus is more on the supply viewpoint, in terms of reviewing research articles related to Halal certification, and Halal logistics (HL) and Halal supply chain (HSC) particularly. The study by Haleem et al. (2020) reports the top researchers in Halal areas, the major sub-research areas and the impact works based on citations and PageRank, and suggests that the main influential publications of Halal are from biological science-related areas. Qurtubi

DOI: 10.4324/9781003223719-6

and Kusrini (2018) studied HL and HSC research papers, and classified them as follows: (1) principles, conceptual model and framework, (2) innovation, development and challenges, (3) critical control point, critical success factors and halal control activities, (4) consumers' willingness to pay, (5) transportation and information technology, (6) strategic approach.

In terms of related theories, the Theory of Planned Behaviour, the Theory of Reasoned Action and Technology Adoption Theory are used for individual units of analysis, not for studies at the organizational unit of analysis; Diffusion of Innovation (DOI), Institutional Theory and the Technology–Organization–Environment (TOE) Framework are the most broadly used theories at the organizational level (Ngah et al., 2019). According to Indarti et al. (2020), most of the HSC studies are organization-level analysis, qualitative interview methods in Muslim-majority countries. Selected international studies applying relevant theories are summarized in Table 4.1. These studies applied theories include Fuzzy Logic Theory, Grounded Theory, Human Capital Theory and Supply Chain Theory.

Research in Halal logistics

The findings by Tieman and Ghazali (2014) show that product characteristics and market requirements affect the weakness of HSC, where the latter is reduced

Table 4.1 Selected Halal certification/logistics/supply chain studies overseas

No.	Halal certification/ logistics/supply chain	Journals	Countries	Theories	Samples
	Halal certification				
1	Rafiki (2016)	Journal of Islamic Marketing	Indonesia	Human Capital Theory	370 samples
2	Shahbaz et al. (2019)	Journal of Modelling in Management	India	Fuzzy DEMATEL Approach	10 experts
	Halal logistics transportation				
3	Lestari et al. (2018)	Journal for Global Business Advancement	Indonesia	Theory of Planned Behaviour	779 samples
	Halal supply chain				
4	McElwee et al. (2017)	Food Policy	United Kingdom	Supply Chain Theory	Qualitative Interviews
5	Randeree (2019)	British Food Journal	United Arab Emirates	Ethnography and Grounded Theory	1,250 samples
6	Shahbaz et al. (2019)	Journal of Islamic Marketing	India	Fuzzy Analytic Hierarchy Process	Experts' assessment

through establishment of Halal control and assurance activities in logistics processes, or avoided by having dedicated logistics infrastructure; for example, a Halal warehouse and nominated transport, or through containerization at a lower level. The review of Talib et al. (2020) reported six tasks, namely, regulation, financial incentives, taxation, infrastructure, guidance and encouragement, and education and labour supply in Halal logistics. On the other hand, Masudin et al. (2018) reviewed client-focused perspectives, the HL performance and customer loyalty.

Research in Halal supply chain

The results of Antonio et al. (2020) showed that the publications on Islamic economics and finance research experienced a significant increase, the highest number of document types are journal articles, and the most popular author is Professor Dr Marco Tieman, while the most popular keywords are Halal, supply and chain. This is also consistent with Omar et al. (2012), who suggest that Halal food supply chain research mostly focused on HL or HSC performance.

A review of literature by Zulfakar et al. (2012) highlights Halal food supply chain management and issues on Halal integrity, and factors affecting Halal food supply chain integrity such as traceability, asset specificity, quality assurance and trust and commitment. In addition, the review of Mohamed et al. (2016) focuses on Malaysia Halal food traceability concerning Halal integrity, while Zailani et al. (2010) highlight the Halal traceability and Halal tracking for Halal food products.

The Halal research studies can be classified into respective categories. Wahyuni et al. (2018) report four main clusters of food safety and two clusters of Halal food in supply chain research as the brightest future research areas. Omar et al. (2012) classify Halal food studies into eight research areas: the concept of Halal, Halal certification, Halal product attributes, consumer awareness of Halal, Halal marketing, information technology adoption in Halal, Halal integrity and Halal food supply chain management.

Models reviewed by Saifudin et al. (2018) are Halal traceability and tracking activity, Halal certification and labelling process, Halal facilities segregation and Halal food quality management. Shahbaz et al. (2019) determine five research clusters, that is, Halal food and the role of certifications, Halal food and awareness, Halal food production and quality, Halal food in tourism management and Halal food and the supply chain. Indarti et al. (2020) suggest five themes of studies: the engagement process, quality control assurance, critical success factors, the production and distribution process and HSC operations support.

Talib et al. (2015) suggest that government support, transportation planning, information technology, human resource management, collaborative relationships, Halal certification and Halal traceability are the critical success factors for the HSC. In the era of the digital revolution, the Internet of Things (IoT) presents five major benefits for the Halal food supply chain: traceability of products, enhancement of supply chain efficiencies, facilitation of livestock management, authentication of foods' Halal status, and monitoring of Halal certifications. On the other hand, challenges identified include the technical limitations of IoT devices, technological immaturity, lack of user acceptance and cost and regulatory barriers (Rejeb et al., 2021).

Review method

With the review keywords HL and HSC on hand, the research articles were searched. Initially, the articles were mainly sourced from Scopus databases. The second step was article selection. The data analysis was selected by evaluating the articles from the keywords of HL and HSC. It was acknowledged by previous researchers that the Scopus database includes the most journals indexed in the Web of Science (Mongeon and Paul-Hus, 2016). The third step was data analysis. This was performed from the perspective of publication source, location of the research by country and theories applied in the previous researches. The selected studies were then analysed and synthesized into respective themes.

Data analysis and findings

Data was analysed from the articles listed in the Scopus database using the refine results value and content analysis. The findings are discussed below.

Halal logistics

The first analysis that was performed was examining the trend of Halal logistics articles published in the Scopus database. There are 122 articles related to 'Halal logistics' published in the Scopus database from 2007 to 2020. The annual Halal logistics articles published in Scopus are shown in Figure 4.1. The result indicates an upward trend in the frequency of Halal logistics articles published, with the highest number of articles being in 2020 with a total of 23 articles.

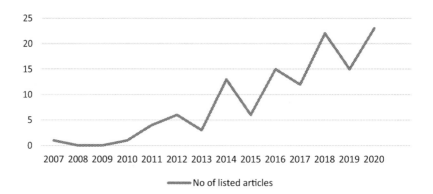

Figure 4.1 Frequency of Halal logistics articles in Scopus database.
Source: Scopus.

This finding reflects the increasing interest in research related to this area. This is also supported by the escalating demand for Halal products by Muslim consumers and interest on behalf of logistics providers in ensuring the integrity of Halal products (Aziz and Zailani, 2016). Notwithstanding that, the market size of Halal products is also getting bigger across the globe. Based on a market analysis report published by Grand View Research in December 2020 suggests that the worldwide Halal logistics market size will develop at a compound annual growth rate of 8.4% for the period of 2020–2027.

The second analysis was on evaluating the publication source. The top ten journals that published articles for Halal logistics were *Journal of Islamic Marketing, International Journal of Supply Chain Management, British Food Journal, IOP Conference Series Materials Science and Engineering, ACM International Conference Proceeding Series, IEEE International Conference on Industrial Engineering and Engineering Management, Journal of Critical Reviews, Asian Social Science, Journal of Food Products Marketing* and *Pertanika Journal of Social Sciences and Humanities*. The results displayed in Figure 4.2 show that the *Journal of Islamic Marketing* has published the largest number of articles on Halal logistics. This is appropriate with the aims of that journal to cover Islamic marketing research. Other publication sources also have provided the opportunity for researchers to explore a new path in the marketing research field. This signals a positive acceptance of Halal logistics research among publishers.

The third analysis was identifying the top ten countries that researched the Halal logistics field. The result is depicted in Figure 4.3. The outcome shows that the number of journals on Halal logistics by Malaysian researchers is far ahead compared to other countries. It shows that Malaysia has produced many researchers in Halal logistics. This is sustained by Malaysia's reputation for Halal logistics providers in the ASEAN market. Notwithstanding that, continuous support by the Malaysian government on Halal logistics through education funding or grants reinforces the research activities this area. It encourages the researchers to conduct an in-depth study that is able to produce high-quality Halal logistics professionals.

The fourth analysis was on the theories applied by previous researchers in conducting Halal logistics research. By evaluating the content analysis of the published articles on Halal logistics, the results show that there are limited theories applied in this area. The most prominent theories are Diffusion on Innovation (DOI) Theory, Technology Acceptance Model (TAM), Resource-Based View (RBV), Institutional Theory, Theory of Planned Behaviour (TPB) Theory of Reasoned Action (TRA) and Technology–Organization–Environment (TOE). The results are presented in Table 4.2.

DOI and TAM were applied by Yunan et al. (2020) as an underlying theory in exploring the causes for maintaining the Halal integrity intention in Malaysia's food industry. They have selected relative advantage, ease of use, compatibility as the factors that contributed to the intention in maintaining Halal integrity. TAM has been used widely as a primary theory to examine the acceptance of new technology containing two specific beliefs; perceived ease of use and perceived

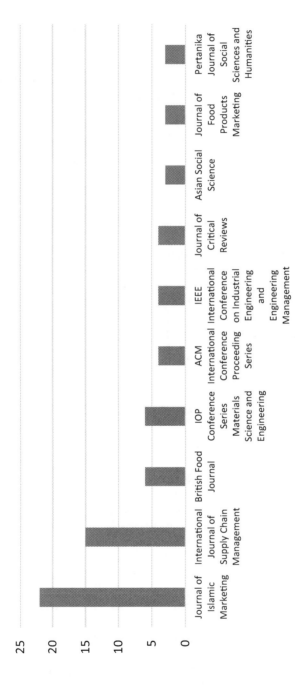

Figure 4.2 Number of Halal logistics articles in top ten journals.
Source: Scopus.

Theories used in Halal logistics studies 51

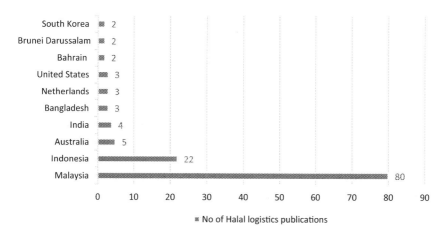

Figure 4.3 Number of Halal logistics publication by country.
Source: Scopus.

Table 4.2 Theories applied in Halal logistics research

Theories applied	Location	Research titles
Diffusion of Innovation Theory	Malaysia	Determinant factors towards the adoption of Halal logistics services among Malaysian Halal small medium enterprises (SMEs) (Husny et al., 2018)
Diffusion of Innovation Theory	Malaysia	Factors behind third-party logistics providers' readiness towards Halal logistics (Tarmizi et al., 2014)
Diffusion of Innovation Theory	Malaysia	Factors that influence the intention to adopt Halal logistics services among Malaysian SMEs: formation of hypotheses and research model (Husny et al., 2016)
Diffusion of Innovation Theory	Malaysia	Service innovation: Halal logistics intention adoption model (Hamid et al., 2017)
Diffusion of Innovation Theory and Technology Acceptance Model	Malaysia	Safeguarding Halal integrity through Halal logistics adoption: a case of food manufacturers (Yunan et al., 2020)
Resource-Based View	Indonesia	Determinants on the obtainment of Halal certification among small firms (Rafiki, 2014)
Resource-Based View	Malaysia	Assessing Halal logistics competence: an Islamic based and resource-based view (Karia et al., 2015)

(*continued*)

Table 4.2 Cont.

Theories applied	Location	Research titles
Resource-Based View	Malaysia	Developing Halal logistics framework: an innovation approach (Karia and Asaari, 2020)
Resource-Based View	Malaysia	The influence of knowledge, attitude and sensitivity to government policies in Halal certification process on organizational performance (Othman et al., 2017)
Resource-Based View and Institutional Theory	Korea	Optimal design for the Halal food logistics network (Kwag and Ko, 2019)
Theory of Planned Behaviour	Malaysia	Applying the Theory of the Planned Behavior on Halal logistics services adoption among food & beverages small and medium enterprises (Mahidin et al., 2019)
Theory of Planned Behaviour	Thailand	Factors influencing the purchase intention of Halal packaged food in Thailand (Syukur and Nimsai, 2017)
Theory of Planned Behaviour and Marketing Mix	Malaysia	The role of firm size and customer orientation on Halal transportation adoption (Yunan et al., 2019)
Theory of Planned Behaviour and Theory of Reasoned Action	Malaysia	Factors influencing manufacturers in implementing Halal logistics (Ustadia et al., 2019)
Technology–Environment–Organization Framework	Malaysia	Modelling the adoption of halal warehousing services among Halal pharmaceutical and cosmetic manufacturers (Ngah et al., 2019)
Technology–Environment–Organization Framework	Malaysia	The role of firm size and customer orientation on Halal transportation adoption (Yunan et al., 2019)

usefulness. The findings of TAM application in this study are in line with the result from research conducted by Huang et al. (2020) who researched the acceptance of open-source learning platform using TAM. On top of that, DOI has been used by Husny et al. (2017) in their research to investigate the factors to adopt Halal logistics among small and medium enterprises. Identically, Tarmizi et al. (2014), adopted DOI in their study to evaluate the readiness of third-party logistics providers in implementing Halal logistics. In essence, DOI has been conceptualized as the fundamental theory in executing a new phenomenon; that is, Halal logistics. Other theories that have been applied in the Halal logistics research field are RBV and Institutional Theory, as used by Kwag and Ko (2019). The authors used RBV and Institutional Theory to explain how Halal certificates became the resource, legitimacy and social pressure that may help the Halal logistics business to flourish.

From another perspective, Karia et al. (2015) have created a resource-based Halal logistics framework inspired by RBV and ascertain five elements of Halal logistics in their framework. Coupled with that Karia, and Asaari (2020) also used RBV in their recent research on the Halal logistics competency framework. The ideology of RBV is the optimum utilization of resources including tangible and intangible resources and thereafter, transformation of it into a competitive advantage and better firm performance (Almarri and Gardiner, 2014). On the other hand, TPB and TRA have been employed by Mahidin et al. (2019), and Ustadia et al. (2019) in supporting their argument that attitudes, subjective norms, perceived behaviour control, Halal integrity, knowledge and perceived usefulness will foster the intention to adopt Halal logistics services and Halal transportation services in Malaysia. In this regard, the components of TPB and TRA have been visualized as the causes fostering the intention to adopt Halal logistics.

The finding of TPB application is also supported by other Halal research fields as demonstrated by Alam and Sayuti (2011) in purchasing Halal food, Weng et al. (2017) in Halal meat purchasing behaviour and Khalek and Ismail (2015) in Halal food consumption. Apart from the above, TOE has been applied by Ngah et al. (2019) in examining the causes for using Halal warehousing services among pharmaceutical and cosmetics producers. Comparatively, the components of TOE have been employed in the research on the acceptance of HL by adding the firm magnitude and customer orientation as the predictors in their proposed framework (Yunan et al., 2019). In a nutshell, the previous studies embrace Halal logistics as an emerging business. DOI, TAM and TPB become the theoretical frameworks to determine the notion in the adoption of Halal logistics while RBV and TOE are used to explain the resources to adopt Halal logistics.

Halal supply chain

The first analysis for the Halal supply chain is on determining its publication trend. Based on the keywords "Halal supply chain", 194 articles have been published for Halal supply chain in the Scopus database from 2008 to 2020. The highest number of publications is in 2020 with 50 articles being published. The results can be viewed in Figure 4.4. Figure 4.4 shows an increasing trend of the research on the Halal supply chain from 2008 to 2020. It implies the increasing attention on the research related to the HSC as resulted from the globalization of production that exposes the goods to risks of contamination with the Haram product (Jaafar et al., 2016).

The second analysis is on evaluating the publication source for the Halal supply chain. The top ten journals that published articles related to the HSC are *International Journal of Supply Chain Management*, *Journal of Islamic Marketing*, *IOP Conference Series Materials Science and Engineering*, *British Food Journal*, *ACM International Conference Proceeding Series*, *Food Research*, *IEEE International Conference on Industrial Engineering and Engineering Management*, *International Business Management*, *International Food Research Journal* and *Journal of Critical Reviews*. The outcomes are presented in Figure 4.5.

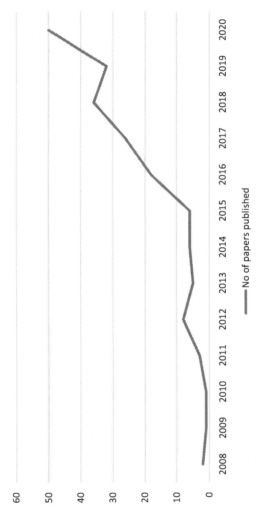

Figure 4.4 Frequency of Halal supply chain articles in Scopus database.
Source: Scopus.

Theories used in Halal logistics studies 55

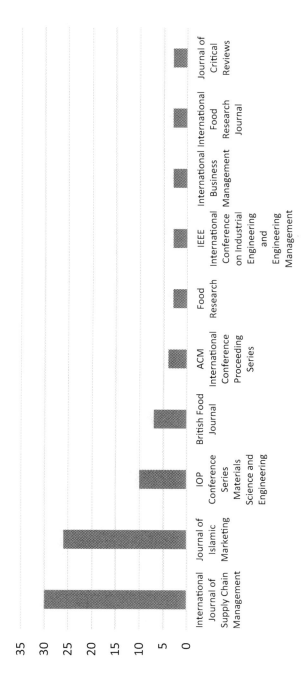

Figure 4.5 Number of Halal supply chain articles in top ten journals.
Source: Scopus.

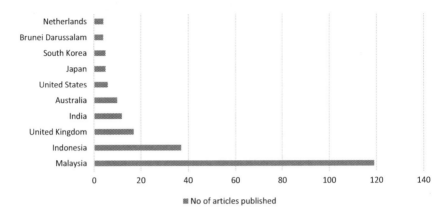

Figure 4.6 Number of Halal supply chain publications by country.
Source: Scopus.

The highest number of articles on the HSC is published by the *International Journal of Supply Chain Management* which is 30. The journal has enhanced the opportunity to explore and publish the articles within the scope of the supply chain including the Halal perspective. It offers the theoretical and practical prospect for the Halal supply chain.

Further analysis was conducted on the countries that published articles related to the Halal supply chain. The result is shown in Figure 4.6. The findings reveal that Malaysia has the highest number of articles published on the Halal supply chain with 119 articles. The research in this area is supported by the Malaysian government and various programmes that develop knowledge and consideration of the Halal view. Thorough research has been performed to stimulate Malaysia to be a Halal hub in a global marketplace and various initiatives have been implemented to comply with the Shariah law.

Finally, content analysis has been performed to determine the theories that have been applied in Halal supply chain researches. The results are presented in Table 4.3. In research conducted by Hew et al. (2020), DOI and Institutional Theory have been utilized as the theoretical framework. The researchers idealized the three components of Institutional Theory isomorphism, namely coercive isomorphism, mimetic isomorphism and normative isomorphism will lead to perceived desirability and subsequently resulted in the intention to participate in blockchain Halal traceability-based systems. They conceptualized that the components of DOI that include complexity, comparability and relative advantage will also lead to the intention to participate in blockchain Halal-based systems. In other research, Azmi et al. (2018) used DOI theory and the Technology–Organization–Environment (TOE) Framework to express the individuals' decision on the adoption of Halal supply.

Table 4.3 Theories applied in Halal supply chain research

Theories applied	Location	Research titles
Adaptive Structuration Theory	Malaysia	The impact of external integration on Halal food integrity (Tan et al., 2017)
Agency Theory	Malaysia	The mediating impact of Halal logistics on supply chain resilience: an agency perspective (Aigbogun et al., 2016)
Diffusion of Innovation Theory and Technological-Organizational-Environmental Framework.	Malaysia	The adoption of Halal food supply chain towards the performance of food manufacturing in Malaysia (Azmi et al., 2018)
Theory of Planned Behaviour	Malaysia	Halal food supply chain knowledge and purchase intention (Yusoff et al., 2015)
Theory of Planned Behaviour	Malaysia	Willingness to pay for Halal transportation cost: the moderating effect of knowledge on the Theory of Planned Behavior (Ngah et al., 2020)

Generally, DOI was applied to determine how people adapt to a new idea or concept over some time. Specifically, in the context of HSC research, the application of DOI denotes the spread of a new business approach into a wider market that connected one product to another product and one business to another business. Coupled with DOI, Azmi et al. (2018) used TOE as the basic philosophy to explain the adoption factors from the aspect of technology, organization and environment. In their study they suggested compatibility as one of the technological aspects, management support as an organizational aspect, and pressure from consumer and competitors as environment aspect. Their findings reveal that the elements in TOE are able to improve the Halal manufacturers' performance.

From another perspective, Yusoff et al. (2015) employed TPB by applying the TPB's components of attitude, subjective norm and perceived behaviour control to the knowledge of Halal supply chain dimensions. The findings from their study express that knowledge in the Halal supply chain is crucial in influencing the consumer to purchase Halal food. This is due to the linkage in the process to produce Halal food that should comply with the Halal-Toyyiban conditions and required appropriate knowledge to handle it. Other than that, Agency Theory also has been utilized as the fundamental theory in Halal supply chain study. Aigbogun et al. (2016) made use of Agency Theory to explain the multi-principal and agent relationship. In Agency Theory, the relationship between principal and agents should be monitored to align the interest of all parties and to manage the potential risks exposed to all actors. Previous research also shows that Adaptive Saturation Theory (AST) is one of the theories applied in HSC research (Tan et al., 2017). The theory illustrates the relationship between the businesses and the ability of the actors in the chain to adopt the Halal supply chain businesses.

AST has been viewed as the interaction between group and organization in saturation process to adapt to the new technology. In essence, the findings imply that DOI, Institutional Theory, TPB, Agency Theory and AST have been used by the previous researchers in explaining the widespread of the HSC, institutional forces to adopt HSC, the factors fostering the adoption of the HSC, monitoring the interest of various parties in HSC and the saturation process among and group and business in the Halal supply chain.

Conclusion

This chapter attempted with available literature to explore the new research areas of HL and HSC. This chapter reported an overview of the distribution of HL and HSC. A set of 122 articles published on Halal logistics and 119 articles published on Halal supply chain research were selected by searching the Scopus database using predefined keywords. Article titles and contents were analysed, and those that were irrelevant were removed to safeguard the validity of the analysis. The established publication source, location of the research by country and theories applied in the previous researches have been isolated to allow for an analytical approach. Based on the findings, it can be concluded that the number of publications on HL and HSC has shown an upward trend for the past 20 years. The number of highest publications for Halal logistics is from the *Journal of Islamic Marketing* while the number of highest publications for research in the Halal supply chain is from the *International Journal of Supply Management*. Parallel with the initiative to become the Halal hub country and supported by many grants for the Halal research field, Malaysia has produced the greatest number of publications in both Halal logistics and Halal supply chain studies. This study further concluded that DOI, RBV, TOE, TAM, TPB, Institutional Theory, Agency Theory and AST are the theories that have been applied in various aspects of investigation in HL and HSC. These results yield especially the relevant theories applied in the literature, which could be used as a benchmark for scholars to obtain further insights relating to the emerging research areas in Halal logistics and Halal supply chain.

Research implications

The potential of the Muslim market is huge. Hence, the review of articles carried out in this chapter brings major implications to scholars, practitioners as well as authorities.

Implications for scholars

The coverage of Scopus academic databases was focused, and it gave the top related specialized journals concentrating on HL and HSC as *Supply Chain Management – An International Journal*, *British Food Journal* and *Journal of Islamic Marketing*. Besides DOI, Institutional Theory, TOE Framework, TPB and TRA, other theories found to be applied in these HL and HSC studies include Fuzzy Logic Theory, Grounded Theory, Human Capital Theory, RBV, Supply Chain Theory and TAM. This chapter adds to the increasing collection of HL and HSC studies. This enriches the Halal research disciplines in the Halal economy. Scholars interested in these research areas should search and study publications and theories used in these journals.

Implications for practitioners

With the background of a relatively high growth rate of the Muslim population, this is a market that practitioners cannot ignore. Products conforming to Halal requirements will facilitate entrance into the expanding Muslim market. The findings of this review could be referenced by managers for strategic policy-making and effective implementation of HL and HSC. The chapter will also provide firms with the bright prospects of the Halal industry's global market. Having growing promotion of the Halal industry, this chapter encourages Halal practices and invites more firms to undertake HL and HSC.

Implications for authorities/public sectors

Scholars from Malaysia have published the highest number of publications both in HL and HSC studies, followed by Indonesia, the largest Muslim country in the world. It is understood that the Department of Islamic Development Malaysia is recognized as one of the main Halal certification bodies worldwide.

Limitations and recommendations

There are a few limitations in this study. First, the current study only focuses on the Scopus database in reviewing the papers on HL and HSC. It is suggested that future studies may also include coverage of article publications in journals listed in Web of Science (WoS) on top of the Scopus database. The review from the lens of WoS will be more comprehensive and inclusive. Second, the current study only reviews the aspect of a trend of publication, publication sources, research location and theories applied in the HL and HSC. Future researchers may review other aspects such as the components in HL and HSC and methodology that have been applied. This chapter shows that the perception of the Muslim consumer is important to address in the Halal industry, and hence, more studies are required on HL and HSC research. This chapter provides the deepening of information through the use of Halal concept into logistics and supply chain practices.

References

Aigbogun, O., Ghazali, Z. and Razali, R. (2016). The mediating impact of Halal logistics on supply chain resilience: an agency perspective. *International Review of Management and Marketing*, 6(4S), pp. 209–216.

Alam, S. S. and Sayuti, N. M. (2011). Applying the Theory of Planned Behavior (TPB) in Halal food purchasing. *International Journal of Commerce and Management*, 21(1), pp. 8–20.

Almarri, K. and Gardiner, P. (2014). Application of resource-based view to project management research: supporters and opponents. *Procedia-Social and Behavioral Sciences*, 119, pp. 437–445.

Antonio, M. S., Rusydiana, A., Laila, N., Hidayat, Y. R. and Marlina, L. (2020). Halal value chain: a bibliometric review using R. *Library Philosophy and Practice*. https://digitalcommons.unl.edu/libphilprac/4606

Aziz, A. A. and Zailani, S. (2016). Halal logistics: the role of ports, issues and challenges. In D. S. Mutum, M. M. Butt and M. Rashid (Eds.), *Advances in Islamic Finance, Marketing, and Management*. Bingley: Emerald Group Publishing Limited, pp. 309–321.

Azmi, F., Abdullah, A., Bakri, M., Musa, H. and Jayakrishnan, M. (2018). The adoption of Halal food supply chain towards the performance of food manufacturing in Malaysia. *Management Science Letters*, 8(7), pp. 755–766.

Haleem, A, Imran, M. K., Shahbaz, K. and Jami, A. R. (2020). Research status in Halal: a review and bibliometric analysis. *Modern Supply Chain Research and Applications*, 2(1), pp. 23–41.

Hamid, Z. J. M. H., Hussien, M. Z. S. M. and Tan, M. I. I. (2017). Service innovation: Halal logistics intention adoption model. *International Journal of Supply Chain Management*, 6(1).

Hew, J. J., Wong, L. W., Tan, G. W. H., Ooi, K. B. and Lin, B. (2020). The blockchain-based Halal traceability systems: a hype or reality? *Supply Chain Management: An International Journal*, 25(6), pp. 863–879.

Huang, C. Y., Wang, H. Y., Yang, C. L. and Shiau, S. J. (2020). A derivation of factors influencing the diffusion and adoption of an open source learning platform. *Sustainability*, 12(18), 7532.

Husny, Z. J. M., Hussein, M. Z. S. M. and Tan, M. I. I. (2016). Factors that influence the intention to adopt Halal logistics services among Malaysian SMEs: formation of hypotheses and research model. *Asian Social Science*, 7(12).

Husny, Z. J. M., Hussein, M. Z. S. M. and Tan, M. I. I. (2017). Service innovation: Halal logistics intention adoption model. *International Journal of Supply Chain Management*, 6(1), pp. 146-154.

Husny, Z. J. M., Hussein, M. Z. S. M. and Tan, M. I. I. (2018). Determinant factors towards the adoption of Halal logistics services among Malaysian Halal small medium enterprises (SMEs). *Research Journal of Applied Sciences*, 8(11), pp. 608–616.

Indarti, N., Lukito-Budi, A. S. and Islam, A. M. (2020). A systematic review of Halal supply chain research: to where shall we go? *Journal of Islamic Marketing*. doi 10.1108/JIMA-05-2020-0161

Jaafar H. S., Faisol N., Rahman F. A. and Muhammad A. (2016) Halal logistics versus Halal supply chain: a preliminary insight. In S. A. Manan, F. A. Rahman and M. Sahri (Eds.), *Contemporary Issues and Development in the Global Halal Industry*. Singapore: Springer, pp. 579–588.

Karia, N. and Asaari, M. H. A. H. (2020). Developing Halal logistics framework: an innovation approach. In K. S. Soliman (Ed.), *Vision 2020: Sustainable Growth, Economic Development and Global Competitiveness*. Kula Lumpur: IBIMA, pp. 328–334.

Karia, N., Asaari, M. H. A. H., Mohamad, N. and Kamaruddin, S. (2015). Assessing Halal logistics competence: an Islamic-based and resource-based view. In *2015 International*

Conference on *Industrial Engineering and Operations Management (IEOM)*. IEEE, pp. 1–6.

Khalek, A. A. and Ismail, S. H. S. (2015). Why are we eating Halal? Using the Theory of Planned Behavior in predicting Halal food consumption among Generation Y in Malaysia. *International Journal of Social Science and Humanity*, 5(7), pp. 608–612.

Kwag, S. I. and Ko, Y. D. (2019). Optimal design for the Halal food logistics network. *Transportation Research Part E: Logistics and Transportation Review*, 128, pp. 212–228.

Lestari, Y. D., Susanto, J. M., Simatupang, T. M. and Yudoko, G. (2018). Intention towards Halal logistics: a case study of Indonesian consumers. *Journal for Global Business Advancement*, 11(1), pp. 22–40.

Mahidin, N., Mustafar, M., Elias, E. M. and Bakar, A. S. (2019). Applying the Theory of the Planned Behavior on Halal logistics services adoption among food & beverages small and medium enterprises. *International Journal of Supply Chain Management (IJSCM)*, 8(4), pp. 1039–1046.

Masudin, I. Fernanda, F. W. and Widayat, W. (2018). Halal logistics performance and customer loyalty: from the literature review to a conceptual framework. *International journal of Technology*, 5, pp. 1072–1084.

McElwee, G., Smith, R. and Lever, J. (2017). Illegal activity in the UK Halal (sheep) supply chain: towards greater understanding. *Food Policy*, 69, pp. 166–175.

Mohamed, Y. H., Rahim, A. R. A., Ma'ram, A. and Hamza, M. G. (2016). Halal traceability in enhancing Halal integrity for food industry in Malaysia – a review. *International Research Journal of Engineering and Technology (IRJET)*, 3(3), pp. 68–74.

Mongeon, P. and Paul-Hus, A. (2016). The journal coverage of Web of Science and Scopus: a comparative analysis. *Scientometrics*, 106(1), pp. 213–228.

Ngah, A. H., Ramayah, T., Aziz, N. A., Ali, H. and Khan, M. I. (2019). Modelling the adoption of Halal warehousing services among Halal pharmaceutical and cosmetic manufacturers. *Journal of Sustainability Science and Management*, 14(6), pp. 103–116.

Ngah, A. H., Jeevan, J., Salleh, N. H. M. and Tae, T. (2020). Willingness to pay for Halal transportation cost: the moderating effect of knowledge on the Theory of Planned Behavior. *Journal of Environmental Treatment Techniques*, 8(1), pp. 13–22.

Omar, W. M. W., Rahman, S. and Jie, F. (2012). Halal food chain management: a systematic review of literature and future research directions. *13th ANZAM Operations, Supply Chain and Services Management Symposium*. Melbourne: RMIT University.

Othman, B., Shaarani, S. M. and Bahron, A. (2017). The influence of knowledge, attitude and sensitivity to government policies in Halal certification process on organizational performance. *Journal of Islamic Marketing*, 8(2).

Pew Research Centre (2019). *The Countries with the 10 Largest Christian Populations and the 10 Largest Muslim Populations*. Retrieved from: www.pewresearch.org/fact-tank/2019/04/01/the-countries-with-the-10-largest-christian-populations-and-the-10-largest-muslim-populations/ (accessed 15 August 2021).

Qurtubi and Kusrini, E. (2018). Research in Halal logistics and Halal supply chain: issue and area development. *MATEC Web of Conferences*, 154, 01096.

Radzman, N. W. S., Muhammad, A., Mohamad, S. and Jaafar, H. S. (2016). Halal transportation providers for supply chain management in Halal industry: a review. *Journal of Hospitality and Networks*, 1, pp. 1–12.

Rafiki, A. (2014). Determinants on the obtainment of Halal certification among small firms. *World Applied Sciences Journal*, 32(1), pp. 47–55.

Rafiki, A. (2016). The human capital and the obtainment of Halal certification. *Journal of Islamic Marketing*, 7(2), pp. 134–147.

Randeree, K. (2019). Challenges in Halal food ecosystems: the case of the United Arab Emirates. *British Food Journal*, 121(5), pp. 1154–1167.

Rejeb, A., Rejeb, K., Zailani, S., Treiblmaier, H. and Hand, K. J. (2021). Integrating the Internet of Things in the Halal food supply chain: a systematic literature review and research agenda. *Internet of Things*, 13, 100361.

Saifudin, A. M., Zainuddin, N., Elias, E. M., Samsuddin, S. N. F. and Osman, A. A. (2018). Reviewing the contributors towards the performance of the new Islamic supply chain model in Malaysia using robust econometric regression *International Supply Chain Management*, 7(4), pp. 151–157.

Shahbaz, K., Haleem, A., Imran, M. K., Abidi, M. H., and Al-Ahmari, A. R. (2018). Implementing traceability systems in specific supply chain management (SCM) through critical success factors (CSFs). *Sustainability*, 10, 204.

Shahbaz, K., Imran, M. K. and Haleem, A. (2019). Evaluation of barriers in the adoption of Halal certification: a Fuzzy DEMATEL Approach. *Journal of Modelling in Management*, 14(1), pp. 153–174.

Syukur, M. and Nimsai, S. (2017). Factors influencing the purchase intention of Halal packaged food in Thailand. *International Journal of Supply Chain Management*, 7(4).

Talib, M. S. A., Hamid, A. B. A. and Zulfakar, M. H. (2015). Halal supply chain critical success factors: a literature review, *Journal of Islamic Marketing*, 6(1), pp. 44–71.

Talib, M. S. A., Pang, L. L. and Ngah, A. H. (2020). The role of government in promoting Halal logistics: a systematic literature review. *Journal of Islamic Marketing*. doi: 10.1108/JIMA-05-2020-0124

Tan, K. H., Ali, M. H., Makhbul, Z. M. and Ismail, A. (2017). The impact of external integration on Halal food integrity. *Supply Chain Management*, 22(2), pp. 186–199.

Tarmizi, H. A., Kamarulzaman, N. H. and Latiff, I. A. (2014). Factors behind third-party logistics providers' readiness towards Halal logistics. *International Journal of Supply Chain Management*, 3(2), pp. 53–62.

Tieman, M. and Ghazali, C. (2014). Halal control activities and assurance activities in halal food logistics. *Procedia – Social and Behavioural Sciences*, 121, pp. 44–57.

Ustadia, M. N., Rasib, R. Z. R. M. and Osmanc, S. (2019). Factors influencing manufacturers in implementing Halal logistics. *International Journal of Innovation, Creativity and Change*, 10(8), pp. 43–54.

Wahyuni, H. C., Vananvy, I. and Ciptomulyono, U. (2018). Identifying risk event in Indonesian fresh meat supply chain. *IOP Conference Series Materials Science and Engineering*, 337(1), 012031.

Weng, T. F., Khatibi, A. and Azam, S. F. (2017). Applying the Theory of Planned Behavior (TPB) in green & halal chicken meat purchasing behavior of Malaysian consumers. *Proceeding International Conference on Humanities, Language, Culture & Business, (2nd ICoHLCB)*. Cameron Highlands Pahang, 22–23 April 2017, pp. 20–35.

Yunan, Y. S. M., Ali, M. H. and Alam, S. S. (2019). The role of firm size and customer orientation on Halal transportation adoption. *International Journal of Supply Chain Management*, 8(2), pp. 1028–1034.

Yunan, Y. S. M., Ali, M. H. and Alam, S. S. (2020). Safeguarding Halal integrity through Halal logistics adoption: a case of food manufacturers. *Institutions and Economies*, 12(3), pp. 19–41.

Yusoff, F. A. M., Yusof, R. N. R. and Hussin, S. R. (2015). Halal food supply chain knowledge and purchase intention. *International Journal of Economics & Management*, 9(S), pp. 155–172.

Zailani, S., Arrifin, Z., Wahid, N. A., Othman, R. and Fernando, Y. (2010). Halal traceability and Halal tracking systems in strengthening Halal food supply chain for food industry in Malaysia: a review. *Journal of Food Technology*. 8(3), pp. 74–81.

Zawya (2016). *State of the Global Islamic Economy Report 2016/17*. Retrieved from: www.zawya.com/mena/en/ifg-publications/280916063519J/ (accessed 24 November 2021).

Zulfakar, M. H., Jie, F. and Chan, C. (2012). Halal food supply chain integrity: from a literature review to a conceptual framework. *10th ANZAM Operations, Supply Chain and Services Management Symposium*, Melbourne.

Part II
Technology applications and sustainability

5 Traceability technology in Halal logistics and supply chain
Critical success factors

Zuhra Junaida Binti Ir Mohamad Husny Hamid and Mohd Iskandar bin Illyas Tan

Introduction

In recent decades, increasing attention has been paid to Halal products and services by various countries across the globe in realization that the Halal industry provides a potential source of national income. This attention had led to the emergence of Halal logistics and supply chain management. This concept is known as Halalan Toyyiban. It focuses on the management of the Halal network to maintain the Halal product integrity from raw material to the point of purchase by consumers (Tieman et al., 2012). The goal of Halal logistics and supply chain is to safeguard the Halal integrity. This includes the physical activities such as transporting and storing, which require a set of data for communication and management among successive links, upstream and downstream along the product supply chain (Kamaruddin et al., 2012). This data enables tracing and tracking of Halal products to guarantee that no risk of cross-contamination occurs along the supply chain (Jaafar et al., 2013). This must tally with the Muslim consumers' expectations and must not build unnecessary costs for customers and industry (Tieman, 2011).

Any kind of activity involved throughout the supply chain, such as product handling, storing, warehousing and distributing, should comply to Shariah law. The concept of Halalan Toyyiban alongside the supply chain starts from sourcing the raw material and ends at the point of consumers' consumption. In each activity all aspects of Halal and Toyyiban must be considered (everything should be Halal and Toyyiban) to guarantee the end consumer attains the expected quality and status of Halal products as assured. Halal logistics is the part of Halal supply chain where these standards are upheld. Because of this, and taking into consideration the increase in Halal product demand, the fields of Halal logistics and supply chain are vitally important to support the global Halal market.

The Malaysian government in particular began implementing Halal regulation back in the 1960s. In the beginning, the regulation was created to protect the interests and concerns of the Muslim people, who represent the majority of the Malaysian population. Looking at the increasing demand for Halal products worldwide, the Malaysian government took a step further in becoming the

DOI: 10.4324/9781003223719-8

Halal hub for the region as well as the world. In being the world Halal hub, Malaysia has to also be at the forefront for Halal logistics and supply chain, where a proper control can be placed to avoid the Halal products' integrity from being compromised. This can be done by having the control of the whole process, from sourcing of raw material, through production, storage, transportation and monitoring the suppliers' uses of certain products. The government views the Halal logistics and supply chain as vital and their implementation as necessary in the Halal control system.

A Halal trace and tracking system has emerged as profitable field in the world Halal market. A traceability and tracking system that is effective is vital to alleviate the risks associated with Halal that could potentially upset the global trade of Halal products. This system serves as an instrument of communication which makes the required information available throughout the supply chain.

The main problems regarding Halal product traceability were the unethical acts of Halal product manufacturers who, intentionally or unintentionally, failed to comply with the Malaysia Halal authority's regulation. One of the most recent scandals that became the talk of the town was a meat cartel that had been aggressively smuggling Haram or non-Halal certified meat into Malaysia which was later sold as Halal certified beef (Amir, 2020). This caused such a degree of turmoil that Malaysian Muslim consumers began to question the effectiveness of the Halal product traceability system in Malaysia. Another huge issue on Halal integrity that shocked the country was the discovery of two Cadbury chocolate products, Dairy Milk and Dairy Milk Hazelnut Roasted Almond, reported to contain porcine DNA after a random testing done by the Malaysian Ministry of Health on the product taken from the shelves in Perlis and Kedah (*Straits Times Asia*, 2014). This angered the Muslim community in Malaysia and resulted in a loss of trust for the product and consequently a loss of millions of ringgits by the company.

Halal integrity

Halal integrity does not only concern Halal and Haram food, but also the Halal status of the products' raw materials and these standards must not be breached at any stage in the process of reaching the end customer. In other words, there must be no cross-contamination with Haram products, substance or methods, and also with no wrong intentions (Soon et al., 2017). Halal integrity also implies that the product will still remain Halal starting upstream until downstream of the product supply chain. It will also be free from any process that potentially breaches the Halal status, whether intentionally or unintentionally. With current technology advancement in the food industry, a great deal of genetically modified food has been developed. Likewise, the production of food has become a complex process with many different stages, many changes of hands and travel from and to different geographical location before it is able to get to the final stage as a finished good.

Halal integrity is also the key properties and unique traits of a Halal product. In relation with others, Halal products are made concurring to the Islamic needs based on the concept of Halalan Toyyiban which, in accordance to Shariah laws, means a product is safe and high in quality. This concept obliges the products to comply with the critical components of Halal and wholesome (Toyyib), which represent high quality for human consumption (Mohamed et al., 2016). This is an Islamic holistic concept not only focusing on the physical characteristics of the product but also emphasizing the moral behaviour that is involved throughout the entire Halal product supply chain.

Traceability in Halal logistics and supply chain

According to the International Organization of Standardization (n.d.), ISO 12875:2011, clause 3.1, defines traceability as the ability to trace the history, application or location of that which is under consideration. The Codex Alimentarius defines traceability as the ability to follow the movement of a food through specified stages of production, processing and distribution (Food and Agriculture Organization, 2004). In Halal, the issue of traceability is most related to consumable product, and food integrity is comparable to product (food) safety issues. However, in Halal there is an additional requirement, which is compliance to Shariah/Islamic law.

According to Arienzo et al. (2008), food traceability insinuates an ability to track any food, animal feed, animal produced food or material that will be used at the point of consumption, across all phases of production, processing and distribution. Bahrudin et al. (2011) stated that traceability signifies the capability to locate records of origins and history of a food product from material genetics to the plate. This tracing includes identifying all related procedures and practices that will impact the product's life cycle. All of this information will be delivered and documented and made available to the customer or any other partakers in the product supply chain to view when needed. This view is supported by Meuwissen et al. (2003), who stated that traceability encourages transparency throughout the product supply chain, which decreases the risk of product recalls on top of liability claims towards the manufacturers or producers.

Therefore, Halal traceability is a system ensuring the physical separation of Halal products from non Halal products in transit to prevent cross-contamination, remove the possibility of human error and make certain that the transport system is in line with Muslim consumers' expectations (Tieman, 2011). It is also a form of communication and tracking instrument to make sure all required information is visible and accessible throughout the Halal product supply chain (Zailani et al., 2010). In other words, tracing aims to obtain the product history, for example, to identify the source or the point of cross-contamination (Meuwissen et al., 2003), whereas tracking is the capability to track the goods along the downstream of the supply chain as they are redistributed amongst business partners. It is clear that food is to maintained as safe and Halal in all conditions. Physical segregation from Haram substance is mandatory not only during procuring and preparation of the product but also during packaging, labelling, storing and transporting.

In the Malaysian perspective, the Department of Islamic Development Malaysia (Jabatan Kemajuan Islam Malaysia, JAKIM, n.d.a, n.d.b) is a federal government agency that administers all Islamic affairs for the country. In JAKIM there is a division known as Halal Management Division that responsible for conducting Halal certification in Malaysia together with the Islamic religious departments of the states (Jabatan Agama Islam Negeri, JAIN). This division has established procedures and guidelines for which all Halal applicants of Malaysian Halal certification are obliged to comply. Among those procedures and guidelines are the Manual Prosidur Pensijilan Halal Malaysia (MPPHM 2020) and the Malaysian Halal Management System (MHMS 2020) (JAKIM, n.d.a, n.d.b). According to MPPHM 2020, the organization shall be able to: describe the process of raw material retrieval, suppliers, customers and finished products; explain the work process exactly as practised in the field; and this must be recorded, documented and be able to be reviewed during the audit or monitoring of Malaysian Halal certification. In extension to this requirement, MHMS 2020 also stresses the need to establish Halal traceability in companies' Halal assurance systems (for medium-sized and above companies) or internal Halal control systems (for smaller companies). This requirement is mentioned in section 5(9) and section 6(3) respectively.

As regards ensuring the Halal control continues along the product supply chain, companies should also set up and employ a traceability system in their logistics services. The system should enable the identification of the inbound goods which is the processing stage by the immediate vendors and the delivery routes. This includes the containers used to carry goods and/or cargo. The containers should be explicitly identifiable, appropriately constructed and made from impermeable materials where required. They should also be well secured to avoid any mischievous or accidental adulteration to the product from handling activities during transportation of the goods.

Halal traceability should be developed with one aim, which is to improve the transparency of the Halal production chain. The increment on transparency may boost consumers' trust of the integrity of the Halal product. Consumers will have peace of mind if they able to acquire more information on the production processes and food safety controls. This would, among other things, increase the Halal level of the food and result in good information flow along the chain (Zailani et al., 2010).

Technology application in Halal logistics and supply chain traceability

In modern society, where technology is rapidly and constantly evolving, the application of technology in supply chain management is also changing at a brisk pace. As we know, supply chain management is the distribution network of raw materials, processed through different intermediaries and utilized by end-consumers. Traditionally, the supply chain pattern is more tolerant. This results in consequences such as non-transparency, possible intervention, loss, defects, etc. This situation has been detrimental to industry due to loss of trust from customer as a result of lack of information communicated.

It is very clear that the role of technology is extremely important to resolving this issue, particularly regarding the traceability of the product supply chain. This is also a major factor in the Halal industry. There are several technologies that are already available that can be adopted by industry. Some are already stable and mature while others are still in the early stage of implementation. Among the technology related to traceability are: barcode and QR codes, radio frequency identification (RFID), tracing and tracking systems and blockchain.

Barcodes and QR codes

According to Encyclopedia Britannica (n.d.), the information from a barcode is presented in the form of a printed series of parallel bars or lines of varying widths, which is read by an optical scanner that is a part of a computerized system. To scan the barcode, a handheld scanner or barcode pen is pointed at or moved across the barcodes, or the barcodes are moved towards or across a built-in scanner at, for example, checkout counters. This barcoding system was introduced back in the 1970s and today it has become an everyday part of regular business transactions. The foremost advantage of the barcode system is that it allows user to process detailed information while the barcode is being scanned, storing the needed information later for processing. The functions of barcodes and QR codes are similar. The main dissimilarity between barcodes and QR codes are the physical dimensions of the codes. Barcodes are scanned in a line, which means that data is limited to what can be placed within that stretch of stripes. Whereas for QR codes, another dimension is added for which information can be written and also scanned (Insight Works, 2021).

In logistics, this technology is highly used in inventory and asset traceability. Traceability in inventory represents the capability to track all stages of the production process as well as the components, from raw materials, ingredients, parts, work-in-progress products, packaging and other processes involved in producing the finished product. There are two methods of traceability: backward and forward. In backward traceability, the flow of tracing is from finished product back to the supplier. That is to say, tracing all ingredients back to their origin. Information is provided for each product regarding where each component came from, who the vendors are, when it was produced, when it was received, and many other considerations that vary depending on each business requirements. In forward traceability, the tracing flow is from finished product to customer or distributor. It means finding all products that contain a specific ingredient or part, locating these products and their status, such as in progress, stored in warehouse, sold to the customer, etc., so that obtaining a list of distributors or customers who are in possession of these products will be done easily. This can be adapted to Halal product tracking and tracing by adding information on critical ingredient and Halal certificates to the barcodes or QR codes.

Radio frequency identification (RFID)

In the early twentieth century, RFID technology has been well accepted for a well-designed traceability system on collecting data on humans or animals and tracking products (Sahin et al., 2002). RFID is a wireless technology that utilizes the transmitted radio signals to tag a product in order to track and trace its movement with no human involvement. It has outstanding abilities as compared to barcodes and it is able to provide many benefits to supply chain activities, such as reductions in shortages, efficiency in material handling, increases in product availability and improvement in asset management (Li and Visich, 2006; Angeles, 2005; Taghaboni-Dutta and Velthouse, 2006). To date, RFID has been applied in many industry applications such as retail, logistics, healthcare, data management and many more. Using RFID to track and monitor goods as they travel along the supply chain can potentially be used in Halal product supply chain control.

In logistics, Ngai et al. (2007), stated that the development of an RFID system when combined with mobile commerce in a container yard, will be capable of, first, keeping track of stackers' and containers' locations; second, providing better transparency of operation data; and third, enhancing the monitoring processes. Shi et al. (2009) concurred that RFID is the great technology for tracking containers. It is able to track the operation, prevent loss due to theft and damage of the containers, and increase business revenue as well as promote efficiency.

Tracing and tracking system

The basic technology behind a tracing and tracking system is quite simple. When a tracked product arrives at a predefined location in the logistics network, its arrival is noted and a message sent to a tracking database (Kärkkäinen et al., 2003; Loebbecke and Powell, 1998; Tausz, 1994). The message received comprises three basic pieces of information on products or shipments, which are: predefined identity, location and arrival time (Stefansson and Tilanus, 2001). There may also be other related information on the shipments, such as the item's quality and quantity and its previous and next distribution points.

In order to implement the tracking and tracing system, the shipped item or product needs to codified based on its particular functionality in the logistics network, such as transportation tracking, item storage and recall, products or product sorting, work in progress tracking, etc. Codifying the product is to ensure easy facilitation during data exchange between the business partners within the supply chain (Shamsuzzoha and Helo, 2011).

In this tracing and tracking system, software, coding equipment and a scanner are needed for the system to work. The current obtainable technologies for tracking and tracing include a barcode, RFID, magnetic strip, voice and vision systems, optical character recognition and biometrics. Tracking information collected from scanners is centralized to the tracking service provider. This information will be interfaced or integrated with the tracking system and able to be accessed by customers. This system can be used to support Halal product traceability by adding additional information on Halal product status at the coding stage. This information is crucial to ensure the status of the Halal product is maintained while it is being distributed. Some concerns in the matter of container sharing in the case of less than container load (both Halal and non Halal product in the same container) are: history of each vendor, history of container up-keeping, and most significantly the allocation of space between Halal and non-Halal product in same container as means of segregation. This is to avoid the risk of contamination, in order to prevent the integrity of Halal products from being compromised. With this information, immediate action will be able to be taken whenever the Halal status of the products is contaminated. For example, data on the ritual cleansing (Samak services) of the container would improve the information flow between supplier and customer (Husny et al., 2012).

Blockchain

Blockchain is another technology that can assist the Halal industry in terms of providing traceability in the supply chain. This technology provides tamper-proof data with strong authentication where the information about all the products is encrypted. This cryptography-based record-keeping system can be utilized to make sure the integrity of the global Halal food and its safety in the distribution chain is upheld. If implemented well, the Halal authority can issue Halal certificates with blockchain technology that can include production and distribution records from Halal product producers or manufactures. Blockchained Halal certificates could not be falsified without leaving a trail of evidence that allows Halal product producers and Halal regulators to promptly trace products back to their source, allowing for immediate product recall and removal in the case of Halal violation or fraud (Tan and Husny, 2020). The blockchain technology is integrated with the Internet of Things to provide the increased transparency and efficiency in supply chain.

The critical success factors for Halal logistics and supply chain traceability technology application

According to Daniel (1961), management approaches must be aligned with factors that are significant to the success of the organization. This view is similar to Digman (1990), who stated that critical success factors (CSFs) are the areas where things must go well in order for a business to flourish. Therefore, to ensure a higher chance of success in implementation of any system or technology, identifying the CSFs is crucial. In the Halal industry, safeguarding the integrity of Halal through the traceability system is obligatory throughout the supply chain. Nevertheless, employment of an effective Halal traceability system is complicated. CSFs of the implementation of traceability systems could be very useful to reduce, if not overcome the complexities.

Table 5.1 The CSFs selected by respondents

No	Critical success factors	Percentage
1	Top management support and commitment	100
2	Islamic values and monitoring practices (Halal compliance)	88
3	Clear vision, goal and objectives	88
4	Project management	75
5	Education on new business process, training, knowledge transfer	63
6	Careful change management	63
7	Communication among the implementation team members	63
8	Vendors and customer partnership	63
9	Business process reengineering	50
10	Date exchange and information quality	50
11	Implementation strategies and process	50
12	IT infrastructure and technologies	50
13	Project team composition, skills and teamwork	50

Source: Marjudi et al., 2017.

According to Marjudi et al. (2017), as shown in Table 5.1, the top ten most required CSFs for Halal SCM technology implementation, listed starting from the highest rank are: top management support and commitment, Islamic values and monitoring practices (Halal compliance), clear vision, goals and objectives, project management, education on new business process, training, knowledge transfer, careful change management, communication among the implementation team members, vendors and customer partnership, business process reengineering and data exchange and information quality.

Marjudi et al. (2017) also stated that top management support and commitment is the most critical factor for the success of technology or system implementation in an organization. Azam (2016) support that finding by stating that top management of a leading manufacturing industry has recognized traceability systems as an instrument to conform with law and regulation and to obtain consumer trust in Halal products or services. This also applicable to smaller companies like Halal SMEs. Second in rank is awareness of Islamic values and monitoring practices. This supports statement by Al-Qaradawi (1993), as Shariah practices are required to be fully understand by the product participants; as for Muslims Halal is part of the way of life. If a company or organization fully understands and applies Islamic values in the workplace, it is also important for the company to apply the means (in this case, the technology) to assure the integrity of Halal is safeguarded.

Other than top management support, a study by Khan et al. (2018) suggested that government support and awareness about Halal products is also a major driver that will influence the organization in implementing traceability systems on the Halal supply chain. He also said that selection of apt technology is a vital issue to achieve required transparency and the seamless information transfer among the supply chain players. As a result, Halal integrity is assured, which in turn will satisfy the customer and subsequently the firm will be able to maintain a competitive advantage. Communication with the customer and other stakeholders will also be improved.

Conclusion

The issue of food safety issue has been dealt with in a comparable manner to the issue of food integrity. Food integrity involves food safety, wellbeing, quality and nutrition. This applies the same to Halal, as the concept of Halal is not restricted to food safety and its quality but also comprises the process control, packaging, storage and delivery. Ever since the scandals related to the authenticity of Halal products occurred, it has raised concerns among Muslims consumers. The integrity of the Halal product should be monitored and be able to be traced and tracked and the information must be accessible to the consumers. This way, consumers will able to put their trust in the authenticity of Halal products. This can be achieved by implementing a traceability system. An effective traceability system of Halal products requires the whole chain of Halal supply to be in communication and transparent to the industry players. Information on the history of upstream and downstream material flow can be made available to consumers and business partners. The ability to trace and track the product or, in the Halal case, the ingredient of a Halal product and provide the customer access to that information is a competitive advantage. This is crucial for a company to survive not only in the Halal market but also in the global product market. Halal traceability also allows industry partners to trace and track important information at every stage of production and reduce product withdrawal and the number of non-compliances found by Halal certification bodies or authorities. Thus, removal the product from the market can be reduced.

Among the most mentioned critical success factors in implementing a traceability system by previous studies are receiving support from the company's top management, support by the government in form of initiatives, policy, etc., and awareness among Halal product producer and consumers regarding violation of Halal practices in supply chain operations. Companies need to start realizing that traceability is a tool to increase consumer confidence in the Halal product. It is suggested that safeguarding Halal integrity, especially in an uncertain environment, can be achieved through the proper selection of traceability technology and effective communication with the consumers in regards to the product information.

References

Al-Qaradawi, Y. (1993). *The Lawful and Prohibited in Islam*. Lahore: Islamic Publications.

Amir, A. (2020). Jakim announces action plan to tackle meat cartel scandal. *New Strait Times*. Retrieved from: www.nst.com.my/news/nation/2020/12/653040/jakim-announces-action-plan-tackle-meat-cartel-scandal (accessed 24 November 2021).

Angeles, R. (2005). RFID technologies: supply-chain applications and implementation issues. *Information Systems Management*, 22(1), pp. 51–65.

Arienzo, A., Coff, C. and Barling, D. (2008). The European Union and the regulation of food traceability: from risk management to informed choice? In C. Coff, D. Barling, M. Korthals and T. Nielsen (Eds.), *Ethical Traceability and Communicating Food: The International Library of Environmental, Agricultural and Food Ethics*. Dordrecht: Springer, pp. 23–42.

Azam, A. (2016). An empirical study on non-Muslim's packaged Halal food manufacturers: Saudi Arabian consumers' purchase intention. *Journal of Islamic Marketing*, 7, pp. 441–460.

Bahrudin, S. S. M., Tan, M. I. b. I. and Desa, M. I. (2011). Tracking and tracing technology for Halal product integrity over the supply chain. *Proceedings of the 2011 International Conference on Electrical Engineering and Informatics*, 2011, pp. 1–78.

Daniel, D. R. (1961). Management information crisis. *Harvard Business Review*, 39, pp. 111–121.

Digman, L. A. (1990). *Strategic Management: Concepts, Decisions, Cases*. Boston, MA: BPI/Irwin.

Encyclopedia Britannica (n.d.). *Barcode*. Retrieved from: www.britannica.com/technology/barcode (accessed 24 November 2021).

Food and Agriculture Organization (FAO) (2004). *Codex Alimentarius Commission: Report of the Twenty-Seventh Session*. Retrieved from: www.fao.org/3/y5549e/y5549e0l.htm (accessed 24 November 2021).

Husny, Z. J., Razali, R. N. and Tan, M. I. B. I. (2012). Halal Traceability Container System (Halal TraCS) using radio frequency identification (RFID) technology for Malaysian Halal logistics. *International Conference on Information Technology 2012*, Madrid, 28–29 March.

Insight Works (2021). *Barcodes vs. QR codes: Which Is Better for Manufacturers?* Retrieved from: www.dmsiworks.com/resources/erp-news/inventory-management/barcodes-vs-qr-codes-which-is-better-for-manufacturers/ (accessed 24 November 2021).

International Organization of Standardization (ISO) (n.d.). *ISO 12875:2011, Traceability of Finfish Products: Specification on the Information to be Recorded in Captured Finfish Distribution Chains*. Geneva: ISO Central Secretariat.

Jaafar, H. S., Omar, E. N., Osman, M. R., and Faisol, N. (2013). The concept of Halal logistics – an insight. *International Conference on Logistics and Transport*. Kyoto: Doshisha University, Kyoto.

Jabatan Kemajuan Islam Malaysia (JAKIM) (n.d.a). *Malaysian Halal Management System, MHMS 2020*. Retrieved from: www.halal@gov.my (accessed 24 November 2021).

Jabatan Kemajuan Islam Malaysia (JAKIM) (n.d.b). *Manual Prosidur Pensijilan Halal Malaysia (Domestik) MPPHM 2020*. Retrieved from: www.halal@gov.my (accessed 24 November 2021).

Kamaruddin, R., Iberahim, H. and Shabudin, A. (2012). Willingness to pay for Halal logistics: the lifestyle choice. *Procedia – Social and Behavioral Sciences*, 50, pp. 722–729.

Kärkkäinen, M., Holmström, J., Främling, K. and Artto, K. (2003). Intelligent products: a step towards a more effective project delivery chain. *Computers in Industry*, 50(2), pp. 141–51.

Khan, S., Haleem, A., Khan, M. I., Abidi, M. H. and Al-Ahmari, A. (2018). Implementing traceability systems in specific supply chain management (SCM) through critical success factors (CSFs). *Sustainability*, 10, 204.

Li, S. and Visich, J. K. (2006). Radio frequency identification: supply chain impact and implementation challenges. *International Journal of Integrated Supply Management*, 2(4), 24407424.

Loebbecke, C. and Powell, P. (1998). Competitive advantage from IT in logistics: the integrated transport tracking system. *International Journal of Information Management*, 18(1), pp. 17–27.

Marjudi, S., Hassan, W. A. W., Ahmad, R. M. T. R. L., Hamid, A. and Zainuddin, N. M. M. (2017). The critical success factors of Halal SCM systems for Malaysian SMEs. *The 69th IRES International Conference*, Jeddah, 24–25 May.

Meuwissen, M. P., Velthuis, A. G., Hogeveen, H. and Huirne, R. B. (2003). Traceability and certification in meat supply chains. *Journal of Agribusiness*, 21(2), pp. 167–182.

Mohamed, Y. H., Rahim, A. R. A., Ma'ram, A. B. and Hamza, M. G. (2016). Halal traceability in enhancing Halal integrity for food industry in Malaysia – a review. *International Research Journal of Engineering and Technology (IRJET)*, 3(3), pp. 68–74.

Ngai, E. W. T., Cheng, T. C. E., Au, S. and Lai, K-h. (2007). Mobile commerce integrated with RFID technology in a container depot. *Decision Support Systems*, 43(1), pp. 62–76.

Sahin, E., Dallery, Y. and Gershwin, S. (2002). Performance evaluation of a traceability system: an application to the radio frequency identification technology. *IEEE International Conference on Systems, Man and Cybernetics*, 3. doi: 10.1109/ICSMC.2002.1176118

Shamsuzzoha, A. H. M. and Helo, P. T. (2011). Real-time tracking and tracing systems: potentials for the logistics network. *International Conference on Industrial Engineering and Operations Management*, Kuala Lumpur, 22–24 January.

Shi, Y.-D., Pan, Y.-Y. and Lang, W.-M. (2009). The RFID application in logistics and supply chain management. *Research Journal of Applied Sciences*, 4(1), pp. 57–61.

Soon, J. M., Chandia, M. and Regenstein, J. M. (2017). Halal integrity in the food supply chain, *British Food Journal*, 119(1), pp. 39–51.

Stefansson, G. and Tilanus, B. (2001). Tracking and tracing: principles and practice. *International Journal of Services Technology and Management*, 2(3/4), pp. 187–206.

Straits Times Asia (2014). Cadbury Malaysia reviews supply chain after pork DNA found in two products. Straits Times Asia. Retrieved from: www.straitstimes.com/asia/se-asia/cadbury-malaysia-reviews-supply-chain-after-pork-dna-found-in-two-products (accessed 24 November 2021).

Taghaboni-Dutta, F. and Velthouse, B. (2006). RFID technology is revolutionary: who should be involved in this game of tag? *Academy of Management Perspectives*, 20(4), pp. 65–78.

Tan, M. I. I. and Husny, Z. J. I. M. (2020). Digital innovation, Halal industry and the Fourth Industrial Revolution. In N. A. A. Rahman, A. Hassan and M. F. Mohammad (Eds.), *Halal Logistics and Supply Chain Management in Southeast Asia*. Abingdon: Routledge.

Tausz, A. (1994). The high stakes game of keeping tabs. *Distribution*, 93(13), 54–57.

Tieman, M. (2011). The application of Halal in supply chain management: in-depth interview. *Journal of Islamic Marketing*, 2(2), pp. 186–195.

Tieman, M., van der Vorst, J. G. A. J. and Che Ghazali, M. (2012). Principles in Halal supply chain management. *Journal of Islamic Marketing*, 3(3), pp. 217–243.

Zailani, S., Arrifin, Z., Abd Wahid, N., Othman, R. and Fernando, Y. (2010). Halal traceability and Halal tracking systems in strengthening Halal food supply chains for food industry in Malaysia (a review). *Journal of Food Technology*, 8(3), pp. 74–81.

6 Technology and traceability in Halal logistics

Critical success factors

Mohd Farid Shamsudin and Hajjah Zawiah Abdul Majid

Introduction

Halal products are now getting a place in the world consumer market. The definition of Halal alone can be used as a measuring stick to the quality of the products produced and also the services. Halal status is an important symbol of Muslim consumers' highest beliefs and values worldwide (Memon et al., 2019). There are almost two billion Muslims in the world. Meanwhile, non-Muslim consumers are attracted to consume Halal products because of their religious factor promoting hygienic products (Garg and Joshi, 2018).

As of 2020, millions of Halal products and services have been produced by thousands of companies from around the world (Fatmi et al., 2020). The problem is that they have different processes compared to one another. This difference occurs because the companies that manufacture Halal products are in different locations, with cultures and standards of operation, etc. The same issues currently exist regarding the Halal logo and certification (Aziz and Chok, 2013).

However, that does not stop the high demand from Muslim consumers from increasing in number every year. The growth implications have increased demand for products and services from Muslim consumers worldwide (Pradana et al., 2019). Based on the growing demand worldwide, emphasis should also be placed on the whole process, including logistics. Growing technology has helped the ability for Halal logistics to be tracked transparently as part of the effort to comply with the full Halal compliance process (Poniman et al., 2018).

Supply chain partners can track their goods using advanced traceable technologies (such as GPS, RFID and barcode). The technology-based applications and solutions enhance information collection and transmission of quality data with the speed required by the administrations (Rasul et al., 2018). Those technologies help improve the overall inventory system and management. The following are among the popular solutions used by the logistics sectors especially related to Halal.

Track and trace

The development of technology in the twenty-first century has enabled various GPS and internet-based equipment and applications such as "tracking and tracing"

DOI: 10.4324/9781003223719-9

or "track and trace" to be created. Track and trace is one of the technologies that allows supply companies to monitor a trip without stopping (Zainuddin et al., 2020). With track and trace, delivery and product supply companies can ensure that travel and transportation processes in the value chain can be tracked and monitored (Mohamed et al., 2016). This is following the implementation of the Halal process to guarantee and eliminate doubts among consumers.

There is no doubt that track and trace is a great solution that can revolutionize the transportation industry and the supply chain. The technology has begun to be accepted and adopted around the world. The technology accommodates the supplier to track and know exactly the route and status of a shipment and control from web-based platforms. Customers are sometimes given access to information so that they can monitor the delivery. The solutions create a confident relationship and show the supplier's commitment (Saifudin et al., 2018).

Track and trace is not only for domestic or national use but can also work across international borders. This great feature gives an advantage to suppliers where they can give an accurate picture of the trip, including the estimated time of arrival to a destination (Saifudin et al., 2018). The company can also track the entire trip both in terms of stopover, speed and several other activities such as container door alerts and so on. Track and trace allow tracking to be done on vehicles and track containers and pallets.

Track and trace works by providing GPS-based location and movement information (Mohamad et al., 2016). Transmission of data can be done according to the agreed time interval. The transmission of data from the device to the headquarters or any customer server is via the internet from the track and trace tool installed on the vehicle or any part of the object to be tracked (Rohmah et al., 2020). Apart from that, most of the track and trace devices also come with other sensor facilities that can be used to detect other movements such as opening doors, filling fuel, fuel level, temperature level and others. Everything is easier with technology.

RFID

Radio frequency identification (RFID) is not a new concept. It is now being used in various sectors, including manufacturing, to handle products and inventory and to classify data in travel documents such as passports and airline-operated luggage (Lathifah and Narulidea, 2017).

The majority of us already use RFID without realizing it, such as credit cards that can be used exclusively with scanners to make purchases (Herrojo et al., 2019). This device can also create office or vehicle access cards for residential areas.

The extensive use of RFID systems across multiple platforms is unsurprising, given that these systems provide a reliable signal with rapid response times (Landaluce et al., 2020). Simultaneously, it is cost-effective to use. The range of the RFID scanner can be extended, but this is still dependent on the device and its specifications (Van Hoek, 2019).

RFID refers to radio frequency IDs. The tags used were encoded digitally to provide information using the radio waves (Denuwara et al., 2019). RFID tags are available in different types depending on the appropriateness of an item or substance to be detected. Tags are normally attached to items and can be read from several feet away. Furthermore, marks do not need to be directly targeted to start interactions.

The RFID function works very closely with the barcode scheme because a computer (scanner) reads the data from a label and sends it to a database (Duroc and Tedjini, 2018). RFID tags are a simple way to provide an item with a unique identity. They don't need an internal power source. Simultaneously, as long as the tag can store information for monitoring purposes, the tag can be as small as possible.

The embedded transmitter and receiver of RFID tags are available. The basic RFID portion of the tag includes two parts: a built-in storage and processing circuit and an antenna to receive and transmit signals (McGee et al., 2019). RFID tags feature unfixed memory storage used to process transfers and sensor data via fixed logic or programmable logic. RFID is among the flexible applications to be combined with other solutions. RFID is also among the solutions required to meet ISO compliance requirements especially concerning food movement and information (Usama and Ramish, 2020). RFID is already widely used to help ensure the level of logistical security. It is also one of the solutions used in supply chain security to provide or monitor the processes that go through the supply chain (Bibi et al., 2017). Manufacturers and suppliers must always use efficient methods to ensure smooth operations and give confidence to customers, especially Halal products so that they believe and trust in the seriousness of suppliers and manufacturers in ensuring that Halal goals are achieved.

Barcodes

Despite the progress of RFID as a technological tool used in track and trace, we must not forget the barcode, which is one of the earliest developments in track and trace management. Barcodes are still used and function in contributing services to identify objects and their identities (Razak and Katuk, 2017). This is because barcodes are among the cheapest and easiest solutions to use compared to other applications. Technically, the barcode serves as an informant of the identity and information of the object or product to be detected. It is very suitable for use in reading product data (Ahmad et al., 2017). It is cheaper and can be read using a scanner or smartphone camera.

Barcodes only need to be printed on the required labels before affixing to the object or product. There are no specific barriers in the type of label or printer used as long as the barcode successfully displays the barcode line obtained from the system to be read by the barcode user (Muliansyah et al., 2020).

In the context of Halal, barcodes are very suitable for consumers to use to find out the status of the product they want to buy. Users can get accurate information about the product and data related to the product by scanning the barcode using a smartphone. In this way, the track and trace process from the beginning of the journey of the factory goods to the consumer can be detected and monitored to ensure compliance with the Halal process itself.

Critical success factors in technology and traceability in Halal logistics

Legislation

Several countries have mandatory rules regarding the supply chain, especially traceability device regulations (Zainuddin et al., 2020). Traceability implementation thus constitutes an organization's regulatory requirement. One of the methods to ensure compliance with the rules is through mandatory regulations. Such a thing is necessary to ensure that Halal's main goals are adhered to, especially from the suppliers (Mohamed et al., 2016). In general, not all suppliers or transport providers consist of Muslims who adhere to the interests of Halal requirements themselves.

Some countries such as Australia, Brunei, Indonesia, Malaysia, Pakistan and the USA have mandatory regulations related to the supply chain, especially those related to tracking device regulations (Kawata and Salman, 2020). Therefore, the implementation of tracking is a condition of organizational rules. The Halal industry promises a broad market around the world. Still, the implementation of mandatory requirements towards the Halal process compliance process is relatively less well-received except with the involvement of government intervention through mandatory requirements and strict monitoring (Othman et al., 2016). Several countries impose mandatory conditions on compliance, such as track and trace equipment, accompanied by government agencies' cooperation in determining whether industry players are ready to enter the Halal market (Lee et al., 2019). All industry players need to comply with the law so that supply chain systems can be identified. Legislation is important to ensure that the conditions in force comply with the Halal system and process framework. The effect of legislation can be seen in most developed countries where implementing technology-based equipment helps the track and trace process itself (Aslan and Aslan, 2016).

All industry players need to comply with the law to identify supply chain systems. Legislation is important to ensure that the conditions in force comply with the Halal system and process framework. The effect of legislation can be seen in most developed countries where implementing technology-based equipment helps the track and trace process itself. Good rules related to a matter from the government are very important in ensuring the success of an endeavour (Othman et al., 2016). Keep in mind that legislation is important in terms of promoting a rule. Industry players will see the seriousness of the government in enforcing when legislation is applied. Apart from that, the legislation can also show the government's transparency towards the steps and efforts in achieving a goal.

ICT systems

ICT systems are collections of components needed for efficient data production and processing. In the supply chain, ICT generates data used to build a product traceability scheme. In general, ICT systems are among the components required by any organization for efficient data production and processing. This process is aided by appropriate applications followed by equipment used to help the smoothness and ability to do something more efficient and beneficial for industry players. In the context of the supply chain, ICT generates data used to build product tracking schemes. In contrast, applications such as RFID and barcodes help streamline delivering the data in an orderly and meaningful manner. Apart from that, ICT also helps make the data collected material that is easy to understand and that can be used by certain parties to achieve their goals.

In product tracking and supply chain, ICT is a very important platform in achieving such effectiveness towards strengthening the Halal process. With the availability of ICT, we can use the website, one of the channels, to obtain information. Here, ICT facilitates the manufacturers and gives users access to receive information. ICT is also one of the factors in the development of technology in any country. ICT allows for more rapid growth involving database systems, automation and other applications that help the entire organization, including developing Halal. Among the benefits of ICT to the smoothness of technology and traceability in Halal logistics is developing technologies such as track and trace that make it easier for all manufacturers, suppliers and consumers to access more accurate and convenient information.

ICT also facilitates the development of applications or systems that comply with regulatory requirements and the purpose of the observation made. ICT also allows access to data through computers and not limited to smartphones, tablets and other suitable gadgets. ICT also provides a facility where data can be communicated easily through various means and methods. Apart from that, the data can also be stored and processed according to the wishes of the authorities following the needs, especially those involving Halal itself. Technology and data have been used for the Halal certification system in Malaysia. The cooperation of all parties and the strength of ICT, and the rapid growth of technology development helps government agencies succeed in the Halal process for all, especially in Malaysia, where most of the population is Muslim.

Quality of information

Information quality involves completeness, uniqueness, timeliness, data validity and consistency (Jusop et al., 2020). It involves the selection of the type of ICT and equipment used to perform an activity.

Equipment

This refers to the data obtained from the application and the delivery and storage methods provided. Overall, completeness refers to 100% of the data obtained based on the requirements required to process the data (Ahmad et al., 2019). For example, in RFID, the data stored must be complete to understand subsequent processes. The data stored should be exclusive to the actual needs to measure the success or effectiveness of the activity, such as slaughterhouse code, date and hour of slaughter, breeding farm code, etc.

Uniqueness

This refers to the efficiency of quality data delivery. The data provided is by the requirements of the next process (Jalil et al., 2018). The data collected and sent meets the needs of the next study while not overlapping with any data that can confuse users.

Punctuality

In the use of track and trace, for example, punctuality is very important. The application used should send data as specified in the settings section (Noordin et al., 2014). Data should be sent promptly to avoid confusion at the management level. For example, track and trace on a set to send data every five seconds should always send data at the set time. This enables the application to send reports related to other matters such as current travel, vehicle safety and driver efficiency.

Validity

The Halal system requires accurate data and information and must be following the syntax (format, type, range) set.

Accuracy

The application user should send accurate data so that it is easy to maintain. Track and trace services, for example, have many alert systems such as geo-fencing, emergency breaks, and even some companies that have started to track the activities performed by drivers (Jalil et al., 2018).

Consistency

This refers to the efficiency of the data being transmitted accurately. It depends on many factors (Nugroho et al., 2018). It is important to produce consistent data as proof that a system is accurate.

Certification

Many of the certification systems, such as "organic", "fair trade", "supportability" and "Halal", require a broad array of product and process details. To obtain these certifications, a manufacturer must document their entire process in detail, as origin, ingredients, manufacturing and logistics activity must all be in order (Othman et al., 2016). Therefore, the traceability framework in the supply chain is necessary to obtain this type of information (Aslan and Aslan, 2016). These certification schemes lead to the implementation of the traceability framework by the supply chain partners, which will achieve greater sustainability and competitiveness. Malaysian Halal certification is currently regarded among the best in the international arena (Tieman, 2019). Primarily it was because Malaysia aims to be a global Halal hub. As such, they are now exploring all the possible efforts to accomplish this.

Halal certification is a document issued by an official party or Islamic body that certifies that a product adheres to the Islamic dietary guidelines, designed to ensure that products do not contain prohibited ingredients such as pork. In general, when it comes to Halal certification requirements, applicants (particularly operators or restaurant owners) must adhere to and follow all standards and instructions established by law or in the halal certification processing manual. Jabatan Kemajuan Islam Malaysia (JAKIM) and the State Islamic Religious Department are the primary bodies that issue Halal certification in Malaysia (Jabatan Agama Islam Negeri, JAIN). Additionally, non-governmental organizations such as IFANCA USA, IFANCA Canada, Japan Muslim Association, Islamic Food Research Center Asia (IFRC Asia), Hong Kong and Kuala Lumpur issue Halal certificates. These organizations are associated with the international World Halal Council (WHC). Additionally, there are Islamic bodies in every country that grant Halal certificates, such as the Australian Halal Food Services (AHFS), the Islamic Center of the Argentine Republic (Centro Islamico de la Republica Argentina), and others. In most countries, applications for Halal certification are optional and not obligatory for the industry (Zakaria et al., 2018). Halal certification is granted to food, beverages, Islamic consumer goods, pharmaceuticals and slaughterhouses. Halal logistics and traceability are two critical concerns that will be tested before certification.

Competitive advantage

The application of traceability increases product acceptance and process knowledge (i.e., good manufacturing practices/good agricultural practices), offers the company a competitive advantage and promotes customer buying decisions (Memon et al., 2019). From the customer perspective, the manufacturer that focused on Halal traceability is serious in delivering the top quality and compliance products to the end-users (Zakaria et al., 2018). Indirectly it will increase the relationship between customers and manufacturers. At the same time, it can also increase the engagement between them. It is also a symbol of compliance from the manufacturer as part of their obligations in delivering the products that meet the Halal regulations (Mutmainah, 2018). The effort made by the manufacturer and the logistic providers indicates that they are focused on their commitments in fulfilling the requirements or legislations of Halal status products. Customers perceived that manufacturers that apply transparency on their overall Halal process including logistics were more trustworthy. This will indirectly increase brand trust and create a new market among Muslims, particularly on the overall Halal process. It will also add a competitive advantage among the industry players.

Information sharing

There is no doubt that the global market for Halal products is growing. Indirectly, this has resulted in the Halal industry being one of the fastest-growing sectors in the world. Halal food can reach a broader segment of the world's population, as it is not limited to Muslim consumers. Traceability information is critical for Halal enforcement, as it increases accountability in the chain of production (Rashid et al., 2018). Increased transparency or details encourage customers to trust the product's protection. As a result, increasing the amount of knowledge available about the manufacturing process, safety controls, animal living conditions and medications is critical for food supply. Traceability also adds integrity to the Halal product's supply chain. Traceability indirectly contributes to increased accountability in the supply chain (Ma'rifat et al., 2017). It builds trust in manufacturers' commitment to achieving maximum Halal compliance. Traceability enhances communication among supply chain stakeholders, which results in precise monitoring of output with improved internal management and reduces unwanted information recording (Poniman et al., 2018). Traceability enables information sharing across the supply chain, thereby improving cooperation between especially important supply chain partners: trace the product's origins, identify delivery network leaks, prevent forgery, and as a means of attracting customers to the commodity.

Conclusion

In practice, technology allows for more effective development of alternative planning schemes and comprehension of potential traceability solutions. The benefits of technology in logistics are required to meet the needs and demand of the Halal industry, especially in the food sectors. Technology-enabled hardware, equipment and software for processing and storing data for the Halal industry enable traceability functions to improve logistics performance. The use of technology integration allows users to obtain accurate, available, reliable and timely information. The incorporation of technology and traceability in the Halal industry assists Halal stakeholders in evaluating the efficacy of various information technology systems in logistics. Finally, the technology applies to the industry in terms of data source reliability and reliability.

References

Ahmad, M. F., Samsi, S. Z. M. and Hui, L. T. (2017). Halascan: Halal brand personality screening process using camera phone barcode scanning. *International Journal of Academic Research in Business and Social Sciences*, 7(10), pp. 291–302.

Ahmad, H., Sabar, R., Udin, Z. M., Abd Latif, M. F. and Zainuddin, N. (2019). Quality management of internal supply chain in Halal food manufacturer. *International Journal of Supply Chain Management*, 8(4), pp. 1047–1052.

Aslan, I. and Aslan, H. (2016). Halal foods awarness and future challenges. *British Journal of Economics, Management and Trade*, 12(3), pp. 1–20.

Aziz, Y. A. and Chok, N. V. (2013). The role of Halal awareness, Halal certification, and marketing components in determining Halal purchase intention among non-Muslims in Malaysia: a structural equation modeling approach. *Journal of International Food and Agribusiness Marketing*, 25(1), pp. 1–23.

Bibi, F., Guillaume, C., Gontard, N. and Sorli, B. (2017). A review: RFID technology having sensing aptitudes for food industry and their contribution to tracking and monitoring of food products. *Trends in Food Science and Technology*, 62, pp. 91–103.

Denuwara, N., Maijala, J. and Hakovirta, M. (2019). Sustainability benefits of RFID technology in the apparel industry. *Sustainability*, 11(22), 6477.

Duroc, Y. and Tedjini, S. (2018). RFID: A key technology for humanity. *Comptes Rendus Physique*, 19(1–2), pp. 64–71.

Fatmi, F. O., Ahmad, A. N. and Kartika, B. (2020). Determinants affecting purchase intention of Halal products: an article review. *Journal of Halal Product and Research*, 3(2), pp. 64–79.

Garg, P. and Joshi, R. (2018). Purchase intention of "Halal" brands in India: the mediating effect of attitude. *Journal of Islamic Marketing*, 9(3), pp. 683–694.

Herrojo, C., Paredes, F., Mata-Contreras, J. and Martín, F. (2019). Chipless-RFID: a review and recent developments. *Sensors*, 19(15), 3385.

Jalil, N. S. A., Tawde, A. V., Zito, S., Sinclair, M., Fryer, C., Idrus, Z. and Phillips, C. J. C. (2018). Attitudes of the public towards Halal food and associated animal welfare issues in two countries with predominantly Muslim and non-Muslim populations. *PLoS ONE*, 13(10), e0204094.

Jusop, M., Ismail, R. M. and Ismail, N. A. (2020). Managing information quality in B2C companies: an empirical investigation on Halal e-commerce websites. *International Journal of Interactive Mobile Technologies*, 14(17), pp. 97–112.

Kawata, Y. and Salman, S. A. (2020). Do different Halal certificates have different impacts on Muslims? *Journal of Emerging Economies and Islamic Research*, 8(3), pp. 26–39.

Landaluce, H., Arjona, L., Perallos, A., Falcone, F., Angulo, I. and Muralter, F. (2020). A review of IoT sensing applications and challenges using RFID and wireless sensor networks. *Sensors*, 20(9), 2495.

Lathifah, A. and Narulidea, W. (2017). Business model financially viable for a radio frequency identification (RFID) application to Halal food system. *Jurnal Ekonomi Dan Bisnis Islam (Journal of Islamic Economics and Business)*, 3(1), pp. 12–25.

Lee, H. Y., Hwang, H. J. and Kim, D. H. (2019). Issues of Halal supply chain management: suggestion for Korean traders. *Journal of Korea Trade*, 23(8), pp. 132–144.

Ma'rifat, T. N., Purwanto, S. and Windarwati, S. (2017). Perception on Halal traceability on chicken meat supply chain. *Agroindustrial Technology Journal*, 1(1), pp. 33–41.

McGee, K., Anandarajah, P. and Collins, D. (2019). A review of chipless remote sensing solutions based on RFID technology. *Sensors*, 19(22), 4829.

Memon, Y. J., Azhar, S. M., Haque, R. and Bhutto, N. A. (2019). Religiosity as a moderator between Theory of Planned Behavior and Halal purchase intention. *Journal of Islamic Marketing*, 11(6), pp. 1821–1836.

Mohamad, M. A., Mansor, S., Ahmad, N., Adnan, W. A. W. and Wali, I. M. (2016). The reliability of Halal product transportation using GPS tracking system. *Journal of Theoretical and Applied Information Technology*, 90(2), pp. 188–196.

Mohamed, Y. H., Rahim, A. R. A., Ma'ram, A. B. and Hamza, M. G. (2016). Halal traceability in enhancing Halal integrity for food industry in Malaysia – a review. *International Research Journal of Engineering and Technology*, 3(3), pp. 68–74.

Muliansyah, D., Rahmayanti, R. and Nurhidayah, R. (2020). Halal and non-Halal product recognition systems. *International Journal of Innovation, Creativity and Change*, 12(9), pp. 255–270.

Mutmainah, L. (2018). The role of religiosity, Halal awareness, Halal certification, and food ingredients on purchase intention of Halal food. *Ihtifaz: Journal of Islamic Economics, Finance, and Banking*, 1(1), pp. 33–50.

Noordin, N., Noor, N. L. M. and Samicho, Z. (2014). Strategic approach to Halal certification system: an ecosystem perspective. *Procedia – Social and Behavioral Sciences*, 121, pp. 79–95.

Nugroho, A. J. S., Andadari, R. K., and Aribowo, E. K. (2018). Supply chain and purchasing behavior of Halal chicken meat. *Share: Jurnal Ekonomi Dan Keuangan Islam*, 7(2), pp. 162–179.

Othman, B., Shaarani, S. M. and Bahron, A. (2016). The potential of ASEAN in Halal certification implementation: a review. *Pertanika Journal of Social Sciences and Humanities*, 24(1), pp. 1–24.

Poniman, D., Purchase, S. and Sneddon, J. (2018). Traceability in Halal food supply chains from a business network perspective. *Information Processing in Agriculture*. Retrieved from: www.impgroup.org/uploads/papers/7855.pdf (accessed 24 November 2021).

Pradana, M., Syarifuddin, S., Hafid, H., Gilang, A. and Diandri, M. (2019). Purchase intention determinants of Halal food in secular countries. *International Journal of Supply Chain Management*, 8(4), pp. 83–89.

Rashid, N. A., Supian, K. and Bojei, J. (2018). Relationship between Halal traceability system adoptions on halal food supply chain integrity and performance. *International Journal of Asian Social Science*, 8(8), pp. 569–579.

Rasul, T., Ashaduzzaman, M. and Jebarajakirthy, C. (2018). How do Muslim consumers arrive at Halal purchase decisions in online food consumption context? *Proceedings of the 20th Australia and New Zealand Marketing Academy Conference (ANZMAC)*, Adelaide, 3–5 December.

Razak, M. N. F. A. and Katuk, N. (2017). Barcode scanning mobile application for searching Halal information of food products. In J. Zulikha and N. H. Zakaria (Eds.), *Proceedings of the 6th International Conference of Computing & Informatics*. Sintok: School of Computing, pp. 418–425.

Rohmah, D., Maharani, S., Kholis, M., Taqwa, S. and Setyaningrum, H. (2020). *Traceability and Tracking Systems of Halal Food Using Blockchain Technology to Improve Food Industry Competitiveness*. Retrieved from: https://eudl.eu/pdf/10.4108/eai.13-2-2019.2286199 (accessed 24 November 2021).

Saifudin, A. M., Zainuddin, N., Elias, E. M., Samsuddin, S. N. F. and Osman, A. A. (2018). Reviewing the contributors towards the performance of the new Islamic supply chain model. *International Journal of Supply Chain Management*, 7(4), pp. 151–157.

Tieman, M. (2019). Branding Halal: a delicate balance. *ICR Journal*, pp. 283–287.

Usama, M., and Ramish, A. (2020). Towards a sustainable reverse logistics framework/typologies based on radio frequency identification (RFID). *Operations and Supply Chain Management*, 13(3), pp. 222–232.

Van Hoek, R. (2019). Exploring blockchain implementation in the supply chain: learning from pioneers and RFID research. *International Journal of Operations and Production Management*, 39(6/7/8), pp. 829–859.

Zainuddin, N., Saifudin, A. M., Deraman, N. and Osman, A. A. (2020). The effect of Halal traceability system on Halal supply chain performance. *International Journal of Supply Chain Management*, 9(1), pp. 490–498.

Zakaria, Z, Majid, M. D. A. Jusoh, Z. A. Z. and Zakaria, N. Z. (2018). Influence of Halal certification on customers' purchase intention. *Journal of Fundamental and Applied Sciences*, 9(5S), pp. 772–787.

7 Halal logistics sustainability
A conceptual framework

Haliza Mohd Zahari, Ruzaidin Mohammed Zain and Nur Hidayah Binti Azhar

Introduction

Islam not only teaches its Ummah to do good deeds, but it is also a way of life. It emphasizes Halal and haram as a principle guideline based on Al-Quran and Hadis. Halal is a term that can be defined as permissible, allowed or lawful, while Haram means unlawful and in violation of the Islamic principle. In addition, Islam strongly advocates Halal and encourages Toyyiban, which indicates a standard of quality, safety, hygiene and cleanliness (Haleem et al., 2020; Surjandari et al., 2021; Susanty et al., 2021). Tieman et al. (2012) indicate that Halal and Toyyiban are not only evaluated from the point of the final product, but it is all started from the beginning; obtaining raw materials, producing the product until it is handed over to the consumer. The concept of Halal starts from production and continues to the point of consumption (Susanty et al., 2021). Therefore, the Halal supply chain (SC) is inextricably linked to the planning, implementation and control of storing Halal-certified products efficiently from the point of origin to the point of consumption. Surjandari et al. (2021), as well as Susanty et al. (2021) add that the entire process of purchasing, transporting, storing, attaining spare parts, handling materials, works-in-progress, finished inventory and livestock should all be properly documented and conducted to adhere to Halal and Toyyiban standards. It is the responsibility of the producing company to be committed and have the integrity and morale justifiable in Halal principles and values (Susanty et al., 2021). Furthermore, to prevent any cross-contamination, which can make it product Haram or non-Halal, the integrity of the Halal food products need to be safeguarded in the whole process in the SC. Therefore, the product must be Halal from the beginning, all the way through the SC, until it reaches its final destination (Rahim et al., 2016).

Halal markets expansion, Muslim lifestyle offerings and recently the Halal product ecosystems have dominated the global market, raising safety and quality standards (Susanty et al., 2021). Currently, there are more than 300 companies that have been certified Halal (Chandra et al., 2019), which is demonstrated by the abundance of Halal certified products sold in Muslim and non-Muslim countries alike (Mutsikiwa and Basera, 2012). Halal products are no longer categorized as only for Muslim communities; non-Muslims have also preferred

DOI: 10.4324/9781003223719-10

Halal products, especially the Halal food, due to the food products being much tastier, healthier and cleaner (Susanty et al., 2021).

Even though Halal products have a good reputation and support from the consumer, there are also many considerations for the Halal SC, such as raw materials from the original source, ingredients, materials and flavourings, slaughtering methods, contamination during production and manufacturing, usage of equipment, storage, packaging and transportation, as well as an emphasis on safety and quality aspects. On the other hand, there are also issues related to Halal global standardization, which is very hard to achieve due to different cultures and behaviours from many other countries (Chandra et al., 2019).

Many studies have been conducted on Halal and Toyyiban focusing on food; however, not many understand the concept of Halal and Toyyiban. Therefore, this study was carried out to examine the concept of Halal, explore the current Halal practices in logistics and develop a reliable and transparent Halal logistics sustainability conceptual framework, which will assist in understanding the Halal and Toyyiban concept to comply with the Halal standard and restrictions.

The nature of Halal logistics

Halal has turned out to be a symbol not only for religious matters but is related to ethical practices, integrity, safety and hygiene (Susanty et al., 2021). The manufacturing of Halal products and services is related to a process-oriented approach (Khan et al., 2018). Bonne and Verbeke (2008) stated that Halal is not only related to the process but also to the nature and origin of the products and services. The integrity of the whole process indicates Halal originality. Based on this, the Halal certificate can be issued to the company that comply with this requirement. According to Surjandari et al. (2021), issuing a Halal certificate to those who comply is proof that a product or service is following Islamic law besides being safe and acceptable. Products and services with Halal certificates make consumers feel safe and give them confidence in consumption as well as in using a product or service (Haleem et al., 2020). Auditing of Halal certificates is performed to check the integrity of foods and whether or not it is contaminated, which can easily happen along the process. Therefore, it is important to monitor the process for ensuring the Halal products' and services' integrity from the beginning until the point of consumption. Halal logistics involves storage, warehousing, material handling, packaging, inventory and transporting. The main concern in Halal logistics is whether or not the products and services could reach the consumer at the right time and place as well as adhering to Shariah law. Therefore, it is crucial to ensure that the products and services do not compromise Halal integrity. The Halal concern should not be put solely on the Halal manufacturer but also on the Halal logistics provider.

Halal warehousing and transportation

The warehouse has three primary functions: receiving materials, storing them and issuing inventory out of the warehouse, including distribution to customers. In these three warehouse functions, the concept of Halal plays a significant role in emphasizing the separation of Halal and non-Halal products throughout the warehouse processes (Khairuddin et al., 2018). During the inbound and outbound phases, the product must not have been processed on equipment contaminated with non-Halal items as defined by Islamic religious law (Ikram et al., 2013). In a study conducted by Ngah et al. (2017), the challenges in applying Halal warehouse standards involve high costs. To maintain integrity throughout the process, the products must be segregated from entering the SC process separately from the non-Halal products. The segregation process during transportation will protect the integrity of the Halal status and preserve the product from becoming Haram or contaminated by "Najs" before reaching consumers (Yaacob et al., 2018). The critical point is that all products enter the warehouse at the same point in the SC process (Ngah et al., 2017). Meanwhile, Halal transportation is critical for the integrity of Halal products. Halal transport highlights the shipping process as the products will pass through a few locations before reaching their final destination (Ngah et al., 2019). Halal transportation provides a higher level of service by ensuring that the Halal characteristics of the products are maintained. Unlike conventional transportation, Halal transportation is concerned with maintaining Halal integrity by separating Halal and non-Halal products from contamination, which may incur a higher cost than conventional transportation that seeks efficiency and effectiveness on transporting full loads of products to reduce cost and maximize profit.

Halal packaging

Although Halal packaging seems easy as it only involves packaging, it is a starting point to attract consumers to buy Halal goods. The packaging can be defined as all items of any kind used for containing material for safety, storage, distribution, from raw materials to processed goods, and also contributes to the outer appearance of goods (Abdelsamie et al., 2014). In other words, the packaging is a material used to contain, protect and handle goods. According to the Malaysian Food Act of 1983, "packaged food" means any tray, basket, pail or container of any sort, whether opened or closed, in which food is solely or partly cased, wrapped, contained, mounted, enclosed or otherwise packaged in any way. Packaging can also play various roles in logistics, according to Talib and Johan (2012), which include keeping products enclosed and secure while being shipped and distributed. It is also used to secure employees when handling dangerous items such as fluids, chemicals or loose products. Furthermore, packaging can eliminate or mitigate the risk of injury, spoilage, misplacement or theft during the logistics process. Packaging will shield products from cross-contamination between Halal and non-Halal substances. Packaging is also used to distinguish Halal and non-Halal goods during transportation and delivery, either using a different carrier or a different compartment in the same carrier.

Packaging is mainly used in promoting products for sales and to draw the attention and interest of the final buyers, as well as improving the brand value of a product. Packaging in the perspective of Halal includes the elements of Halal certification or logo, a list of ingredients and the origin of the commodity. Placing the Halal brand in the minds of consumers is known as the best positioning in Halal food marketing, which is a strategy in a competitive marketplace. Product packaging and labelling must also create awareness of health and Halal. Manufacturers, distributors and retailers should concentrate on ensuring that their goods are Halal-certified to benefit from the demand in the worldwide market, especially the Muslim market. The most essential factor in deciding whether a product is Halal or not is the Halal logo, and Muslims are very particular about purchasing Halal products, particularly food (Talib and Johan, 2012). On top of that, the most important factor considered by Muslim consumers before deciding to purchase a product was the Halal logo. Food product packaging is a big concern for Muslim communities and must be certified Halal and healthy to the consumers. This is because Halal products are often considered very clean and of high quality, not only on the product itself but also in terms of packaging. Product packaging such as "Jawi"/Arabic writing symbolizes the purity of the product.

Talib et al. (2010) argued that the origination of packaging comes from materials that are sometimes animal products whose Halal status is mistrusted, making Halal packaging status questionable. They mentioned that separating sealed Halal and non-Halal goods during transportation is unnecessary. However, if any material, such as meat juices, leak from the product, it must be isolated. Soong (2007) reported Halal quality in the food service industry taking a different approach, claiming any food that does not comply with Shariah law must be segregated during packaging and shipping activities as the commodity is deemed unclean. Hazair (2007, as cited in Talib and Johan, 2012) indicated that the packaging of Halal products must show and indicate the aspect of Shariah, such as that images printed onto the packaging must not violate Halal concepts, elicit any negative feelings or trigger sensitivity. Specific and pertinent details such as the recognized Halal logo should be made available. The Halal logo on food packaging is very important to customers (Shafie and Othman, 2006). According to Soong (2007), packaging of Halal products must include the product's name or brand, minimum content in matric, the manufacturer's or distributor's name and address, the ingredients, the production batch codes or numbers, the expiry date and a Halal logo from a recognized certification agency.

Halal retailing

The Halal retailer completes an end-to-end Halal SC by handing over the Halal product to the customer after payment. The point of customer purchase is another name for this exchange. The mission of Halal retailing is to ensure the Halal credibility at the point of purchase by ensuring that the Halal SC processes are under strict control (Tieman and Ruiz-bejarano, 2020). According to Hashim et al. (2014), retailers need to have a reassuring atmosphere for their customers. Halal itself has displayed the purity in which retailers show their Halal products clearly in their stores using Halal certifications. Products that have been approved as Halal at earlier stages of the SC must retain their validity until the end (retail). The Malaysian Department of Standards published the world's first Halal retailing standard in 2010, entitled "MS 2400-3:2010: Management System Requirements for Retailing". This Halal retailing standard aims to guarantee Halal integrity in goods, products and cargo at the retail phase. It sets out the framework that a retailer should put in place to comply with Halal regulations in managing and handling of Halal products and goods during receiving, loading and delivery activities.

Tieman and Ruiz-bejarano (2020) stated that there are three Halal retailing formulas:

Halal-exclusive retailer

This is where a store only sells Halal products. This Halal category is developed to cater to the local Muslim community's unique needs and Halal requirements. The Halal-exclusive retailer only sells products that are Halal according to Islamic law and local customs. Hence, non-Halal goods should be kept out of the SC where these standards rules apply in some of the countries in the world.

Halal-segregated retailer

This refers to a store that sells both Halal and non-Halal items, both of which are clearly labelled and physically separated on the shelves to address contamination risks and perception problems through clear signage and displays. This Halal category is intended to provide the mainstream Muslim consumers with as complete a Halal category as possible. A Halal-segregated retailer sells some non-Halal products; however, it specifically distinguishes them and separates their processes and physical flows to ensure Halal integrity. For alcoholic drinks and other non-Halal food items, the retailer should have designated "non-Halal areas" with clear signage and display. However, managing contamination is a very challenging task and hard to avoid due to the criticality, difficulty and interconnectivity of the food SC, making Shariah compliance with food an interesting and demanding process (Chandra et al., 2019).

Halal-mixed retailer

This is where a store sells both Halal and non-Halal products, but neither is clearly labelled nor physically separated. In short, the Halal category is not recognized by the retailer. This formula implies that Halal integrity is not guaranteed until the point of customer purchase with the determination of Halal's right to the consumer's discretion based on the product label. Although the study has streamlined the retailing layout for a store that sells Halal and non-Halal goods, there is also an argument about the use of consumer goods trolleys and payment counters which do not separate the purchase of Halal and non-Halal goods. Therefore, in Malaysia, there is a grocery shop that sells special Halal goods such as Az Zain Mart and Elewsmart run by the preacher Ebit Lew. These stores adopt the concept of selling Halal products only so that consumers are no longer hesitant in purchasing Halal grocery items.

Halal SC

The term Halal SC refers to the process that begins at the point of origin or raw material source and ends at the point of consumption, involving a variety of parties in the SC, for instance, the raw material suppliers to the end-users, also known as the consumers. Source identification such as the source of produce from crops and secondary processing, sorting, warehousing, transportation, product handling, inventory management, procurement, order management and marketing are all activities that must adhere to Shariah law general principles, which ensure that products and services produced are in good condition and Halal (Sukati and Bawaain, 2019). In the context of food security, it considers factors such as health and safety, product origins and ethical considerations (Susanty et al., 2021). It is comparable to the concept of Halal food that inculcates humanitarian values in society with spiritual and moral considerations as well as food safety regulations (Surjandari et al., 2021). This also encompasses of Islamic way of slaughtering and storage (Chandra et al., 2019). The principles of Toyyiban or food ethics applied to the slaughtering process involves treating the animal humanely before slaughter (Haleem et al., 2020). Three elements need to be complied with within the whole process: Halal control, Halal monitoring and Halal certification. According to Zulfakar et al. (2012), traceability and quality assurance are the critical components in ensuring Halal integrity in the Halal food SC.

Issues in Halal logistics

According to Susanty et al. (2021) and Tieman and Darun, (2017), there are five major issues in Halal logistics, namely traceability (the ability to determine the origin and location of a product); guidelines regarding product withdrawal due to Halal requirements; integrity of the Halal SC from manufacturer to customer; incompatible systems and divergent clarifications of the Halal SC; and absence of technological integration. The traceability issues can be found in producing Halal foods. Many studies discuss the concerns regarding Haram ingredients in food production; however, the sources of material used in manufacturing Halal food are also critical in determining the food status (Ikram et al., 2013). There are not many markets that offer Halal raw material (Chandra et al., 2019), especially Halal foods that take into consideration characteristics regarding proper slaughtering, preparation, storage, hygiene and sanitation. On top of that, there are few delimited markets that offer the Halal ingredients crucial for Muslim consumers.

Halal warehouse issues concern the storage of Halal and non-Halal products to avoid the products from being contaminated in the warehouse (Khairuddin et al., 2018; Ghani et al., 2015), during transport and before retailing (Susanty et al., 2021). Businesses are responsible for establishing a storage management system to prevent contamination with Haram or prohibited materials under Islamic religious law (Ikram et al., 2013). Even with proper isolation of Halal and non-Halal products in the warehouse, products may lose their Halal status if they are contaminated during transportation and storage (Khairuddin et al., 2018).

The challenges faced in Halal packaging are quite different from other activities in Halal logistics. Halal packaging focuses on packaging issues as well as Halal logos. Often the problem faced in Halal packaging is the authenticity of the Halal logo on the product packaging (Sumpin et al., 2019). There have been complaints from consumers that the Halal logo displayed was fake and there was also the issue of uncertainty of the Halal logo for products imported from abroad.

Halal food is being manufactured and imported from all over the world; whether or not the items are Halal continues to preoccupy the minds of the consumers, which is particularly true among Muslim communities (Rahim et al., 2016). Contamination of food with non-Halal materials or products is a significant issue in the Halal food SC. Due to the low margins in retailing, conventional emphasis has been put on achieving cost savings in logistics employing consolidation (Tieman and Ruiz-bejarano, 2020). To save logistical costs, consolidation happens as much as possible in transportation, sea containers, air freight pallets (and unit load devices) and trucks. Consolidation also refers to the grouping of items based on their temperature specifications, rather than their Halal status. As a result, mixing Halal and non-Halal foods may be an unintended consequence. Lack of awareness by the retailer on the importance of Halal management practice in the retail stores also imposes major issues in Halal retailing (Rahim et al., 2016). To prevent and minimize the risk of Halal product contamination, retailers must have additional expertise and understanding of management practices.

Therefore, many issues emerge in Halal logistics, especially when the authenticity of the product cannot be ascertained. However, the issues are dissimilar in every process of the SC. Based on the Halal logistics discussed, it is important to ensure that the goods that reach the consumer are truly Halal depending on all logistics activities carried out after the Halal product has been produced. Although each activity complied with the Shariah, the product can only be certified Halal when it has completed all processes and logistics activities until it reaches the consumers. This indicates that managing Halal requires a good SC management approach throughout the product's life cycle, from conception to final consumption or disposition.

Research methodology

This study was conducted using qualitative methodology. An extensive literature search was carried out from the beginning of this study to explore and develop a better understanding of Halal logistics. Then, the literature continued with searching for the issues in Halal logistics application in the industries. The literature review was obtained from the leading database. Using content analysis, the authors developed the Halal logistics theme. Finally, based on the analysis, a Halal logistics sustainability conceptual framework was developed to understand managing the Halal products and services from the beginning until reaching the consumers.

Existing Halal framework

Most Halal related frameworks typically focus on the Halal process framework as in Figure 7.1 and 7.2. There are also numbers of framework that provide Halal standards and guidelines. Their contribution is mostly focused on specific processes and activities in the Halal SC. For this study, it was found that the framework by Zulfakar et al. (2012) describes the integrity of the Halal food SC as in Figure 7.3, compared to other frameworks which focus on individual process in the SC. The available framework is generally comprehensive; however, it is not holistic. Zulfakar et al. (2012) identified that traceability, assets specificity, quality assurance, trust and commitment are involved in the Halal food SC integrity. Since the existing framework is insufficient and does not adequately address the processes that must be passed and the level of integrity that must be maintained, the following section describes the conceptual framework developed with the level of integrity requirements for each process and how it is improved by utilizing technology as an enabler that complements Halal logistics.

A framework for Halal logistics sustainability

The problems faced in Halal logistics revolve around the issues of Halal validity for each activity and process. Halal industries require a better framework that can help provide products and services that are guaranteed with Halal authenticity.

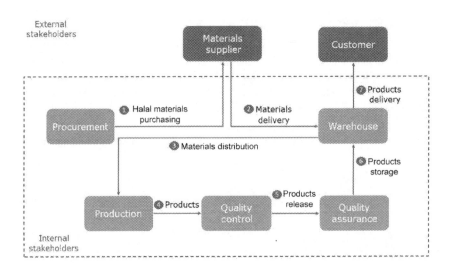

Figure 7.1 Halal pharmaceutical framework.
Source: Ghani et al., 2015.

Halal logistics sustainability 97

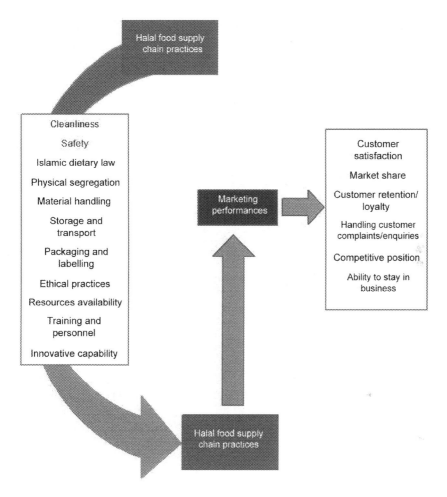

Figure 7.2 Halal food SC framework.
Source: Sukati and Bawaain, 2019.

Therefore, to help the authorities and consumers know the validity of the Halal status of a service or product, the use of technology can help Halal tracking for each process and logistics activity passed. This concept is used to form the Halal logistics framework, which is important in safeguarding the integrity of Halal when the product is being consumed. This is dependent not only on the product's manufacturing process, but also on the logistics management of the product. Therefore, the authenticity of Halal products can only be achieved when all the processes and stages are handled properly and passed, meeting the requirements of Shariah. So with this, it can be said that a product is Halal after it has been through all the Halal logistics processes. The framework for Halal logistics is crucial when Halal integrity is at stake.

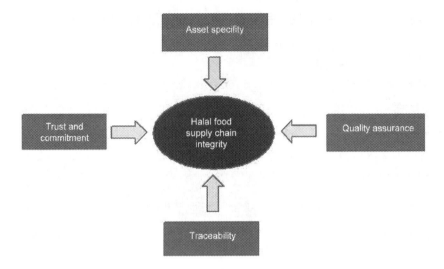

Figure 7.3 Factors influencing the integrity of the Halal food SC.
Source: Zulfakar et al., 2012.

Based on the review of the existing Halal framework, several attributes are important in determining the concept of Halal applied in each process, whether it is Halal manufacturing, warehouse, transportation, packaging or retailing. To become sustainable in the Halal market, the product must have the characteristics of uniqueness, quality and competitiveness (Kuncoro and Suriani, 2018). With these characteristics, a product can belong in the market and achieve long-term success (Hoffman, 2000; Kuncoro and Suriani, 2018) since it is not easily imitated. Hoffman, (2000) added that the sustainability of a product strongly depends on both the trust and commitment of the company. This trust and commitment in Halal products can be applied if companies can conform with the Halal standards of procedure, process and quality assurance, and retain high integrity in the whole process.

On top of that, technology has been used for a long time to achieve effective SC where the information gathered from the technology is used to integrate all components in the SC (de Camargo Fiorini and Jabbour, 2017). Technology captures vast amounts of information. With a wide-range information, technology can also assist in tracking the Halal status of a product. Although JAKIM has introduced a standard procedure, it does not guarantee that the producer and the marketer will follow it. Therefore, the standard of procedure must be followed to minimize the misuse of the Halal status and reduce the concern of Malaysian Muslims on Halal products in Malaysia.

The Halal logistics sustainability conceptual framework in Figure 7.4 presents a complete activity that must be adhered to by all manufacturers in order to succeed in the Halal market. Figure 7.4 shows the processes, activities and

HALAL LOGISTICS SUSTAINABILITY CONCEPTUAL FRAMEWORK

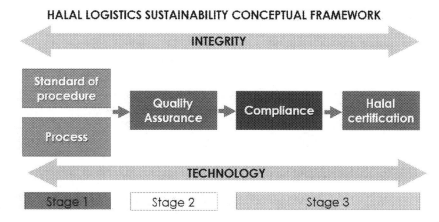

Figure 7.4 Halal logistics sustainability conceptual framework.

stages that all manufacturers need to go through in ensuring that the products produced are truly Halal. This process ends when the product reaches the hands of consumers.

The Halal logistics sustainability conceptual framework has three stages; in the first stage, the manufacturer must comply with the standard of procedure and process that has been set. In the second stage, the manufacturer must comply with all processes not only in the manufacture of products but also Halal compliance in all logistics processes before the product reaches the consumers. When all these processes are followed, then the product is eligible to be given a Halal certification.

Stage 1

Standard of procedure

Malaysia Halal standard of procedure and Halal certification is issued by the certification body, the Department of Islamic Development Malaysia (JAKIM). It is the responsibility of JAKIM to issue Halal certificates for all local products and products imported from abroad after going through the standard of procedure that have been set (Ahmad et al., 2017). The standard encompasses the entire SC, from raw materials to packaging, labelling and transportation. Compliance with the standard of the procedure is the first, and most important, process applied, before other rules that must be adhered to. The process of obtaining a Halal food certificate entails several steps carried out by Shariah and technical auditors from JAKIM (Arif and Sidek, 2015).

The standard of procedure stated bellow is used by JAKIM to regulate Halal compliance and issue the Halal certificate:

- Food Acts 1983 and Food Regulations 1985
- Manual Procedure of Halal Certification Malaysia
- Malaysian Standard MS 1480:2007 Food Safety According to Hazard Analysis and Critical Control Point (HACCP) System (First Revision)
- Malaysian Standard MS 1514:2009 Good Manufacturing Practice (GMP) For Food (First Revision)
- Malaysian Standard MS 1500:2009 Halal Food – Production, Preparation, Handling and Storage General Guidelines (Second Revision).

Although some feel that the standard of procedure (SOP) is very complicated, it is found that the existing SOP is very clear. The company needs to adhere to the SOPs that have been set, and it is the most important step before moving on to the next process. JAKIM's role in enhancing the Halal in the SC is significant because it enacts a law requiring all industries on Halal certificates for medicines, pharmaceutical, cosmetics, food and other products.

Process

According to Arif and Sidek (2015), the certification process for Halal food begins when manufacturers or industries submit an application to JAKIM. They must submit together on the information about the ingredients, the list of suppliers for the ingredients, the ingredients' original Halal status as evidenced by a Halal certificate issued by recognized Islamic bodies or product specification, as well as manufacturing processes and procedures such as HACCP and GMP (Arif and Sidek, 2015). To obtain Halal food certification, applicants must adhere to all procedure outlined in the Halal food standard, the GMP standard, the HACCP standard and the manual. Apart from conducting interviews with Shariah auditors and technical auditors from JAKIM's Department of Halal Hub, applicants may also be required to consult with the major agencies involved in the Halal food certification process led by JAKIM. Considering the Halal certificate application process, companies need to submit all Halal certificates from the use of raw materials to products. Companies also need to submit a list of suppliers.

Stage 2

Quality assurance

Halal products and services are in high demand, not only in Muslim countries but all around the world. Therefore, many agencies chose to comply with the Halal requirements in order to have the opportunity of expanding their market. Quality is measured by conformance of a standard or benchmark, which is a condition that must be adhered to by programmes or institutions to be accredited (Elassy, 2015). When an organization has set a standard of quality, it should be continuously assessed, monitored, maintained and improved, which also known as quality assurance (Vlăsceanu et al., 2007). In Halal logistics, quality measurement and assurance is crucial. It is a process of assessment before accreditation and certification.

Most businesses are unaware of the importance of Halal audits (Talib et al., 2008). The traceability or audit trail on qualification of raw materials and manufacturers will be assessed to determine the Halal authenticity of a product (Ikram et al., 2013). The traceability system can detect all the data linked to the product from its origin to the last nodes of distribution before it is consumed (Zulfakar et al., 2012). Briefly, tracing is the process of determining the information on the product history while tracking is the capability to track food ingredients forward along the production chain. However, the tracing and tracking discussed in the previous studies only focused on the food SC since they only deliberated on the food production from raw materials until it becomes food to be consumed.

Process tracking and tracing should be more holistic not only on food preparation but also cover the logistics processes involved such as storage warehousing, transportation, packaging and retailing. It is a long process and involves a variety of information that needs to be stored and analysed. Since it is a very long process, technology is crucial for the tracking and tracing process to gather all necessary information (Susanty et al., 2021).

Stage 3

Compliance

Halal logistics process has five activities: Halal certification application, on-site inspection, panel decision, certification issuance and Halal compliance (Hassan et al., 2017). Halal compliance is frequently associated with adhering to specific requirements or guidelines regarding its sources and preparation following Islamic laws, which implicitly brings Halal-certified or compliant businesses closer to achieving Halal certification (Ramli, 2020). Halal compliance can be verified using a Halal certificate, a declaration of Halal compliance, material specifications, an analysis certificate, or by determining the manufacturing process (Ikram et al., 2013). To obtain Halal certification, a certain level of compliance is required to verify the extent of Halal implementation (Ramli, 2020). However, a Halal certificate is insufficient to strengthen Halal logistics (Susanty et al., 2021).

Certification

The Halal certification is issued by a Malaysian government-authorized body. The government maintains control of the system with the assistance of multiple agencies led by JAKIM. JAKIM is a body that is instrumental in Malaysia's Halal certification efforts. Currently, the Halal Industry Development Corporation (HDC) has been appointed as a body to manage the Halal certification process. The certification can only be issued once all the five standards of procedure have been complied with. In addition, the attribute that makes up the developed framework requires technological elements to support the efficiency of Halal logistics management sustainability and at the same time indirectly strengthens the Halal integrity of each logistics stage where each process is recorded using technology for ease of the tracking and tracing processes later on and can be used during the audit trail. As discussed, in Stage 1 to Stage 3, there are many process and activities that must be completed before the final Halal Certification process. During the process and activities integrity plays a major role in determining the Halal authenticity.

Integrity in the process

Integrity plays a very important role in the whole Halal logistics stages. It is defined as a commitment to a set of morally justifiable principles and values in thoughts and actions (Soon et al., 2017). Even though JAKIM and other agencies have been given authority in Halal certification, this is only focused on Halal food. Other logistics activities must be adhered to with Halal compliance to ensure integrity. One of the main principles to sustain the Halal SC of the product and services is by having integrity in the whole process until the point of consumption (Haleem et al., 2020). For example, material may be ordered from multiple manufacturers, and each material must be inspected for Halal compliance, which varies by manufacturer. Therefore, every process must be monitored and controlled to avoid contamination, which will lead to non-Halal products and services (Ikram et al., 2013). It is an end-to-end Halal SC integrity process (Susanty et al., 2021). Based on the current process, integrity is lacking in Halal logistics.

Every stage in the logistics processes must have criticality in awareness for Halal integrity within the SC. Integrity here means plainly stating the particulars of the Halal status and ensuring that the stated Halal requirements are met (Soon et al., 2017). Therefore, checkpoints should be established upon receipt of raw materials, during production and packaging, and until the product is distributed to customers (Susanty et al., 2021). Logistics service providers must understand the Halal process that needs to be followed at all times. They are required to know that the processes of warehousing, storage and transportation of Halal products are Shariah-compliant; the services provided need to be segregated from non-Halal products as this is the demand in the Halal logistics process to maintain integrity. Hence, maintaining the Halal integrity of the entire SC requires constant monitoring of all resources. Surjandari et al. (2021) added that the entire process of acquiring the raw materials, production, distribution and up to reaching the consumer must be well documented following the standard to fit the Halal and Toyyiban requirements for traceability when related to Halal quality assurance and certification. Integrity in the Halal SC is usually questioned when involving the audit trail. Here, tracking and tracing the Halal status of all elements and logistics of the product involves heavy data and many sources. Therefore, the role of technology is crucial in order to have fast and accurate information.

Technology

Consumers usually use technology in Halal logistics for searching, purchasing and reviewing products. It helps the community make a decision and influences consumer expectations based on the reviews shared. Therefore, transparency is the main concern. However, in the perspective of the Halal SC, another important concern is integrity in each process. Since Halal validity is a major issue in production and services, technology is very important in the process of tracing, and tracking can be done back to each stage of handling (Zulfakar et al., 2012). Lack of integration on technology application in the SC may bring inconsistency in information and data gathering. It is best in Halal logistics to integrate technology for information exchange throughout the tracking and tracing process. This is related to getting the relevant information (Surjandari et al., 2021; Tieman and Darun, 2017). There have been many new technologies introduced in recent years, including blockchain and devices connected to the Internet of Things (IoT), which enable automated data collection and uploading to the network without human involvement, which will assist in collecting data and providing access to secure trusted and indisputable information (Chandra et al., 2019). On top of that, several blockchain-related aspects can help improve Halal SC, including validating transaction processes and speed tracing entire transactions (Susanty et al., 2021). The technology connects SC partners responsible for ensuring Halal compliance at each link in the Halal SC. It has the potential to create high-performance Halal SC networks (Tieman and Darun, 2017). This technology can evaluate all transactions concurrently and in real-time, which will ensure transparency, security, validity and audibility. Other disruptive technologies such as artificial intelligence enable stakeholders to retrieve the high-quality information necessary to make more informed decisions (Chandra et al., 2019). This can be done by scanning the QR barcodes on the final product with a mobile app to find the product's origin, the Halal status and Shariah compliance. Additionally, feedback and ratings can be gathered and stored on the blockchain in order for all prospective stakeholders to view and improve their service.

Since blockchain is a distributed database, many Halal issues related to quality assurance can be solved by utilizing blockchain technology, such as big data for data analysis (Surjandari et al., 2021). Chandra et al. (2019) added that blockchain could also provide solutions, assurance and access to trusted, secure and irreversible information besides enabling real-time recording and viewing of transactions, creating an audit trail that can be used to verify product background and Shariah compliance throughout the manufacturing and the logistics processes. For example, a computerized trigger will be used to prevent Halal items from being moved to a non-Halal storage area. This is to ensure that material segregation is defined properly and to avoid contamination with non-Halal materials. Each item must have a traceable identification, and the system must be able to determine the item's Halal status at the time of receipt. This further increases the SC efficiency, improves the process and creates higher transparency and assurance of

Halal compliance. Therefore, blockchain technology has the potential to close that gap by increasing transparency and ensuring Halal compliance (Chandra et al., 2019).

The use of available technology such as IoT, RFID and blockchain is very helpful in data collection and information analysis, especially in tracing and tracking in the logistics processes if they involve possible contamination issues. This information is very important not only to the enforcement agencies such as JAKIM but also to consumers to eliminate doubts about Halal authenticity. Without the use of data collection technology, the implementation of the tracing and tracking process would have to be implemented manually, which is quite difficult because it involves very large data analysis.

Conclusion

Halal certification is on a voluntary basis; however, Halal compliance with Halal requirements should be looked at as a business opportunity to sustain as it represents a significant source of consumer trust and confidence besides verifying that the products are free of impurities and unlawful substances. There are many products and services in Malaysia; however, Halal compliance and obtaining Halal certification are entirely voluntary. Therefore, not many manufacturers are keen on going through the Halal certification process. Halal certification is inadequate to prove the Halal status of a product and service despite the standard of procedure for Halal certification that has been developed in Malaysia to ensure compliance with the Halal status of each product. In terms of applying for Halal status, it was found that Malaysia has a very strict process where monitoring and auditing are carried out on participating companies to ensure that they maintain their Halal status as reported. However, it was found that all the processes available only focus on Halal products, especially Halal food. What is lacking is the process or logistics stages, which are the support processes to ensure that the product is truly Halal and uncontaminated when it reaches the consumers.

It was proposed that all stages in logistics should comply with Halal procedures and should be streamlined in the form of the standard of procedure and regulated by enforcement agencies such as JAKIM. With this, the accuracy of the Halal status of a product will not only depend on the manufacturing process of the product but will also become comprehensive considering the logistical process that must be passed by a product before it is marketed to consumers. As shown in the Halal logistics sustainability conceptual framework, technology plays a very important role in aiding the process of tracing and tracking a product from its production processes until it reaches the consumers. All these can be realized with the help of technology applications. If such technology can be developed in the form of applications, information can be displayed to users at their fingertips. This chapter has shown that the ideas of Halal and Haram are both clearly understood by the manufacturers and the enforcement agencies. Additionally, emerging technology is being utilized to identify loopholes and improve SCs in order to increase the transparency and consumer confidence that may assist the Halal issuance to be more holistic and more significant, not only for the manufacturers and enforcement agencies but also for the consumers regarding the Halal status of a product.

References

Abdelsamie, M. A. A., Rahman, R. A. and Mustafa, S. (2014). Pyramid shape power as a new Halal-compliant food preservation and packaging technique. *Procedia – Social and Behavioral Sciences*, 121, pp. 232–242.

Ahmad, A. N., Rahman, R. A., Othman, M. and Abidin, U. F. U. Z. (2017). Critical success factors affecting the implementation of Halal food management systems: perspective of Halal executives, consultants and auditors. *Food Control*, 74, pp. 70–78.

Arif, S. and Sidek, S. (2015). Application of Halalan tayyiban in the standard reference for determining Malaysian Halal food. *Asian Social Science*, 11(17), pp. 116–129.

Bonne, K. and Verbeke, W. (2008). Muslim consumer trust in Halal meat status and control in Belgium. *Meat Science*, 79, pp. 113–123.

Chandra, G. R., Liaqat, I. A. and Sharma, B. (2019). Blockchain redefining: the Halal food sector. *Proceedings – 2019 Amity International Conference on Artificial Intelligence, AICAI 2019*, pp. 349–354.

de Camargo Fiorini, P. and Jabbour, C. J. C. (2017). Information systems and sustainable supply chain management towards a more sustainable society: where we are and where we are going? *International Journal of Information Management*, 37(4), pp. 241–249.

Elassy, N. (2015). The concepts of quality, quality assurance and quality enhancement. *Quality Assurance in Education*, 23(3), pp. 250–261.

Ghani, M. K. A., Ikram, R. R. R. and Basari, A. S. H. (2015). Computerised systems framework for the Halal pharmaceuticals. *International Journal of Telemedicine and Clinical Practices*, 1(1), pp. 77–93.

Haleem, A., Khan, M. I., Khan, S. and Jami, A. R. (2020). Research status in Halal: a review and bibliometric analysis. *Modern Supply Chain Research and Applications*, 2(1), pp. 23–41.

Hashim, H., Hussin, S. R. and Zainal, N. N. (2014). Exploring Islamic retailer store attributes from consumers perspectives: an empirical investigation. *International Journal of Economics and Management*, 8(S), pp. 117–136.

Hassan, W. A. W., Ahmad, R. M. T. R. L., Marjudi, S., Hamid, A. and Zainuddin, N. M. M. (2017). The implementation framework of Halal supply chain management systems. *Indian Journal of Science and Technology*, 10(48), pp. 1–9.

Hoffman, N. (2000). An examination of the "sustainable competitive advantage" concept: past, present, and future. *Academy of Marketing Science Review*, 2000(4).

Khairuddin, M. M., Rahman, N. A. A., Mohammad, M. F., Majid, Z. A. and Ahmad, M. F. (2018). Regulator perspective on Halal air cargo warehouse compliance. *International Journal of Supply Chain Management*, 7(3), pp. 202–207.

Khan, M. I., Haleem, A. and Khan, S. (2018). Defining Halal supply chain management. *Supply Chain Forum: An International Journal*, 19(2), 122–131.

Kuncoro, W. and Suriani, W. O. (2018). Achieving sustainable competitive advantage through product innovation and market driving. *Asia Pacific Management Review*, 23(3), pp. 186–192.

Mutsikiwa, M. and Basera, C. H. (2012). The influence of socio-cultural variables on consumers' perception of Halal food products: a case of Masvingo urban, Zimbabwe. *International Journal of Business and Management*, 7(20), pp. 112–119.

Ngah, A. H., Ramayah, T., Ali, M. H. and Khan, M. I. (2019). Halal transportation adoption among pharmaceuticals and comestics manufacturers. *Journal of Islamic Marketing*, 11(6), pp. 1619–1639.

Ngah, A. H., Zainuddin, Y. and Thurasamy, R. (2017). Applying the TOE framework in the Halal warehouse adoption study. *Journal of Islamic Accounting and Business Research*, 8(2), pp. 161–181.

Rahim, N. H. M., Zainuddin, A. and Shariff, S. M. (2016). Retailing layouts for Halal food supply chain: issues and challenges. *ScienceInternational*, 28(2), pp. 1941–1947.

Ramli, J. A. (2020). The influence of internal governance on Halal compliance of Malaysian food industry: preliminary study. *Global Business and Management Research: An International Journal*, 12(4), pp. 712–720.

Ikram, R. R. B. R., Ghani, M. K. B. A. and Basari, A. S. H. (2013). Novel computerized Halal Pharmaceuticals supply chain framework for warehouse and procurement. *International Journal of Computer Applications*, 70(10), pp. 22–27.

Shafie, S. and Othman, M. N. (2006). *Halal Certiification: An International Marketing Issues and Challenges*. Retrieved from: https://bit.ly/3xlFIpm (accessed 24 November 2021).

Soon, J. M., Chandia, M. and Regenstein, J. M. (2017). Halal integrity in the food supply chain. *British Food Journal*, 119(1), pp. 39–51.

Soong, S. F. V. (2007). *Managing Halal Quality in Food Service Industry*. UNLV Theses, Dissertations, Professional Papers, and Capstones. Singapore: University of Nevada Las Vegas.

Sukati, I. and Bawaain, A. (2019). The practices of Halal foods and beverages supply chain on marketing performance: a conceptual framework. *International Journal of Business and Social Science*, 10(8), pp. 110–117.

Sumpin, N. A., Kassim, N. F., Zaki, M. I. M., Piah, Z. H. M. and Majid, M. A. A. (2019). Will the real Halal logo please stand up? *International Journal of Academic Research in Business and Social Sciences*, 9(9), pp. 1226–1234.

Surjandari, I., Yusuf, H., Laoh, E. and Maulida, R. (2021). Designing a permissioned blockchain network for the Halal industry using hyperledger fabric with multiple channels and the raft consensus mechanism. *Journal of Big Data*, 8(10). https://doi.org/10.1186/s40537-020-00405-7

Susanty, A., Puspitasari, N. B., Jati, S. and Selvina, O. (2021). Impact of internal and external factors on Halal logistics implementation. *Journal of Islamic Marketing*. https://doi.org/10.1108/JIMA-09-2020-0293

Talib, M. S. A. and Johan, M. R. M. (2012). Issues in Halal packaging: a conceptual paper. *International Business and Management*, 5(2), pp. 94–98.

Talib, H. H. A., Ali, K. A. M. and Jamaludin, K. R. (2008). Quality assurance in Halal food manufacturing in Malaysia: a preliminary study. *Proceedings of International Conference on Mechanical & Manufacturing Engineering (ICME2008)*, Johor Bahru, 21–23 May.

Talib, Z., Zailani, S. and Zainuddin, Y. (2010). Conceptualizations on the dimensions for Halal orientation for food manufacturers: a study in the context of Malaysia. *Pakistan Journal of Social Sciences*, 7(2), pp. 56–61.

Tieman, M. and Darun, M. R. (2017). Leveraging blockchain technology for Halal supply chains. *Islam and Civilisational Renewal*, 8(4), pp. 547–550.

Tieman, M. and Ruiz-bejarano, B. (2020). Halal retailing: closing the last mile in an end-to-end Halal. *Islam and Civilisational Renewal*, 11(1), pp. 147–152.

Tieman, M., van der Vorst, J. G. A. J. and Ghazali, M. C. (2012). Principles in Halal supply chain management. *Journal of Islamic Marketing*, 3(3), pp. 217–243.

Vlăsceanu, L., Grünberg, L. and Pârlea, D. (2007). Quality assurance and accreditation: a glossary of basic terms and definitions. *UNESCO-CEPES 2007*. Retrieved from: https://unesdoc.unesco.org/ark:/48223/pf0000134621 (accessed 24 November 2021).

Yaacob, T. Z., Rahman, F. A. and Jaafar, H. S. (2018). Risk categories in Halal food transportation: a preliminary findings. *International Journal of Supply Chain Management*, 7(6), pp. 453–461.

Zulfakar, M. H., Jie, F. and Chan, C. (2012). Halal food supply chain integrity: from a literature review to a conceptual framework. *Proceedings of the 10th ANZAM Operations, Supply Chain and Services Management Symposium*, 61(4), pp. 1–23.

Part III
Halal meat cartel, transportation, port management and pandemic challenges

8 Exploring the Islamic work ethics and Halal meat supply chain

An insight

Emi Normalina Binti Omar, Nor Bakhriah Sarbani, Ismah Osman, Heizal Hezry Omar and Harlina Suzana Jaafar

Introduction

Towards achieving the Sustainable Development Goals (SDGs) as set up by the United Nations General Assembly, Malaysia also upholds its national development plan in the Malaysia Sustainable Goal which aligned with the 2030 Agenda. In the direction of the 17 SDGs as well as the 2030 Agenda that was listed by the United Nations, Malaysia has prioritized its development plan to align and integrate with the SDGs. The importance of SDGs has been seen in every country in the world, and sustainable supply chain management also is part of the activities that cannot be left behind. The recently established notion of the Halal supply chain has added value to the current supply chain in terms of sustainability. This concept creates innovation to supply chain activities as well as generating a catalyst towards a new era of a competitive global supply chain. Therefore, one of the topics to deliberate on the Halal supply chain is the Halal meat cartel due to recent news related to the movement of Halal meat across borders. Thus, this chapter covers the process of Halal meat movement and import clearance as well as the relevant authorities that are involved in cross-border activities. This chapter also incorporates the Islamic business ethics towards enhancing transparency and accountability of Halal integrity within the supply chain environment to enhancement Malaysia as the global Halal hub.

Halal meat and meat products' import clearance process

The supply chain of the Halal meat process begins with the activities at the border. Import border clearance is an important border activity involving massive security and safety control checking using cargo information, documentation and physical cargo before it is able to enter Malaysia. The formalities are conducted with proper regulatory procedures and process flow involving government agencies and other stakeholders (Melan and Sabar, 2014; Sarbani and Jaafar, 2016). The roles of government agencies involve in this border clearance process also aim to provide trade facilitation towards import processes (Widdowson et al., 2018).

DOI: 10.4324/9781003223719-12

The complexity of the activities depends on the number of stakeholders involved in the supply chain process including physical infrastructure, services and the number of regulatory control imposed on certain trades (Shepherd and Hamanaka, 2015). Thus, the meat import clearance process in Malaysia also involves several stages of data, documentation and physical inspection assessments. As shown in Figure 8.1 the overall clearance is shown in the diagram from process 1 until process 12.

As the above process illustrates, various parties are involved in the Halal meat import process. Their roles and responsibilities are discussed in the nest section.

Authorities and stakeholders involved in meat import clearance

Processes and procedures at the border for the movement of imported cargo need to be done carefully and controlled to ensure that all cargo goes through the proper security screening process as stipulated in the Malaysian import regulations. In the context of importing meat cartels into Malaysia, several agencies have been appointed to regulate the cartel's supply chain starting from origin until it arrives at a designated destination within Malaysia. In the issue of cartel import handling, several authorities and private agencies play an important role in dealing with import clearance at the border. Among the main parties involved are the Royal Malaysian Customs Department (RMCD), the Malaysian Quarantine and Inspection Service (MAQIS), the Food Security and Safety Division (Ministry of Health), the Department of Veterinary Service, the Ministry of Agriculture and Food Industries (DVS), the Department of Islamic Development Malaysia (JAKIM), the import agent and the importer. Their roles are described as follows.

The Royal Malaysian Customs Department (RMCD)

The Royal Malaysian Customs Department is the government organization responsible for regulating the nation's circuitous assess arrangement, border authorization and opiates offences. In matters of meat imports to Malaysia, the RMCD acts as the main agency that regulates import activities. Each import trade must be declared in a system called the Customs Information System and complete trade information will be displayed at each relevant customs station. Through the customs information system, the trade will be assessed through the tariff code declared by the importer or the importer's agent who has been appointed. When the tariff code for meat is selected then other enforcement agencies that regulate food will automatically be notified through the integrated system.

Malaysian Quarantine and Inspection Service (MAQIS)

In a nutshell, the MAQIS Act 2011 mandates MAQIS to guarantee that plants, animals, carcasses, fish, agricultural goods, soil and microorganisms imported into Malaysia are free of pests, illnesses, and pollutants, do not harm the national agricultural industry and conform with health regulations (Hamat et al., 2019). In the

Islamic work ethics and Halal meat supply chain 113

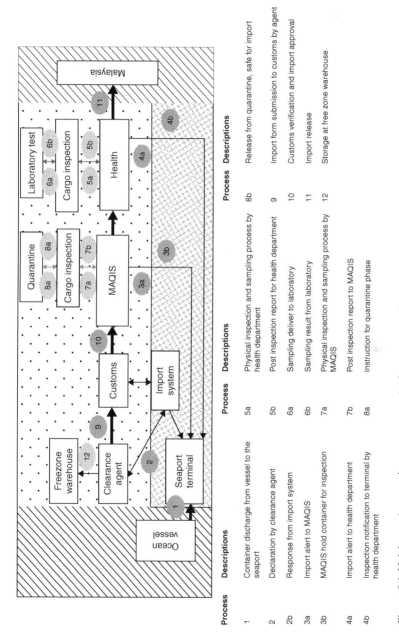

Figure 8.1 Halal meat import clearance process in the seaport environment.
Source: Sarbani (2020).

matter of Halal import, the function of MAQIS is to implement control according to the conditions stated in the meat import permit issued by the DVS, which is to ensure that all imported slaughtered meat must include a Halal certificate from an external Halal certification agency that has been recognized by JAKIM.

Food Security and Safety Division (Ministry of Health)

Imported food control's major goal is to verify that food entering the nation is safe and adheres to the provisions of the Food Act 1983 and its regulations. Imported food control activities carried out at the country's entrance include inspection and sampling of food consignments as well as enforcement activities such as detention, withdrawal, rejection, prosecution and destruction of consignments that violate food legislation. The responsibility of the Food Safety and Quality Division is also to ensure that the content declared on the food label is true to each consignment. In principle, Halal consignment control is not subject to the regulation of this section.

Department of Veterinary Service (DVS), Ministry of Agriculture and Food Industries

Under the Ministerial Functions Act 1969 (Kementerian Dalam Negeri, 2021), the DVS is responsible for supervising the import and export of livestock and animal products, as well as quarantine services. In the context of the supply of Halal meat from abroad, the function of the DVS is to recognize foreign plants that are eligible to supply meat to Malaysia through established meat import procedures. Importers and every international Halal meat processing plant must apply for qualification approval before being eligible to carry out import activities. Eligible importers must apply for a permit for each import and must obtain DVS approval before the import is eligible to be brought into Malaysia. This can be seen in the published list of approved companies and countries in the DVS website for abattoirs and Halal slaughtering plants in foreign countries. Several countries have been acknowledged by the DVS and JAKIM to supply meat and meat products to Malaysia, including South Africa, Australia, Argentina, Belgium, Brazil, Denmark, India, Pakistan, Japan, New Zealand and the United States of America. The role of the DVS is not limited to controlling Halal meat and meat products only, it is also responsible for monitoring other products, including poultry and poultry products, egg and egg products, gelatine from various sources, pork and pork products and dairy and dairy products from various countries including Germany, Korea, Poland, Thailand, Turkey, Spain, Bangladesh, Netherland, China, the UAE, Indonesia Canada, Vietnam and Iran.

Department of Islamic Development Malaysia (JAKIM)

The Halal Management Division of JAKIM is the competent authority in Malaysian Halal Certification, with responsibilities that include Halal certification, inspection and Halal certification of foreign slaughterhouses; product sample analysis; Halal information and advisory services; and enforcement of the Trade Descriptions Act 2011(Sarbani, 2020). The 2011 Trade Description Act amendment also expands the jurisdiction of JAKIM officers in monitoring and law enforcement activities against operators who misuse the Halal logo on their products where JAKIM and MAIN/JAIN officers will be appointed as Assistant Trade Description Officers authorized by the Ministry of Domestics Trade and Consumers Affairs (KPDNHEP) (Sarbani, 2020). JAKIM is also given the same prosecution powers as the KPDNHEP instead of just being a witness, as it was before the 2011 Trade Description Act amendment was made. Nevertheless, in the formalities for Halal meat import from foreign countries, JAKIM remained an unlisted border agency that is not directly involved in the process of regulating import trade at the border. The import control and enforcement tasks are handed over to MAQIS by using import permit requisition approved by the DVS.

Import agents

While all the lenses are focused on the weaknesses of Halal meat control enforcement, the role of importing agents also needs to be addressed. The logistics practitioner is the intermediary agent for the trade clearance process in the border area including pledging and physical handling before it is sent to the importer. Halal meat consignment import agents including the slaughtered meat category are eligible to obtain JAKIM Halal certification through voluntary initiatives by applying certification Halal MS 2400-1:2019 (Transportation), MS 2400-2:2019 (Warehousing) and MS 2400-3:2019 (Retail) (Sarbani, 2020) to ensure that the services delivered comply with Shariah and technical requirements related to Halal logistics as an added value to their services (Department of Standards Malaysia, 2019). However, the number of logistics operators that have obtained Halal certification is very limited and the prices offered to importers are also not competitive. So, most importers continue using agents who are not registered under Halal certification as this is more profitable. This also contributes to the weakness of Halal goods handling operations at the border, as logistics operations are managed by parties that are not sensitive to the needs of Halal trade. The logistics operations of the agents involved influence the pledging activities, the selection of transportation and the equipment used.

Importers

The responsibility of the importer towards the handling of Halal trade ensures the quality of Halal trade throughout the trade clearance activities carried out until it arrives at the premises. It has been found that some of the meat importers appoint non-certified Halal import agent to handle their import clearance. As a result, operations were implemented that were not Shariah compliant. Importers were found to focus only on import permits as a guarantee for import clearance but lacked awareness towards the importance of the continuity of Halal operations post-import clearance process. Importers make decisions regarding logistics operations including storage or value-added activities to trade. So, this is seen as a significant weakness influenced by the knowledge and level of awareness of the importer.

Islamic business ethics: an integrated component within the ecosystem of Halal market

This study encapsulates Islamic ethics as one of the important components within the perspectives of the ecosystem of any business endeavour. Thus, it can incorporate Islamic business ethics in supply chain management activities, which is the main aim of this chapter. Ethics is defined as "the set of moral principles that distinguish what is right from what is wrong" (Beekun et al., 2003; International Islamic University Malaysia, 2021). Work ethic, moreover, is a personality attribute that varies from person to person and develops early in childhood, and it has a substantial effect on the attitudes and behaviours of employees at work (Saks et al., 1996). The uniqueness of ethics and morality, on the other hand, is that they cannot be assessed or imposed by power. While regulations apply to all firms in the same way or must be applied in the same way, ethical norms in various firms might be distinctive and vary.

Conducting operations with integrity and appropriate skill, consideration and diligence, organizing affairs reliably and effectively with adequate risk management systems, adhering to proper market conduct standards, avoiding conflicts of interest and paying attention to the interests of its customers by treating them fairly are all examples of ethical norms for many organizations (Rexhepi and Ramadani, 2016). According to Rizk (2008), ethics is concerned with the formation of broad guidelines for human activity or behaviour. Yousef (2000) asserts that ethics is a system or recognition of a certain social situation that allows one to judge human behaviour in terms of goodness or immorality. Luco (2014) affirms that ethics is a means to evaluate human behaviour in terms of goodness or immorality by way of a system or through recognition of a specific social setting. The distinction between ethics and morality is that morals define their own identity, whereas ethics govern the intricate details of a social structure, and notably originated through moral standards adopted by individuals within a group.

To translate the word ethics, "Akhlaq" is the fitting term in Arabic. Its meaning is derived from the root, which signifies making, moulding, shaping, moulding or generating. The understanding of morality (Ilm al-Akhlaq) can be interpreted as ethics, moral science or moral philosophy, whereas Akhlaq is a plural of "Khuluq", which refers to groups of various personality qualities (Ahmad and Owoyemi, 2012).

Akhlaq differs from Western viewpoints from an Islamic standpoint. According to Western sociologists, determining what is good or terrible is mostly reliant on human viewpoints. However, in Islam, the religious institution is the source of ethics, having received a divine revelation and communicating it to humankind. In other words, the Quran and Sunnah are the automatic sources of Akhlaq in

Islam. Thus, all patterns of behaviour and character qualities draw their virtue or badness from the holy book's sanction or otherwise, as well as the sayings and deeds of the Prophet Muhammad (SAW), who has been called as the ideal model of behaviour for all believers.

Islamic ethics refers to a set of laws that regulate individual and organizational behaviour, with the goal of ensuring compassion, openness and responsibility in behaviour and acts while also protecting society interests. Islamic ethics in the workplace is an attitude that moulds and affects market players' involvement and participation to be honest, accountable and devoted to achieving their own goals without risking the welfare of other players or society (Ahmed and Fatima, 2015). Within the setting of promoting, Islamic ethics looks to maintain dependable conduct based upon religiously authorized information, from the avoidance of double dealing and false behaviour to fortifying straightforward operation and generous behaviour.

Workers are an organization's human capital. Having workers in an organization who are ethically and morally reliable will have a great effect on the organization. There is a veritable conviction that, as a source of happiness and achievement, Islam emphasizes creative and productive efforts. This is in accord with what Allah promises us in the Quran: "Allah has promised you His forgiveness and bounties" (2:2688). The verse says that people who make a concerted effort to do their jobs appropriately will be rewarded and, following the will of Allah, are promised forgiveness and bounties. Instead, Islamic teaching condemns begging and living as a parasite on the labour of others. The Prophet Muhammad (SAW) preached in this regard that: "No one eats food other than what he eats from his labour" (Sahih al-Bukhari, n.d.). Islam sees work as an Ibadah (a religious duty) and Jihad (cause of Allah). The Prophet (SAW) has delivered his message: "The honest, trustworthy, merchant will be with the Prophets, Siddeeqs and martyrs" (At-Tirmidhi, n.d.).

Work is a dedicated effort aimed at advancing one's economic, social and psychological interests, as well as maintaining social status, advancing social welfare and reaffirming religion. Work, in other words, is a means of safeguarding the five primary human needs of "Din" (faith), "Nafs" (human self), "Aql" (intellect), "Nasl" (posterity) and "Mal" (wealth). As a result, human people must pursue whatever labour is available at any given time, subject to Allah's Will, as Allah (SWT) has ordained in the Quran: "disperse through the land and seek of the bounty of Allah" (62:10) (Ali, 1989).

Work as an Ibadah (religious duty) and Jihad (striving for something) demonstrates that participation in economic activities (work) is not just a way of supporting a healthy and wealthy community, but is also a divine imperative. In Islamic work ethics, the worth of work is determined from the associated objectives rather than the employment achievements. As a result, "Niyyah" is the most crucial role in Ibadah and Jihad (intention). In Islam, every man's ultimate aim (Niyyah) for his actions must be completely for Allah (SWT).

As a result, work must be done with sincerity for the sake of Allah's joys (Ikhlas). This is explained in the Quran: "Say, verily, I am commanded to serve

Allah with sincere devotion" (39:14) (Ali, 1989). Sincere intent will guarantee that the task effectively and effectively follows the given instruction, leading to "Falah" (successful in this world and hereafter) (Islamic Markets, 2021).

The Islamic perspective on work is further addressed in work ethics. The Islamic system is comprised of three primary core teachings: "Aqidah" or deep conviction in Allah's Oneness; "Ibadah" or one's surrender and obedience to Allah; and "Akhlaq", or one's submission and obedience to Allah. Ethics in Islam includes not just religious morality in particular actions, but also all elements of life in the physical, spiritual, moral or emotional domains, as well as intellectual, emotional, individual and social components (Yaken, 2006).

"Akhlaq" refers to a person's excellent behaviour, way of thinking, attitude, or ideals as dictated by the Quran and Sunnah. "It is, therefore, subject to the assessment of Allah (SWT): ... the most honoured of you in the sight of Allah is indeed the most righteous of you" (49:13) (Ali, 1989). Imam Al-Ghazali refined the view by recommending three ways of doing good, so that the true meaning of "Akhlaq" is implied. "Akhlaq" differs from the conventional view of "do not harm" because Islam argues that it can also imply that it can be neutral not to harm others in the sense that one cannot do any good either (Al-Shafii et al., 2018).

To begin with and first, one must practise benevolence (Ihsan) toward others. Second, one has to abstain from harming others. Finally, it is considered irreligious and immoral to harm others. The three attributes correspond to the revelation of Allah in the Quran: "We sent yee not, but as a mercy for all creatures" (21:107) (Ali, 1989). To convey the notion of "Akhlaq", Islam utilizes phrases like "Khayr" (goodness), "Birr" (righteousness), "Qist" (equity), "Adl" (justice), "Haqiqah" (truth), "Ma'ruf" (recognized and authorized) and "Taqwa" (piety). As mentioned in the Quran, Islam also gives the most important paradigm for humankind to incorporate "Akhlaq" into every act: "We have indeed in the Apostle of Allah a beautiful pattern of (conduct) for everyone whose hope is in Allah and the Final Day, and who engages much in praise of Allah" (33:21) (Ali, 1989).

In business, Islam considers ethical behaviour to be a critical component of developing connections with both the Creator and other people. Sula and Kartajaya (2006) acknowledge that adopting Islamic values, morality and honesty, as well as other virtuous tenets that are prevalent towards sound business dealings, will drive towards embracing spiritual, ethical, realistic and humanistic constituents. Nonetheless, many firms employ business ethics to promote a favourable image. It is described as a corporation's efforts to encourage customers to engage in socially responsible behaviour while also benefiting the corporation's market position and improving its image. Ali (2005) asserts that marketers confront the density of competition and frequently pursue the profit maximization objective, particularly in the current open market economy. Nevertheless, in an Islamic context, it is pertinent to reinforce customer interactions, as well as the public at large through the propagation of Ihsan, which somehow relates to goodness in morality, consecutively, manifest in the behaviour of an individual, in addition to their connection with other human beings in society (Kadhim et al., 2017).

The distinctive factors of Islamic work ethics

In Islam, ethical behaviour is founded on the belief that humans are obligated to obey God's commands and adhere to Shariah rules (Ernst, 2003). To put it another way, an ethical person must distinguish between what is allowed (Halal) and what is prohibited (Haram). This ethical obligation was allocated at the beginning of creation when the "Ruhu" (soul) of all human beings pledged to fulfil God's orders in their earthly existence (32:71–73, translated by Ali, 1989, 2005). A cursory review of relevant Islamic literature and the guidance given in the Holy Quran and Sunnah led to the conclusion that the main distinguishing factors of Islamic work ethics are the emphasis on Halal and Haram, purity of intention (Niiyat), seeking employment and the nature of the relationship between employer and employee. These factors were put forward by a cursory review of relevant Islamic literature and the guidance given in the Holy Quran and Sunnah.

Employment in Islam

Islam emphasizes the importance of labour for all parts of society, believing that lawful labour is a requirement for individuals to gain rewards and Allah's (SWT) blessings in this world and the next (Ali, 2005). The Prophet Muhammad (SAW) remarked about the employee–employer relationship: "Your brothers are your servants whom Allah has made your subordinate, he should give them to eat for what he eats and wear for what he wears and do not put on them burden of any labour which may exhaust them. And if you give them such task then provide them assistance" (Sahih al-Bukhari, n.d.). The nature of the relationship that should exist between the employer and his or her followers is clarified in this Hadith. The nature of the relationship as indicated is described further down.

Employers should treat their employees like brothers rather than followers, respecting, forgiving and appreciating them. Leaders who see their subordinates as brothers under the banner of Islam or mankind are more likely to be generous, fair and sympathetic when it comes to their responsibilities and rights. As a consequence, employees are more likely to work hard and with honesty, trust and focus to satisfy job objectives, adhere to Islam's spirit of oneness and ultimately receive the Almighty's (SWT) contentment (Ali and Al-Owaihan, 2008).

The previous Hadith explains the essential premise of calculating the minimum salary of the employees inside enterprises. It necessitates companies being very liberal in paying their employees' salaries that are sufficient to suit their wants and expectations. Employees do work hard to assist the company to realize its goals and objectives, as well as a strong market position. As a result, they have the right to seek equitable remuneration from their employer to satisfy their basic needs.

An employee should not be assigned a task that is above their capabilities, or that is likely to cause them significant hardship; and they should not be required to work lengthy hours that are harmful to their health. The Prophet (SAW) said, "Allah (SWT) has no mercy on him who is not merciful to (His) men" (Sahih al-Bukhari, n.d.). He (SAW) again suggested that, "Be merciful to those on earth, that (God Who) is in Heaven will be merciful to you" (At-Tirmidhi., n.d.). Furthermore, an employee who has been assigned a difficult work should be aided by more personnel and cash to lessen their load.

Therefore, integration of Islamic business ethics into the business process particularly Halal meat supply chain management activities can enhance the business to become more transparent and integrity will be achieved in the business. Moreover, it endeavours value added in the import of Halal meat supply chain as well as other business processes.

Conclusion

In conclusion, with the involvement of parties such as RMC, MAQIS, Food Security and Safety Division (Ministry of Health), Department of Veterinary Service, Ministry of Agriculture and Food Industries (DVS), Department of Islamic Development Malaysia (JAKIM), Import Agent and the Importer in the import process of the Halal meat supply chain, and also incorporate the Islamic business ethics in the supply chain environment, this adds value-added as well as strengthen the Halal supply chain in the future. Moreover, it is suggested in future research, in-depth research regarding Islamic business ethics and its effect on the business and supply chain activities should be considered and carried out.

References

Ahmad, S. and Owoyemi, M. Y. (2012). The concept of Islamic work ethic: an analysis of some salient points in the prophetic tradition. *International Journal of Business and Social Science*, 3(20), pp. 116–123.

Ahmed, A. and Fatima, S. (2015). The Holy Quran: text, translation and commentary by Abdullah Yusuf Ali (a critical review). *Al-Adwa*, 44(30).

Al-Shafii, M. M. O., Ali, M. S., Zin, E. I. E. W. and Thoarlim, A. (2018). Al-Akhlaq (ethics) perceptions in Islam: a textual interpretation through Imam Muhammad Al-Ghazali. *International Journal of Academic Research in Business and Social Sciences*, 8(10), pp. 315–329.

Ali, A. Y. (1989). *The Holy Quran: Text, Translation and Commentary* (New Revise). Maryland, MA: Amana Corporation.

Ali, A. J. (2005). *Islamic Perspectives on on Management and Organization*. Cheltenham: Edward Elgar.

Ali, A. J. and Al-Owaihan, A. (2008). Islamic work ethic: a critical review. *Cross Cultural Management: An International Journal*, 15(1), pp. 5–19.

At-Tirmidhi. (n.d.). *Jami' at-Tirmidhi 1209. The Hadith of the Prophet Muhammad.* Retrieved from: Sunnah.com (accessed 24 November 2021).

Beekun, R. I., Stedham, Y. and Yamamura, J. H. (2003). Business ethics in Brazil and the US: a comparative investigation. *Journal of Business Ethics*, 42(3), pp. 267–279.

Department of Standard Malaysia (DSM) (2019). *Department of Standard Malaysia 2400–2019*. Kulala Lumpur: DSM.
Ernst, C. W. (2003). *Following Muhammad: Rethinking Islam in the Contemporary World*. Chapel Hill, NC: University of North Carolina Press.
Hamat, M. A. H. C., Rashid, M. F. and Mohammad, N. B. (2019). Role of freight and forwarding company in facilitating the export-import process in Kelantan Malaysia. *International Journal of Economics and Business Research*, 18(3), pp. 387–398.
International Islamic University Malaysia (2021). *IIUM Repository*. Retrieved from: http://irep.iium.edu.my/ (accessed 24 November 2021).
Islamic Markets (2021). *Navigate the Islamic Economy*. Retrieved from: https://islamicmarkets.com/ (accessed 24 November 2021).
Kadhim, A. S., Ahmad, S., Owoyemi, M. Y. and Ahmad, M. (2017). Islamic ethics: the attributes of Al-Ihsan in the Quran and its effects on Muslim morality. *International Journal of Business and Social Science*, 8(11), pp. 102–107.
Kementerian Dalam Negeri. (2021). *About Us*. Retrieved from: www.kdn.gov.my (accessed 24 November 2021).
Luco, A. (2014). The definition of morality: threading the needle. *Social Theory and Practice*, 40(3), 361–387.
Melan, M. and Sabar, R. (2014). Seamless freights movement towards the quality services at cross border checkpoints between Malaysia and Thailand. *International Journal of Science and Research*, 3(9).
Rexhepi, G. and Ramadani, N. (2016). Ethics and social responsibility in Islamic finance. In V. Ramadani, L. P. Dana, S. Gërguri-Rashiti and V. Ratten (Eds.), *Entrepreneurship and Management in an Islamic Context*. Cham: Springer, pp. 133–142.
Rizk, R. R. (2008). Back to basics: an Islamic perspective on business and work ethics. *Social Responsibility Journal*, 4(1/2), pp. 246–254.
Sahih al-Bukhari. (n.d.). *Sahih al-Bukhari 1979. The Hadith of the Prophet Muhammad*. Retrieved from: sunnah.com (accessed 24 November 2021).
Saks, A. M., Mudrack, P. E. and Ashforth, B. E. (1996). The relationship between the work ethic, job attitudes, intentions to quit, and turnover for temporary service employees. *Canadian Journal of Administrative Sciences*, 13(3), pp. 226–236.
Sarbani, N. B. and Jaafar, H. S. (2016). Facilitation for Halal product supply chain: a conceptual review. *MITRANS Logistics and Transport International Conference*, 6, pp. 12–14.
Shepherd, B. and Hamanaka, S. (2015). Overcoming trade logistics challenges: Asia-Pacific experiences. *Asia Pacific Journal of Marketing and Logistics*, 27(3), pp. 444–466.
Sula, M. S. and Kartajaya, H. (2006). *Syariah Marketing*. Bandung: Mizan Publishing.
Widdowson, D., Short, G., Blegen, B. and Kashubsky, M. (2018). National committees on trade facilitation. *World Customs Journal*, 12(1), pp. 27–48.
Yaken. (2006). *What is the Meaning of My Belong to Islam?* Beirut: Darul Al-Ressalh Publication.
Yousef, D. A. (2000). The Islamic work ethic as a mediator of the relationship between locus of control, role conflict and role ambiguity – a study in an Islamic country setting. *Journal of Managerial Psychology*, 15(4), pp. 283–298.

9 Exploring the Halal meat cartel case

A legal framework and insight from the regulator

Faradina binti Ahmad,
Muhammad Zaly Shah and
Zuhra Junaida Binti Ir Mohamad Husny Hamid

Introduction to Halal integrity in the supply chain

Halal logistics are the chain of procurement, transferring, loading and handling of material parts, cattle and other animals, finished or semi-finished inventory of consumable and non-consumable items, and related documented data and certification flows through the business and the supply chain under the general doctrines of Shariah principles (Tieman and van Nistelrooy, 2014). The same authors also mentioned that Halal logistics and supply chain management (SCM) is an important discipline for the Halal industry in extending the Halal integrity from the source to the point of consumer purchase (Tieman and Ghazali, 2014).

The importance of Halal logistics services are, first, ensure avoidance of cross-contamination (Tieman and Ghazali, 2014; Rashid and Bojei, 2020). Second, to avoid mistakes (Mahidin et al., 2017) and, finally, to ensure the compliance of Shariah thus fulfilling the expectation of Muslims' demand for Halal goods and services (Zaina et al., 2015). Meanwhile, Krishnan et al. (2017) explained that Shariah compliance is synonymous with food safety, including good animal welfare of the animals before they are slaughtered. In order words, Halal logistics is the shield of protection that protects the integrity of the other Halal schemes.

The impact of the Halal meat cartel towards Halal integrity

Halal meat

Halal meat is the type of meat which is slaughtered in accordance with the Shariah requirement, Order 3(1) of the Trade Description (Definition of Halal) Order 2011. Hence, Muslim consumers consider purchasing Halal meat to be part of their act of worship as it satisfies all the elements of "Syarak" under the Shariah laws. As for non-Muslims, according to Ambali and Bakar (2014), they are of the idea that Halal products or food reflect good quality, hygiene and cleanliness, as all aspects of process have to be in accordance to the Halal assurance management system. Furthermore, the idea of Halalan Toyyiban reflects the concept of safety,

DOI: 10.4324/9781003223719-13

which is very attractive to both Muslim and non-Muslim consumers (Ahmad et al., 2017; Alzeer et al., 2018).

Due to the high popularity which led to a demand for the Halal meat, there is an impending need to ensure there is no cross-contamination during the supply chain transaction (Afiq et al., 2009). Nevertheless, due to the high standards requirement, many logistics service providers turn a blind eye towards dedicating warehouses for safekeeping or transport fleets for the Halal meat due to the costs. As a result, instances of combining shipment of Halal meat with non-Halal meat occurred to cut the expenses. Despite the fact that the business is thriving and making profit from the Halal meat business, the industry effort is limited in observing the standard and it seems this cross-contamination can only be minimized but not avoided (Zulfakar et al., 2014).

The supply chain of the Halal meat operation consists of businesses or commercial entities in Halal meat from the point of raising the chattel to the point of slaughtering and distributing to the end consumers. The general rule of having a Halal meat supply chain is to maintain the integrity of the Halalan Toyyiban aspect of the goods; however, recently in Malaysia, news of cross-contamination, fraudulent action and deliberate non-compliance of the Malaysia Standards on Halal has shown otherwise. Table 9.1 are the lists of news from the local Halal meat scene.

Halal integrity – violations of rights of the end user or customers and the accreditation company

By undertaking the right processes, manufacturers as well as consumers will ensure Halal integrity along the supply chain of food and beverages (Mahidin et al., 2017). A formal definition of Halal integrity might be articulated as: the assurance of safe (pure), quality (good) and free from malpractice (lawful) food from farm to fork (Soon et al., 2017). Therefore, this research seeks to identify the effect of the violation of the Halal meat cartel towards the stakeholders.

The stakeholders who are directly affected by the violation of the Halal meat cartel are, first, the customers, second, the accreditation body and, finally, the Halal meat industry in Malaysia. Figure 9.1 shows the related stakeholders of the Halal meat cartel.

The first stakeholder: the consumers

The consumers are the main group who suffers from the fraudulent action in the Halal meat cartel. Their reliance on the Halal logo results in their willingness to part with their hard-earned money in observance of their faith by purchasing this product. In law, they are examined as the group minority of an unequal bargaining power. The law perceives consumers as the minority, defenceless against the mighty corporate business which is armed with expert advisors.

Unfortunately, due to the fact that access or supplies of Halal meat comes from only a selected few firms that have JAKIM Halal certification, the customer

Table 9.1 List of news articles about the Halal meat scandal

News article	Issues
Suhaini, 2017	Suspicions of a mixing of Halal and non-Halal meat in a single container.
Hammim, 2020	A meat distribution company and its two directors pleaded not guilty at the Sessions Court to two charges of using unrecognized Halal logos on its lorries. Raihanah Cold Storage Sdn Bhd and its directors Rahman Sheikh Abdullah and Raihanah Kasim made the plea after the charges were read in front of Judge Mohd Haldar Abd Aziz.
Denin, 2021	All four suspected of involvement in the Halal meat cartel were detained by SPRM Johor and to be charged under Section 117 Penal Code at the Magistrate Court Johor Bahru.
Hammim, 2021	It was recently reported that a cartel has been importing non-certified meat and selling it as Halal meat in Malaysia. The cartel has reportedly been operating for over 40 years and imported meat from non-Halal-certified slaughterhouses in a few countries, such as Brazil, Bolivia, Canada, Colombia, Spain and Mexico. The meat, smuggled out of ports, would be taken to warehouses where it would be mixed with Halal-certified meat and repacked with fake Halal logos, then sold in the market.
Hamid, 2021	The owner of Raihanah Cold Storage Sdn Bhd filed a defamation suit of RM50.0 million and seeks an apology from Facebook's Zaharin Mohd Yasin owner for defaming them in the non-Halal meat cartel case.

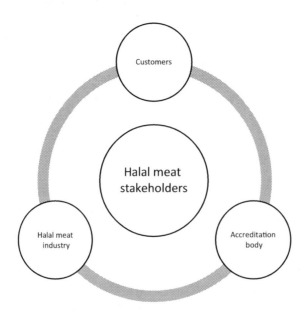

Figure 9.1 Halal meat stakeholders.

has no choice but to rely on the available produce duly certified by JAKIM. They are confident with the JAKIM certification stamped on the packaging. This dependence by the customer on the JAKIM Halal logo raises the duty of care towards the Halal certified company to strictly follow the standards and regulations. According to Rigod and Tovar (2019), it shows the end consumers simply rely on the authorities that certify the Halal label without questioning or investigating further on the safety, quality or Halalan Toyyiban aspect of the products. In addition, once the sense of security is embedded in their mind, the trust level will increase towards the Halal products (Firdausi et al., 2020).

Similarly, an article by Aksoy and Özsönmez (2019) shows evidence that the Millennial generation trust Halal certified products, and are willing to pay premium prices for them. Once this trust is established, these consumers are willing to recommend the food to another (Al-Ansi et al., 2019).

The second stakeholder: the accreditation authorities

The second stakeholder directly affected by the Halal meat cartel is the accreditation authorities. These authorities play a vital role in ensuring the Halal logo and certification instil trust in Muslim and non-Muslim consumers and subsequently support Halal industries (Ahmad et al., 2013). Violation of the Halal meat will directly affect the reputation of the accreditation body.

Under the Trade Descriptions (Certification and Marking of Halal) Order 2011, it is stated that the Department of Islamic Development Malaysia (JAKIM) and the Islamic Religious Council of the States (MAIN) are recognized as the competent authorities to accredit any food, goods or services in relation to food or goods under the Trade Descriptions (Definition of Halal) 2011. Therefore, none of the goods can use the Halal logo unless they are certified as Halal by the competent authorities (JAKIM/MAIN) and properly marked with the logo. The rationale of consumer trust towards the JAKIM Halal logo lies on the fact that the Order clearly states that those who violate the Order are guilty of an offense and upon conviction may be fined up to RM100,000 or imprisoned for a term not exceeding three years or both for the individual. The penalty for a corporate body is a fine of up to RM250,000.

Therefore, the consumers are assured of their rights being protected by the accreditation bodies, be it JAKIM or religious state authorities, as they have the power to regulate the Halal operation within each state (Shariff et al., 2014). Furthermore, JAKIM also has many projects in relation to consumer rights and also awareness of the duties and responsibilities of the certified company. Moreover, JAKIM and state religious bodies are able to monitor import and export activities which justify the reliance of the first stakeholder towards the Halal logo on the meat products (Abdullah et al., 2017).

Finally, violation of the Halal meat chain has resulted in distrust of the consumer towards large business chains. As a consequence, individual purchasers are willing to opt out from buying from large chain markets and instead buy from local farmers who are known to observe the Islamic lifestyle. According to

126 *Ahmad, Shah and Hamid*

Al-Ansi et al. (2019), they are willing to switch to purchase meat in smaller shops as long as the seller is Muslim too; this is the case for Halal meat in the UK.

Exploring the Halal meat cartel case: an insight from the regulator

The legal process framework

So now the main issue is how are these violations being dealt with by the aw? In Malaysia, all Halal operations are governed by the Malaysian Standards on Halal and also Trade Descriptions Act (TDA) 2011 (Yaacob et al., 2016). The legal process framework is laid out in Figure 9.2, and shows that there are two approaches depending on the status of the certification of the company. For the

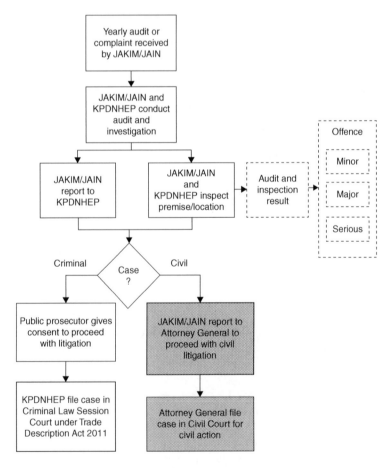

Figure 9.2 Legal process framework for Halal violation.
Source: Ahmad et al., 2020.

company with existing JAKIM Halal certification which is found to be in breach of the standards, the legal enforcement will follow the procedures and the punishment under the standards. On the other hand, if the company did not have JAKIM Halal certification but had used the Halal logo to mislead and make profit from the end user, thus the matter is deal with under TDA 2011.

In relation to the case of mixing Halal and non-Halal meat as recently reported in the local news, the said company is certified Halal by JAKIM. As such, JAKIM or the state religious agency has the jurisdiction to enforce the terms under the Malaysian Standards. Based on Figure 9.2, the violation was the company action of mixing Halal and non-Halal meats in the same warehouse before selling the same under the Halal logo. The Disciplinary Committee of the religious state department may decide that such violation is minor, major or a serious in nature. Next, the sentencing of the violation will depend on the type of wrongdoings as shown in Figure 9.2.

On the other hand, if the Halal meat operator is not certified by JAKIM and is abusing the Halal logo arbitrarily for profit, then the violation falls under the TDA (2011) (Ariffin et al., 2021). Investigation by JAKIM, state religious authorities and KPDNHEP will lead to charges under the TDA 2011. A criminal legal proceeding is next filed into the Session Court, criminal division and prosecution is conducted by KPDNHEP (Zakaria and Zubaidah Ismail, 2014; Ab. Halim and Ahmad, 2014). JAKIM and state religious authorities' officers are witnesses to the proceeding and will later report the outcome of the case to the media. The prosecutor will bear the burden of proving the case beyond reasonable doubt as this is a criminal court and the judge will either find the defendant to be guilty and give a sentence under the TDA 2011 or dismiss the case if the prosecutor fails to prove the evidence of fault. Nevertheless, it seems that despite the available sources of laws in Malaysia, civil law was not included as part of the enforcement tools. This fact has been raised as issue by several existing authors and should be taken into serious consideration (Hasan, 2007; Ab. Halim and Ahmad, 2014).

The analysis and findings

The challenges of the legal enforcement process in the Halal meat cartel under the TDA 2011

The first challenge in a criminal trial is to have a higher burden of proof as compares to a civil proceeding. The case must be proved beyond reasonable doubt for the court to decide in favour of the defendants. As compared to a civil proceeding, which demands for there to be evidence on the balance of probability.

The second challenge is the fact that there is no specific Halal Act to regulate the Halal activities. There has been news of the potential passing of such regulation but to date, the matter has been kept in the dark (Bernama, 2019). Despite having the Trade Descriptions Order (Definition of Halal) 2011, so far there is one pending case under the Order. One convicted cased under the

Trade Descriptions Act 1972 shows the decision of the judge in allowing the conviction for the second charge which is a violation under the Act when the defendant put on display the word Halal on packaged noodles when the product actually contained a non-Halal substance. As for the first charge, the expert statement from the Chemist Ministry was dismissed by the court due to the judge's refusal to accept the evidence to establish the elements of non-Halal substance in the noodles sold to the Muslim consumers (*Malayan Law Journal*, 1986).

Besides that, there are also the issues faced by the legal agencies' officers who are responsible for ensuring compliance of the Halal meat business. In a nutshell, these officers graduate in Islamic studies and not conventional legal study. As such, they do not have the qualifications to conduct an investigation, collect evidence and prepare the charge. They need legal training to conduct an investigation, prepare charges documents, collect evidence and take part in court proceedings (Ab. Halim and Ahmad, 2014; Zaina et al., 2015). There are other challenges that they have to face including the lack of logistics facilities to keep the evidence, the feeling of intimidation due to lack of experience, lack of time and the possibility of a counter-suit.

Finally, the existing legal process does not include all the available sources of law in Malaysia. It is restricted to only criminal laws, disregarding the civil laws and Shariah laws on issues of Halal meat (Ab. Halim et al., 2014). This should not be the case, as applying all the legal tools will heighten compliance, as more operators will become aware of the expensive penalty they might face or the jail time they will have to spend if convicted in the Shariah court.

Conclusion and future research

In conclusion, the Halal meat cartel activities have been discovered by the legal authorities, some of the officers among the operators have been charged, others are being investigated and these enforcements are evidence that JAKIM and the related legal agencies are monitoring the Halal industry closely. Nevertheless, taking into account the challenges discussed, it is important to focus on the protection of the three stakeholders who are directly related to the industry. The consumers, being the stakeholder with the least authority and power, must be protected by the law. JAKIM's goodwill as the accreditation body must also be kept safe from being tarnished by the illegal act of the cartel. Finally, the honest business ventures in the Halal meat industry who are paying for the certification must also be taken into consideration. As such, it can be concluded that current enforcement on the Halal meat cartel is on the right track.

This research opens the possibility of future research with regards to the possibility of the importance of including civil laws and Shariah laws for Halal logistics violations. Besides that, this should also spark interest on the details of evidence and the suitable witnesses to corroborate the expert witnesses from the Ministry of Chemist to determine the elements of Halal and Haram in court.

References

Abdullah, M. S., Salleh, A., Rosman, B. and Mia, M. H. (2017). Halal food and Sufism: introduction of new technology. *Journal of Enginering Technology*, 6(2), pp. 842–852.

Ab. Halim, M. A. and Ahmad, A. A. (2014). Enforcement of consumer protection laws on Halal Products: Malaysian experience. *Asian Social Science*, 10(3), pp. 9–14.

Ab. Halim, M. A. B., Mohd, K. W. B., Salleh, M. M. M., Yalawae, A., Omar, T. S. N. M. S., Ahmad, A., Ahmad, A. A. B. and Kashim, M. I. A. B. M. (2014). Consumer protection of Halal products in Malaysia: a literature highlight. *Procedia – Social and Behavioral Sciences*, 121, pp. 68–78.

Afiq, M., Razak, A., & Ramli, M. A. (2009). *Aplikasi Umum Al-Balwa Dalam Menangani Pencemaran*. www.academia.edu/35881465/Aplikasi_Umum_Al-Balwa_Dalam_Menangani_Pencemaran_Silang_Produk_Makanan?auto=download&email_work_card=download-paper

Ahmad, A. N., Rahman, R. A., Othman, M. and Abidin, U. F. U. Z. (2017). Critical success factors affecting the implementation of Halal food management systems: perspective of Halal executives, consultants and auditors. *Food Control*, 74, pp. 70–78.

Ahmad, F., Shah, M. Z., Junaida, Z., Yazid, M. T., Rozelin, A., Donn, T., Shima, R., Ghazali, M. A. I. and Ramzi, M. (2020). Halal logistics legal framework: Malaysia perspective. *Journal of Critical Reviews*, 7(8), pp. 33–39.

Ahmad, M., Kadir, S. A. and Salehudin, N. A. (2013). Perceptions and behaviors of Muslims and non-Muslims towards Halal products. *Journal of Social and Development Sciences*, 4, pp. 2–6.

Aksoy, H. and Özsönmez, C. (2019). How Millennials' knowledge, trust, and product involvement affect the willingness to pay a premium price for fairtrade products? *Asian Journal of Business Research*, 9(2), pp. 95–112.

Al-Ansi, A., Olya, H. G. T. and Han, H. (2019). Effect of general risk on trust, satisfaction, and recommendation intention for Halal food. *International Journal of Hospitality Management*, 83, pp. 210–219.

Alzeer, J., Rieder, U. and Hadeed, K. A. (2018). Rational and practical aspects of Halal and Tayyib in the context of food safety. *Trends in Food Science and Technology*, 71, pp. 264–267.

Ambali, A. R. and Bakar, A. N. (2014). People's awareness on Halal foods and products: potential issues for policy-makers. *Procedia – Social and Behavioral Sciences*, 121, pp. 3–25.

Ariffin, M. F. M., Riza, N. S. M., Hamid, M. F. A., Awae, F. and Nasir, B. M. (2021). Halal food crime in Malaysia: an analysis on illegal meat cartel issues. *Journal of Contemporary Issues in Business and Government*, 27(2), 1407–1412.

Bernama (2019). Govt to introduce National Halal Council Act in 2019. *News Straits Times*. Retrieved from: www.nst.com.my/news/government-public-policy/2018/10/424023/govt-introduce-national-halal-council-act-2019 (accessed 24 November 2021).

Denin, M. J. A. N. (2021). Isu kartel daging: SPRM kumpul bukti sejak dua minggu lalu. *Harian Metro*. Retrieved from: www.hmetro.com.my/mutakhir/2021/01/660020/isu-kartel-daging-sprm-kumpul-bukti-sejak-dua-minggu-lalu (accessed 24 November 2021).

Firdausi, A. S. M., Farahdiba, D. and Munthe, A. M. (2020). Determining consumers' willingness to buy Halal meat. *Jurnal Bisnis Strategi*, 29(2), pp. 143–162.

Hamid, A. A. (2021). Syarikat pembekal daging tuntut RM50 juta [METROTV]. *Harian Metro*. Retrieved from: www.hmetro.com.my/mutakhir/2021/01/662064/syarikat-pembekal-daging-tuntut-rm50-juta-metrotv (accessed 24 November 2021).

Hammim, R. (2020). Company, two directors plead not guilty to charges of using unrecognised Halal logo. *New Straits Times*. Retrieved from: www.nst.com.my/news/crime-courts/2020/12/653169/company-two-directors-plead-not-guilty-charges-using-unrecognised (accessed 24 November 2021).

Hammim, R. (2021). Meat cartel scandal: three food distribution company execs charged in. *New Straits Times*. Retrieved from: www.nst.com.my/news/crime-courts/2021/02/664430/meat-cartel-scandal-three-food-distribution-company-execs-charged (accessed 24 November 2021).

Hasan, Z. (2007). Undang-Undang Produk Halal di Malaysia: Isu Penguatkuasaan Dan Pendakwaan. Retrieved from: https://zulkiflihasan.files.wordpress.com/2008/06/microsoft-word-halal-di-malaysia1.pdf (accessed 24 November 2021).

Krishnan, S., Haniff, M., Aderis, H. M., Azman, M. N., Nazrin, M. and Kamaluddin, A. (2017). Halal food: study on non-Muslim acceptance. *American Journal of Economics*, 7(1), pp. 41–45.

Mahidin, N., Saifudin, A. M. and Othman, S. N. (2017). Halal food logistics: the challenges among food & beverages small and medium sized manufacturers. *Internal Journal of Supply Chain Management*, 6(3), pp. 337–346.

Malayan Law Journal (1986). Public prosecutor v Wee Mee Industries Co Sdn Bhd. *Malayan Law Journal*.

Rashid, N. A. and Bojei, J. (2020). The relationship between Halal traceability system adoption and environmental factors on Halal food supply chain integrity in Malaysia. *Journal of Islamic Marketing*, 11(1), pp. 117–142.

Rigod, B. and Tovar, P. (2019). Indonesia-chicken: tensions between international trade and domestic food policies? *World Trade Review*, 18(2), pp. 219–243.

Shariff, S. M., Akma, N. and Lah, A. (2014). Halal certification on chocolate products: a case study. *Procedia – Social and Behavioral Sciences*, 121, pp. 104–112.

Soon, J. M., Chandia, M. and Regenstein, J. M. (2017). Halal integrity in the food supply chain. *British Food Journal*, 119, pp. 39–51.

Suhaini, N. A. (2017). 4 kontena daging kambing campur babi dirampas. *Berita Harian Online*. Retrieved from: www.bharian.com.my/berita/nasional/2017/07/303117/4-kontena-daging-kambing-campur-babi-dirampas (accessed 24 November 2021).

Tieman, M. and Ghazali, M. C. (2014). Halal control activities and assurance activities in Halal food logistics. *Procedia – Social and Behavioral Sciences*, 121, pp. 44–57.

Tieman, M. and van Nistelrooy, M. (2014). Perception of Malaysian food manufacturers toward Halal logistics. *Journal of International Food and Agribusiness Marketing*, 26(3), pp. 218–233.

Yaacob, T. Z., Suzana Jaafar, H. and Rahman, F. A. (2016). A review of regulatory framework for Halal meat supply chain: the case of Halal meat based food products in Malaysia. *Journal of Applied Environmntal and Biological Science*, 6(9S), pp. 14–21.

Zaina, C. R. C. M., Rahman, S. A., Mohd., I. Z. and Aziz, S. A. (2015). Jurisdiction and prosecution of Halal related matters in Malaysia: challenges and prospects. *Procedia – Social and Behavioral Sciences*, 172, pp. 294–300.

Zakaria, Z. and Zubaidah Ismail, S. (2014). The Trade Description Act 2011: Regulating "Halal" in Malaysia. *International Conference on Law, Management and Humanities (ICLMH'14)*, 3. https://doi.org/10.15242/ICEHM.ED0614020

Zulfakar, M. H., Chan, C. and Jie, F. (2014). Factors influencing the operations of the Halal meat supply chain in Australia. *Conference: International Symposium on Logistics*, Ho Chi Minh City, 1–8 March.

10 Halal integrity in the supply chain

The impacts of the fake Halal meat cartel scandal towards Halal integrity

Anis Najiha Ahmad, Siti Balqis Zulfigar, Baiduri Zaiyyanna Mohd Farudz and Nur Najihah binti Zulkifli

Introduction

Food fraud has become a widespread global problem. Some foods (such as Halal foods) are more vulnerable than other to fraud. Malaysia has certainly had its fair share of issues related to Halal food fraud, but never to the extent as seen in the recent fake Halal meat cartel. Uncovered in late 2020, the scandal is one of the biggest and most high-profile food fraud cases related to Halal in Malaysia so far. The scandal is associated with a meat cartel who allegedly smuggled non-certified meat from China, Brazil, Canada and Ukraine and sold it as Halal certified meat to unsuspecting Malaysian suppliers.

In a country that attempts to position itself as a global Halal hub with a comprehensive Halal ecosystem, the fact that there is a giant network that has been bypassing the national Halal control system for years is a huge problem. Besides pork, initial reports even linked the imported meat with exotic meats such as kangaroo and horse, although this was later debunked by the authorities. The scandal tainted consumer trust in the Halal industry. There were also concerns regarding Malaysia's reputation as one of the influential players in the Halal market.

This chapter first highlights the chronology of the event to provide background on the issue. Then it discusses the implications of the scandal from multiple perspectives, in addition to considering ways to move forward in terms of managerial and technological approaches. This review provides a reference for Halal supply chain stakeholders to learn about the scandal. Countermeasures suggested could be considered as part of the strategies to circumvent similar occurrences in the future.

Background: Malaysian import meat industry

Malaysia depends heavily on imported meat to meet its domestic needs. It imports approximately 80% of its beef from other countries. The main meat suppliers are from India (77%), Australia (14%) and New Zealand (5%). Meat from India is normally sold at a lower price compared to those sold locally, whereas meats from

DOI: 10.4324/9781003223719-14

Australia and New Zealand are of premium quality, and are pricier (Best Food Importers, 2020).

There are two main sources of imported meat, derived from cattle and buffalo. Frozen buffalo meat is relatively cheaper than beef, thus is often used by Malaysians as a beef substitute. Meat is either chilled or frozen before it is exported to Malaysia. In 2018, frozen beef worth approximately USD 498 million was imported compared to only USD 20 million of fresh or chilled beef. As shown in Figure 10.1, imported beef products are distributed either through traders/wholesalers or directly to markets or institutional buyers.

Chronology of the Halal fake meat cartel

The scandal was first made known to the public on 26 November 2020 through a news report by *Sinar Harian*, a Malay daily. The newspaper reported that it received a tip-off from an anonymous source who alleged that a freight forward company (an intermediary company that arranges export and import) had been smuggling non-Halal certified frozen meat and passing it off as Halal-certified meat. The source also claimed that the practice had been going on for few years, as the company could easily bypass the country port entries, believed to gain access through bribes offered to the port officers in the form of money or sexual favours (Ashman, 2020). This initial news report has caused public uproar as the case was not only associated with fake Halal meat but also tainted with corruption.

A warehouse raid in Senai Industrial Park, Johor, on 1 December 2020 further exposed the illegal activities. The authorities found 1,500 tonnes of smuggled frozen meat worth RM 30 million in the warehouse owned by a meat cartel. Among the modus operandi use by the cartel was to disguise itself as a frozen meat supplier. It was reported that once these unidentified meats entered the Malaysian ports, they were then transported to the warehouse to be repackaged with falsified Halal logos similar to those issued by the Department of Islamic Development Malaysia (JAKIM). The cartel was also discovered to have falsified other related documents such as customs forms, import permits and payment receipts. To conceal its illegal activities, the cartel also imported meat from legal sources.

Further investigation led to the arrest of 11 individuals including five officers from the Department of Malaysian Quarantine Inspection Services (MAQIS), a delivery agent, directors and employees of two importing companies. Police believed that the activity involved larger networks within Malaysia and abroad. The investigation found that besides Johor, the main entrances of the cartel included other Malaysian states such as Kelantan and Sarawak. The cartel used fronts or proxy companies as a medium to bring in the meat supplies. An operation conducted in six states found that 19 cold distribution companies were involved in the cartel's activities. Seven companies were in Johor, four in Kuala Lumpur, four in Selangor, one in Perak, two in Penang and one in Kedah. The chronology of the event is described in detail in Table 10.1.

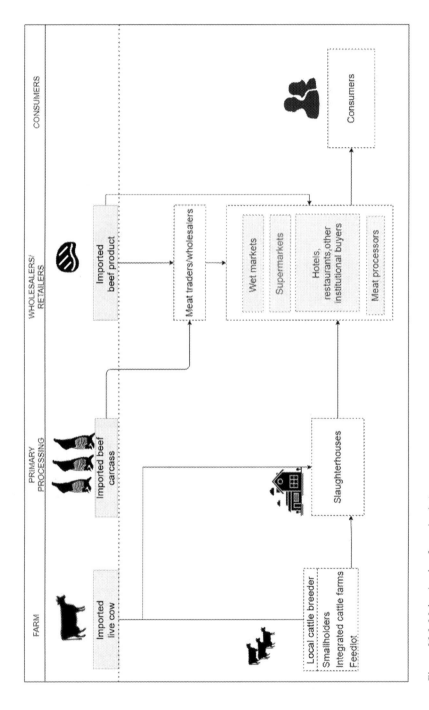

Figure 10.1 Malaysian beef supply chain.
Source: MyCC, 2019.

Table 10.1 Chronology of the event

Newspaper	Date	Event	Reference
Sinar Harian	23 Nov 2020	*Sinar Harian* reported that an anonymous source claimed that a freight company had been importing noncertified Halal frozen meat. Access through port entries were made possible through bribery activities offered to several port officers to turn a blind eye.	(Adam, 2021)
Sinar Harian	1 Dec 2020	A warehouse raided in Senai, Johor, led to the discovery of 1,500 tonnes of imported frozen meat worth RM30 million. The warehouse had been operating as a frozen meat supplier company. Imported meat was stamped with false Halal logos in the warehouse.	(Rozlin and Ramli, 2020)
Sinar Harian	2 Dec 2020	Followed up report from *Sinar Harian* detailed out on how a "cartel" managed to smuggle the non-certified imported frozen meat from China, Ukraine, Brazil and Argentina and repackaged it to be sold all over Malaysia.	(Rozlin and Ramli, 2020)
Sinar Harian	4 Dec 2020	The Department of Islamic Development Malaysia (JAKIM) denied the reports that linked their officers to the meat scandal cartel. The Ministry of Domestic Trade and Consumer Affairs (KPDNHEP) confirmed that there are 30 suppliers involved in the case. The State Religious Affairs Department (JAIN) reported that there was a receipt found relating to the smuggle of swine organ from the premise on 5 November.	(Syaida, 2020)
Sinar Harian	5 Dec 2020	The Department of Homeland Security and Public Order (JKDNKA) revealed that the main access of the cartel imported case was through Kelantan, Johor and Sarawak.	(Syaida, 2020)
Sinar Harian	16 Dec 2020	The KPDNHEP denied the involvement of their officers, saying that the ministry was not involved in the import process.	(Syaida, 2020)

(*continued*)

Table 10.1 Cont.

Newspaper	Date	Event	Reference
Sinar Harian	21 Dec 2020	Another anonymous source claimed at least four government agencies were aiding the cartel and the officers were bribed with cash and women to compensate the activities.	(Syaida, 2020)
NST	22 Dec 2020	The Malaysian Quarantine and Inspection Services Department (MAQIS) denied involvement. An additional allegation was made that the imported meat was not limited to beef, but also included horse and kangaroo meat. It was also reported that beef was obtained from animals of poor quality or even diseased – hence the lower prices.	(Basyir, 2020)
Sinar Harian	28 Dec 2020	JAKIM publishes a list of licensed meat importers	(Syaida, 2020)
Sinar Harian and NST	29 Dec 2020	A committee of legal and Halal enforcement formed by KPDNHEP. JAKIM announced plan to control the issue of the Halal meat cartel. Police believed that the activity involved large networks within Malaysia and abroad. *Sinar Harian* denied reporting about the possibility of kangaroo, horses, and pig meat being smuggled. It also denied reporting that the cartel has been operated for more than 40 years.	(Hibrahim, 2020; Hibrahim and Zulkafli, 2020)
NST	2 Feb 2021	Investigations by the Malaysian Anti-Corruption Commission (MACC) led to the arrest of 11 people including five MAQIS officers, a delivery agent, as well as directors and employees of two importing companies.	(Basyir, 2021)
NST	7 Mar 2021	The cartel uses fronts or proxy companies as a medium to bring in the meat supplies.	(New Straits Times, 2021)
NST	13 Apr 2021	Operation conducted in six states found that 19 cold distribution companies were involved in the cartel's activities.	(Basyir, 2020)
NST	22 Apr 2021	LY Frozen Food Sdn Bhd and its directors charged with abetting and possessing goods prohibited from being imported amounting RM 640,000.	(Hammim, 2021)

The scandal forced many agencies, including JAKIM and the Ministry of Domestic Trade and Consumer Affairs (KPDNHEP), to deny their officials' involvement. In bids to restore consumer confidence, multiple Halal-related agencies came out with statements. For example, Johor Royal Malaysia Police promised to increase food crime investigation and strengthen the enforcement. The Ministry of Agriculture and Food Industry also issued multiple statements. It reassured consumers that only meat from abattoirs recognized as Halal by JAKIM and the Department of Veterinary Services (DVS) would be approved for imports to Malaysia. The ministry also promised to revoke Approved Permits (APs) of meat distributors who violated the import regulations. MAQIS, an agency under the Ministry of Agriculture and Agro-Based Industry, pledged to improve its inspection to curb the smuggling activities of meat and poultry products.

Among these agencies, JAKIM, the highest authority in the Halal industry in Malaysia has perhaps been the main target of criticism since the scandal erupted. It therefore announced several action plans to deal with Halal meat cartel scandal (Ahmad, 2020). The initiatives include:

- Discussion with other Halal-related agencies, such as the Ministry of Domestic Trade and Consumer Affairs (KPDNHEP), the Department of Malaysian Quarantine Inspection Services (MAQIS) and the Royal Malaysian Customs Department (Customs) to outline jurisdiction, steps to be taken to address the issue, as well as to draft a joint action plan on the import process of beef and beef products.
- Roundtable discussion with both industry (both importers and distributers) and Halal-related agencies (KPDNHEP, MAQIS and Customs) on issues faced by the importers and distributors, explanation on the Standard of Operating Procedure (SOP). JAKIM also encouraged the industrial players to apply for the Malaysian Halal Certificate, as well as reiterate the requirement for Malaysian Halal certificate holders to obtain supplies from certified sources only.
- Promotion of an updated list of 84 approved foreign Halal certification bodies. A list of approved foreign Halal certification bodies was updated.
- Augmentation of inspections and visits to the premises of meat import, and slaughterhouses.
- Expedition of the SOP improvement.
- Production of a SOP diagram regarding imported meat and any meat products to Malaysia.

Impacts of meat cartel scandal to stakeholders of Halal supply chain

The meat cartel scandal has huge impacts on different stakeholders in the Halal supply chain, albeit in different ways. To provide context to this discussion, supply chain is defined as a group of "interrelated networks comprised of different stakeholders such as producers, retailers, customers, and facilitators who provide value to the material in ensuring the movement of the chain" (Lu, 2011). When Halal is added into the equation of the supply chain, the stakeholders also need to ensure that the material movement processes, from start to end, are aligned with Islamic law (Shariah) requirements (Mohamed et al., 2020). The impacts of the scandal to selected stakeholders such as consumers, companies (in the supply chain), countries and authorities are discussed in the following sub-sections.

Consumers

The concepts of Halal and Haram are significant for Muslims, they dictate what are permissible and prohibited for Muslims. Muslim consumers thus are inherently sensitive in choosing and purchasing products for consumption. For Muslims, eating Halal food is perceived to be a form of worship (Talib et al., 2015) and being cautious is regarded as a noble attribute (Muhammad Shahrulnizam Muhadi, 2020). Moreover, the religious issues are innately sensitive to Malaysia and could easily trigger dissatisfaction and irritation to many Malaysians (Ashman, 2020).

As such, it is not surprising to observe a drastic fall in consumer confidence in the imported meat products, as reflected by drop in the sales of meat products in the aftermath of the scandal. For instance, AEON, one of the leading retailers in Malaysia reported drop of up to 30–40% in December 2020's sales of meat products, in store areas with a high density of Malays (Ashman, 2021).

The ruling of eating imported meat with a forged Halal logo was issued by the Mufti of Federal Territories of Malaysia to address consumer concerns about the scandal. The ruling stated that consumers who unintentionally purchased and consumed products or food that are non-Halal will not be held accountable or bear any sin. Specifically, consumers are forgiven for unintentionally eating meat which they believed to be Halal certified but later found to be fabricated (Muhammad Shahrulnizam Muhadi, 2020). This is based on the following Quranic verse: "And there is no blame upon you for that in which you have erred but [only for] what your hearts intended. And ever is Allah Forgiving and Merciful" (Surah al-Ahzab, 5).

Nevertheless, it is anticipated that consumers will remain very conscious of what they purchase and consume for some time to come. Temporarily avoiding anything that is "Syubhah" (doubtful), which is the imported meat in this context, is aligned with the principle taught by the Prophet Muhammad (SAW) in the following hadith: "Leave that which makes you doubt for that which does not make you doubt" (Jami' al-Tirmidhi, 2518).

The shift of consumer purchase behaviour is expected, and this includes the shift of demand to alternative products or offerings such as other types of meat (e.g., poultry, fish) or from different supply chains, such as local meat. This indirectly boosts the sale of the local beef industry, even though local meat is more expensive (Zulsyamini and Suhaini, 2020). Some consumers even opt for other meat substitutes such as vegetables (Daniele, 2021). Consumers are also increasingly asking for seller's verbal verification on the authenticity of meat sold, despite the visible Halal logo (Basyir, 2020).

Changes in consumer purchase behaviour after a scandal is not new. Similar consumer avoidance patterns were observed in the aftermath of the 2013 horse meat scandal, whereby foods advertised as containing beef were found to contain horse meat in parts of Europe. In the immediate aftermath, consumers shifted to local butchers and avoided selected supermarket products. There were also long-term changes in consumer behaviour reported, the survey conducted on consumers in 2017, four years after the scandal, found that over two thirds of respondents (70%) would regularly take measures to ensure their food product is authentic, such as reading ingredients or the label of a product. About 17% of respondents reported they will avoid altogether certain foods perceived to susceptible to fraud (FandD Technology, 2017). It will take time to assess the long-term impact of the meat cartel scandal, but the previous horse meat scandal hints a clear message to the industry not to take fraud lightly. Consumer trust is paramount for most businesses. Consumer trust is hard to gain and easy to lose. A trusted market and chain warrants access to foods that fulfil only Halal criteria for consumers.

Companies

The negative implication of the scandal is not only bounded to consumers but naturally extended to companies in the meat supply chain. The scandal is affecting both businesses-to-business (B2B) and business-to-consumers (BC2). In this scandal, the cartel is alleged of using the genuine Halal logo issued by JAKIM to prominent meat companies (such as Allana Group) to deceive their consumers. This forced the affected companies, who are also the largest frozen meat suppliers in Malaysia, to give a public assurance that their products are Halal (Bernama, 2020). The impact on these large businesses is bad enough, but small businesses were similarly affected, in addition to the economic crisis due to the COVID-19 pandemic. Small traders and hawkers who previously opt for imported frozen meat due to the lower prices compared to local meat were among those who were badly impacted by the scandal (Dhesegaan and Solhi, 2020).

When the scandal unfolded, Kuala Lumpur Bumiputera Traders and Hawkers Association, an organization of Malay traders and business associations, immediately urged their members to stop selling the beef-based products, especially meats that were sourced from overseas. The association urged their members to focus on fish- and chicken-based products, as concerns surrounding the Halal status of frozen beef persisted. Their representative stated that halting the sales of beef-based products is a wise decision given the increasing doubt among consumers over the Halal status of frozen beef in the market. As such, continuing to offer beef products will only cause difficulties and affect the income of their members (Ashman, 2021).

As the fake Halal meat could potentially have infiltrated numerous supply chains, many companies including a few giant food retailers in Malaysia such as Mydin, Tesco and AEON, were forced to step forward to convince their consumers that their products were not sourced from the cartel, and thus were safe for consumption. Mydin, for example, claimed that its supermarkets imported meat directly from the suppliers who hold JAKIM Halal certificates. Tesco announced that its frozen meat was approved by both the Department of Veterinary Services Malaysia as well as JAKIM (Mohamed et al., 2020). AEON similarly claimed that its imported meat came with valid Halal documentation. AEON, however, added that the company was now more cautious about the meat's country of origin following the scandal (Ashman, 2021).

While macro companies are adamant in defending their meat sourcing, small companies are not as confident. For example, one frozen food manufacturer mentioned that he was convinced of the status of his meat supplies as they were certified by recognized Halal authority such as JAKIM. However, he expressed his doubts on processed meat products such as minced beef, which were sourced from third-party suppliers (Daniele, 2021).

Authorities

The meat cartel scandal not only undermined consumer confidence on the Halal food chain, but it also affected consumer trust on the competency and credibility of the authorities in governing national Halal affairs. Halal authorities are the first to be held accountable in matters related to breaches of Halal supply integrity such as in the Halal meat cartel scandal. When the scandal broke, JAKIM, the top Halal authority in Malaysia, was targeted by many. The representative from Kuala Lumpur Bumiputera Traders and Hawkers Association, for instance, urged JAKIM to step up and clarify the issue (Basyir, 2020). The Malay Consultative Council (MPM), a civil organization, on the other hand, blasted JAKIM for it described as "a failure in the issuance of Halal certification to meat imports". The same entity also called for a drastic measure, a complete reorganization of JAKIM's administrative structure (Tee and Shahrizam, 2020). Many other direct and non-direct stakeholders including industry and politicians have publicly expressed their dismay and criticized the slow pace of investigations, in addition to the failure of the government to proactively regain consumer confidence in the existing stock of Halal meat sold in the country (Razak, 2021).

In the phase of post-crisis or scandal, effective communication with stakeholders helps provide clarity. When there is a lack of prompt communication, it is not difficult to understand the frustration of these stakeholders. However, the case is not as straightforward, and the initial evidence suggests the complexity of the case may possibly delay prompt communication. The case involved not only massive networks of trading companies, but it is also believed to be operated by local and international syndicates (Ashman, 2020).

What complicated and delayed the prompt communication during the crisis could also be the multiple-agency structure that governed the national Halal control. In a multiple-agency structure, responsibilities are shared between different government ministries (health, agriculture, commerce, environment, trade and industry) and across government agencies at different levels (federal, state, local) (Ahmad et al., 2018; Food and Agriculture Organization, 2006). Aside from JAKIM, other agencies that closely monitor the meat sector include the Ministry of Domestic Trade and Consumer Affairs (KPDNHEP), the Department of Veterinary Services (DVS), the Malaysian Quarantine and Inspection Services (MAQIS), the Ministry of Home Affairs (MHA), the Royal Malaysian Customs Department (RMCD) and the Port Police (PP) (Koya and Anis, 2020). Figure 10.2 shows the process of importing meat to Malaysia and the responsible government agencies for each stage. According to Hopper and Boutrif (2006), there are a few general challenges associated with multiple agencies in national governance, one of them is the lack of overall coordination at national level that affects the overall performance.

Countries

Food fraud can destroy brand reputation and even the reputation of an entire exporting country. It was learnt that the cartel imported meat from non-Halal certified slaughterhouses in several countries abroad such as Brazil, Bolivia, Canada, China, Colombia, Mexico, Spain and Ukraine. AEON, for example, clearly stated that the company was taking cautious measures in importing meat from the stated countries (Ashman, 2021).

One of the biggest concerns from the scandal is its potential impact to the reputation of Malaysia as the global Halal hub. Malaysia has been a prominent figure in pioneering development of the Halal market. It has for years positioned itself as a global hub for the USD 2.02 trillion international Halal market (Islamic Chamber Research & Information Center, 2020). What started as only to ensure safe and reliable consumable products to Malaysian consumers has now turned into one of the economic drivers of Malaysia. In 2017, Malaysia exported about RM 43.3 billion of Halal-certified products to countries such as China, Singapore, the US, Japan and elsewhere (Zainul, 2019). As part of national strategic development, a comprehensive Halal ecosystem has been built, which consists of a Halal assurance system and a national Halal control system.

It is too soon to assess the extent of the impact of the scandal on Malaysia's image and reputation as the world's leading Halal hub, but the concern has been reiterated multiple times by many, including authorities and in the media (Ashman, 2020; Bloomberg and Today Online, 2020). This scandal may not only affect the image of Malaysia, but there is also concern regarding how this scandal is perceived by and affecting neighbouring countries. When the scandal erupted, Singapore, for example, investigated whether the meat had infiltrated their local market, the investigation was taken after the circulation of social media messages concerning the scandal (Channel News Asia, 2020).

Managerial and technological countermeasures

The meat cartel scandal is not the first fraud related to Halal and it certainly will not be the last. Malaysia must take extensive approaches to prevent and handle similar issues relating to food fraud incidents in the future. Countermeasures can help in preventing, detecting and responding effectively to fraud. In the

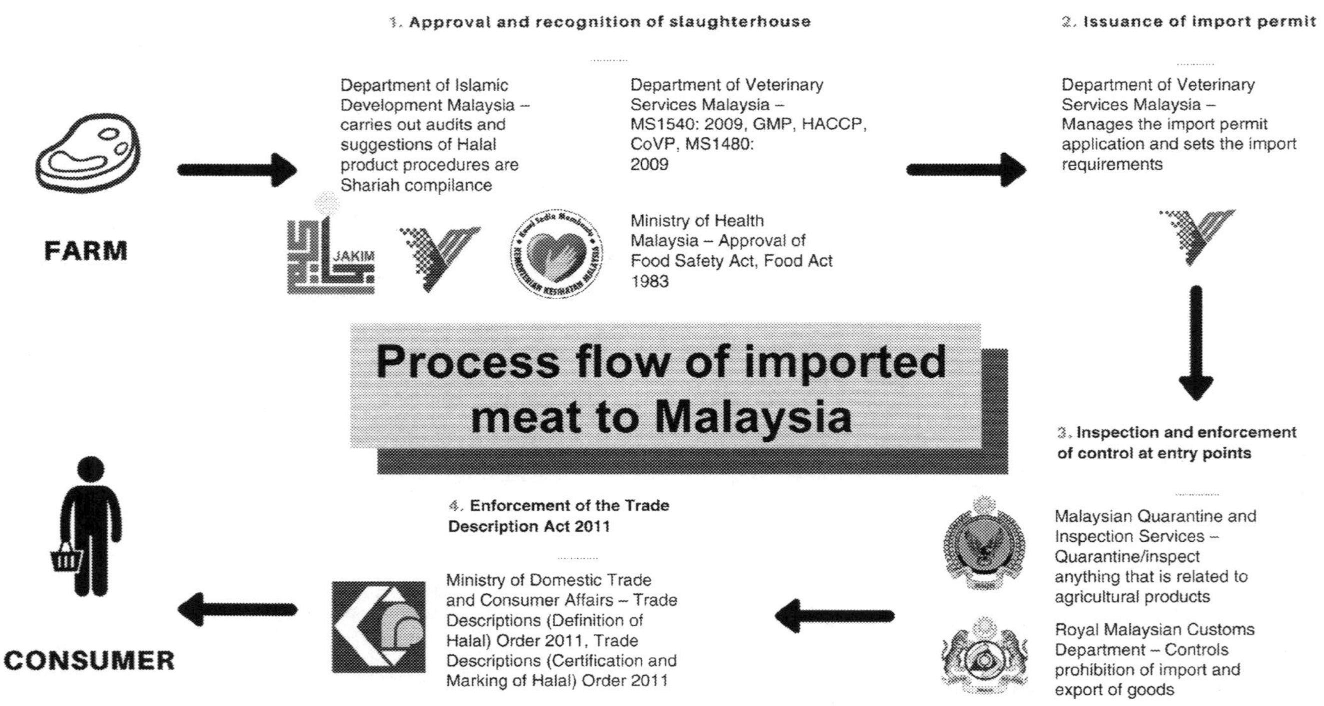

1. Approval and recognition of slaughterhouse

Department of Islamic Development Malaysia – carries out audits and suggestions of Halal product procedures are Shariah compilance

Department of Veterinary Services Malaysia – MS1540: 2009, GMP, HACCP, CoVP, MS1480: 2009

Ministry of Health Malaysia – Approval of Food Safety Act, Food Act 1983

2. Issuance of import permit

Department of Veterinary Services Malaysia – Manages the import permit application and sets the import requirements

3. Inspection and enforcement of control at entry points

Malaysian Quarantine and Inspection Services – Quarantine/inspect anything that is related to agricultural products

Royal Malaysian Customs Department – Controls prohibition of import and export of goods

4. Enforcement of the Trade Description Act 2011

Ministry of Domestic Trade and Consumer Affairs – Trade Descriptions (Definition of Halal) Order 2011, Trade Descriptions (Certification and Marking of Halal) Order 2011

Process flow of imported meat to Malaysia

FARM

CONSUMER

Figure 10.2 Process flow of imported meat to Malaysia.

following sub-sections, managerial and technological countermeasures for fraud are discussed.

Strengthen collaboration between multiple Halal agencies

Multiple agencies involved in monitoring of meat imports possibly leads to role redundancy, which prevents effective monitoring (Ahmad et al., 2018; Fatimah, 2021). The multiple-agency structure also makes the crisis response and communication more challenging. To overcome this issue, better coordination among different agencies involved is needed. This fraud-combating strategy to protect the food chain has been advocated by many food fraud experts. For example, the suggestion was outlined as part of a resolution in 2017's conference of "Safeguarding the Food Chain – Protecting Authenticity and Integrity" held in Dublin. Joint collaboration between government agencies has also been suggested by the Elliott Review, an independent report that proposes measures to address the gap in supply chains in the aftermath of the horse meat scandal (Brooks et al., 2017). Multiple-agency collaboration is not only necessary in preventing and detecting fraud but it is also needed in forming an effective respond to fraud. Multiple-agency response and communication need to be designed to optimize coordination between responding agencies. During the scandal, JAKIM, for example, announced that discussions and meetings with the relevant bodies would continue to be done from time to time. This is a positive step toward better collaboration among multiple Halal agencies.

Industrial–government partnerships and international counterpart collaboration

Collaboration and intelligence gathering and sharing is not only limited to monitoring agencies but also needs to be extended to industry. Industry could collaborate with government agencies for intelligence gathering and sharing as suggested by the Elliott Review (Brooks et al., 2017). It is important to note that the scandal was first exposed due to the tip-off from an anonymous source believed to be from the industry. This implies that information on this illegal practice was known among the industrial players but was never officially shared with the Halal authorities. The Elliott Review suggests the development of a system/channel for industry to collect and disclose information and intelligence related to fraud without fear. This "whistleblowing" channel could also be developed for the Malaysian Halal industry. Besides intelligence gathering and sharing, another industry–government partnership could also be in the form of other knowledge sharing which could contribute to policy development, programmes and implementation of legislative, policy and procedural change to curb Halal food fraud.

It is also important for local government agencies to collaborate with their international counterparts to learn from their experience and expertise in managing and preventing previous food fraud crisis. For example, Malaysia could draw the lessons learnt from United Kingdom and Ireland in connection with the

2013 horsemeat scandal, and recommendations and initiatives from the Elliott Review (Brooks et al., 2017).

Training in Halal food fraud awareness and risk management

Most Halal training offered nowadays in Malaysia focuses on different aspects of Halal such as the fundamentals of Islamic law (Shariah), the certification process, market, consumerism, food safety, quality and management. With an increasing number of fraud cases related to Halal, the scope of the Halal training needs to be further extended to include fraud awareness, and fraud risk management. Fraud awareness exposes employees to the risk of fraud and makes them aware of their obligations concerning fraud and misconduct. This training is the first step towards introducing an effective fraud risk management system. It helps educate employees on the critical role they play in preventing, detecting and deterring fraud (Deloitte, 2014). Fraud risk training allows staff to identify red flags to detect fraud. It informs them on the steps that need to be taken and the reporting procedure. Fraud risk management is a countermeasure that could be applied by the Halal companies to ensure control over fraud. It involves fraud prevention, detection and response. There is an increasing interest in fraud risk management as the food industry has started to grasp the negative effects of fraud (Deloitte, 2014). There is no similar training yet to be offered in the Halal industry context. Awareness and knowledge in fraud risk management could be the first step for the Halal industry toward integrating the system into the Halal management system.

Supplier management

Supplier management practices are crucial for a company to manage fraud. The practices include improvement of transparency and simplifying the upstream supply chain. Simplification could improve traceability, and safety and quality of the products. It also gives fewer opportunities for fraud food/material to infiltrate the supply chain. To ensure supply chain transparency, companies need to make sure their supply chains are visible. As described previously, small companies have indicated their concerns regarding the authenticity of some of their supplies, as they have limited information on their suppliers. Not knowing much about suppliers could expose the companies to risks of purchasing fraudulent supplies. Supply chain simplification processes require companies to know and map their supply chains to eliminate risk. It is important for the companies to understand and assess their supplier suitability if the raw materials are to be procured via an agent/broker (British Retail Consortium, 2016). Although supplier assessment practice is not part of the Halal certification requirements for small companies, a robust supplier approval process based on risks (e.g., raw material risk, location of food safety control measures, supplier performance) could support adulteration prevention efforts. Best practices include gathering supplier information internally via questionnaire, supplier assurance and audit. It is also possible to get external help to verify a supplier or investigate suspicious supplier behaviours or practices, via trade association and informal sharing between different companies in industry (Brooks et al., 2017). Closer supplier relationships are important to lower fraud risks as suppliers readily share information on their supply chain and processes, this also helps to build confidence between both parties.

Food traceability and Halal authentication

The Halal meat scandal has highlighted the importance of two key components from technological perspectives: food traceability and Halal authentication technologies. The combination of both data and scientific provenance is very much needed to ensure Halal integrity parallel to consumers' demand for transparency with regards to their food origin.

According to the Food and Agriculture Organization (2015, p. 1), traceability is defined as the "the ability to follow the movement of a feed or food through specified stage(s) of production, processing and distribution". Compliance with regulations and food fraud are among the issues that could be addressed through traceability systems. These aim to strengthen consumers' trust of the food source, as they could pinpoint the whole supply chain from farm to fork. In the general food supply chain, some retailers have adopted and mandated the application of standardized labelling for product identification by using unique Global Trade Item Numbers (GTIN) via the GS1 Standards (Scholten et al., 2016). These standardized labels will be printed on the products' containers and pallets to enable traceability. The effectiveness of this comprehensive standardized system has enabled rapid product recall where all points of sales can be blocked within 30 minutes if the product is discovered to be unsafe. Although a similar approach seems ideal to be applied in the Halal food supply chain, the involvement of various parties in addition to the complexity of the supply chain limits the effectiveness of this approach.

Blockchain technology, which drives the cryptocurrencies, had found its application in the management of various supply chains including in the food industries (Nakamoto, 2008). Blockchain is defined as networks of information across various parties whereby the data (blocks) can be continuously expanded. The blocks of information are time-stamped and connected through cryptographic hashes, which refers to the digital fingerprints of data in the block (Seebacher and Schüritz, 2017). Meanwhile, a blockchain, according to Raikwar et al. (2019), means a distributed ledger maintaining a continuously growing list of data records that are confirmed by all the participating nodes. Such consensus among participating parties ensures data integrity, making the system immutable and tamper-proof. Powered by the Internet of Things (IoT) with the facilitation of various tracking sensors such as radio frequency identification (RFID), QR codes or artificial intelligence, blockchain allows real-time data retrieval, which empowers consumers in making informed decisions.

The integrity of Halal in meat industries covers all stages of procedures, including pre-slaughtering, slaughtering and post-slaughtering activities. The pre-slaughtering phase involves the activities of animal/livestock rearing and farming. During this initial stage, information regarding the animal's health status including vaccination records, their feed and farm conditions, can be recorded via RFID technologies or 2D barcode and be made available in real-time in the blockchain system (Bahrudin et al., 2011). The data input will be collected by the stakeholders involved and uploaded into the system (Meidayanti et al., 2019). According to Rejeb (2018), five out of ten Halal critical control points in meat processing were identified at the slaughtering stage. During this critical stage, adherence to all Halal criteria can be assured by positioning trained personnel in conducting the slaughtering activity. All data regarding the personnel's competencies, training records, backgrounds and audit findings will be stored in the blockchain system. In addition to these online record keepings, several abattoirs keep records of the slaughtering process in the form of video recordings via IoT sensors to ensure that all Halal criteria are satisfied (Farah, 2021). Similarly, data of the abattoir's facilities, conditions and locations must be made available and transparent through this blockchain system.

Information of carcasses which undergone post-slaughtering procedures such as cleaning, cutting and repackaging will be incorporated in the database to include data on the processing equipment and the specifications, quality control measures and the personnel in charged (Pal and Kant, 2019). Quality checks and Halal authentication analysis can be carried out at this stage through various methods based on DNA, protein or lipid detection analysis to ensure the absence of non-Halal elements. The meat products will be labelled with unique identifiers in the form of either indelible markers or 2D barcodes to ensure traceability (Bahrudin et al., 2011). Meanwhile, cold-chain distribution of the meat products involving service provision by third-party logistics should strictly comply to Halal requirements. The Malaysian Standards (MS) 2400-1:2009 and MS 2400-2:2009 lay out the requirements for the transportation and warehousing of Halal goods. Segregation of Halal from non-Halal products prevents the risk of cross-contamination and these service providers are responsible for providing preferably dedicated transportations for Halal products (Tieman and Ghazali, 2014). Vehicles involved in the transportation of Halal products equipped with Global Positioning System (GPS), enable tracking and mapping of the transportation network to ensure robust traceability system (Iskandar et al., 2012).

Conclusion

The globalization of Halal food market has introduced more frequent food fraud. In a market that is centralized and founded around trust, such as the Halal food market, the loss of trust due to fraud could cracks its foundation. While the impacts of this scandal are huge and extensive, the case also raised the profile of Halal food fraud and crime occurrence within Halal supply chains and illustrated the inherent risks and impacts that come with it. It allows the stakeholders (academic, industry and government) to understand how food fraud incidents can occur in these complex supply chains. The scandal revealed the need for rapid transformation in order to prevent, detect and respond to Halal food fraud – beyond Halal certification.

References

Adam, A. (2021). How Malaysia's "meat cartel" scandal unfolded: a timeline. *Malay Mail*. Retrieved from: www.malaymail.com/news/malaysia/2021/01/04/how-malaysias-meat-cartel-scandal-unfolded-a-timeline/1937007 (accessed 24 November 2021).

Ahmad, A. N., Abidin, U. F. U. Z., Othman, M. and Rahman, R. A. (2018). Overview of Halal food control system in Malaysia. *Food Control*, 90, pp. 352–363.

Ahmad, S. (2020). JAKIM keluarkan 6 pelan tindakan tangani isu halal daging import. *Berita Harian*. Retrieved from: https://bit.ly/2UiRmm4 (accessed 24 November 2021).

Ashman, A. (2020). Cops say "meat cartel" scandal involves massive network, including international syndicates. *Malay Mail*. Retrieved from: www.malaymail.com/news/malaysia/2020/12/29/cops-say-meat-cartel-scandal-involve-massive-network-including-internationa/1935817 (accessed 24 November 2021).

Ashman, A. (2021). Aeon sees sales of red meat plunge after "cartel" scandal: Mydin MD calls for swift action ahead of April fasting month. *Yahoo News*. Retrieved from: https://malaysia.news.yahoo.com/aeon-sees-sales-red-meat-030025910.html (accessed 24 November 2021).

Bahrudin, S. S. M., Illyas, M. I. and Desa, M. I. (2011). Tracking and tracing technology for Halal product integrity over the supply chain. *Proceedings of the 2011 International Conference on Electrical Engineering and Informatics*. doi: 10.1109/ICEEI.2011.6021678

Basyir, M. (2020). Meat cartel scandal: traders group to refrain from selling beef. *New Straits Times*. Retrieved from: www.nst.com.my/news/nation/2020/12/651615/meat-cartel-scandal-traders-group-refrain-selling-beef (accessed 24 November 2021).

Basyir, M. (2021). Meat cartels "exploiting loopholes in the system". *New Straits Times*. Retrieved from: www.nst.com.my/news/nation/2021/02/662044/meat-cartels-exploiting-loopholes-system (accessed 24 November 2021).

Bernama (2020). Malaysia's three largest frozen meat suppliers guaranteed Halal. *New Straits Times*. Retrieved from: www.nst.com.my/news/nation/2020/12/653032/malaysias-three-largest-frozen-meat-suppliers-guaranteed-halal (accessed 24 November 2021).

Best Food Importers (2020). *Malaysia Food Importers and Import Trends 2020 – Best Food Importers*. Retrieved from: https://bestfoodimporters.com/malaysia-food-importers-and-import-trends-2020/ (accessed 24 November 2021).

Bloomberg and Today Online (2020). Malaysian cartel allegedly sold fake Halal meat to Muslims for 40 years. *South China Morning Post*. Retrieved from: www.scmp.com/news/asia/southeast-asia/article/3115837/malaysian-cartel-allegedly-sold-fake-halal-meat-muslims-40 (accessed 24 November 2021).

British Retail Consortium (BRC) (2016). *About*. Retrieved from: https://brcfoodsafety.com/the-british-retail-consortium/ (accessed 24 November 2021).

Brooks, S., Elliott, C. T., Spence, M., Walsh, C. and Dean, M. (2017). Four years post-horsegate: an update of measures and actions put in place following the horsemeat incident of 2013. *NPJ Science of Food*. https://doi.org/10.1038/s41538-017-0007-z

Channel News Asia (2020). SFA, MUIS looking into concerns that alleged Malaysian "meat cartel syndicate" has affected Singapore. *CNA*. Retrieved from: www.channelnewsasia.com/news/singapore/malaysia-meat-cartel-syndicate-muis-sfa-singapore-market-13860308 (accessed 24 November 2021).

Daniele, U. (2021). Malaysia reels from fake Halal meat scandal, consumer mistrust. *Arab News*. Retrieved from: www.arabnews.com/node/1808651/world (accessed 24 November 2021).

Deloitte (2014). *Fraud Risk Management – Providing Insight into Fraud Prevention, Detection and Response*. Retrieved from: www2.deloitte.com/content/dam/Deloitte/in/Documents/finance/Forensic-Proactive-services/in-fa-frm-noexp.pdf (accessed 24 November 2021).

Dhesegaan, B. K. and Solhi. F. (2020). Traders of imported beef "stung" by meat cartel. *New Strait Times*. Retrieved from: www.nst.com.my/news/nation/2020/12/653100/traders-imported-beef-stung-meat-cartel (accessed 24 November 2021).

FandD Technology (2017). Food Fraud Report shows 2/3 of consumers blame producers for food fraud. *Food and Drink Technology*. Retrieved from: www.foodanddrinktechnology.com/news/18367/food-fraud-report-shows-23-consumers-blame-producers-food-fraud/ (accessed 24 November 2021).

Farah, I. (2021). How technology is putting a stop to Halal food fraud. *Halalop*. Retrieved from: https://halalop.com/business/how-technology-stop-halal-food-fraud/ (accessed 24 November 2021).

Fatimah, M. A. (2021). My say: Halal meat fiasco begs a system overhaul. *The Edge Markets*. Retrieved from: https://bit.ly/2V8L0q1 (accessed 24 November 2021).

Food and Agriculture Organization (FAO). (2006). *Strengthening National Food Control Systems: Guidelines to Assess Capacity Building Needs*. Rome: FAO.

Food and Agriculture Organization (FAO) (2015). *Inclusive Business Models: Guidelines for Improving Linkages between Producer and Groups and Buyers of Agricultural Produce*. Rome: FAO.

Hammim, R. (2021). Meat cartel case: frozen food company, two execs charged. *New Straits Times*. Retrieved from: www.nst.com.my/news/crime-courts/2021/04/684411/meat-cartel-case-frozen-food-company-two-execs-charged (accessed 24 November 2021).

Hibrahim, M. A. (2020). Laporan *Sinar Harian* berkenaan isu kartel daging tepat. *Sinar Harian*. Retrieved from: https://bit.ly/36ajTNh (accessed 24 November 2021).

Hibrahim, M. A. and Zulkafli, N. (2020). Sindiket kartel palsu jenama daging hanya libatkan satu syarikat. *Sinar Harian*. Retrieved from: https://bit.ly/369gJcP (accessed 24 November 2021).

Hopper, M. and Boutrif, E. (2006). *Strengthening National Food Control Systems: Guidelines to Assess Capacity Building Needs*. Geneva: FAO.

Iskandar, M., Tan, I., Razali, R. N., and Husny, Z. J. (2012). The adoption of Halal transportations technologies for Halal logistics service providers in Malaysia. *International Journal of Mechanical, Industrial Science and Engineering*, 6(3), pp. 10–17.

Islamic Chamber Research & Information Center (2020). *State of the Global Islamic Economy 2020/21 Report Is Published*. Retrieved from: https://bit.ly/3hfg1Ba (accessed 24 November 2021).

Koya, Z. and Anis, M. N. (2020). Jakim not at fault, say industry players. *The Star*. Retrieved from: www.thestar.com.my/news/nation/2020/12/31/jakim-not-at-fault-say-industry-players (accessed 24 November 2021).

Lu, D. (2011). *Fundamentals of Supply Chain Management.* Bookboon.
Malaysia Competition Commission (MyCC). (2019). *Final Report – Market Review on Food Sector in Malaysia under the Competition Act 2010.* Retrieved from: https://bit.ly/3hcGQ8N (accessed 24 November 2021).
Meidayanti, K., Arkeman, Y. and Sugiarto. (2019). Analysis and design of beef supply chain traceability system based on blockchain technology. *IOP Conference Series: Earth and Environmental Science,* 335, 012012.
Mohamed, Y. H., Abdul Rahim, A. R., and Ma'aram, A. (2020). The effect of Halal supply chain management on Halal integrity assurance for the food industry in Malaysia. *Journal of Islamic Marketing.* https://doi.org/10.1108/JIMA-12-2018-0240
Muhammad Shahrulnizam Muhadi (2020). Bayan Linnas Series 232: the issue of meat cartel which is haram and rulings related to it. *Official Website of Mufti of Federal Territory.* Retrieved from: https://muftiwp.gov.my/en/artikel/bayan-linnas/4642-bayan-linnas-series-232-the-issue-of-meat-cartel-which-is-haram-and-rulings-related-to-it (accessed 24 November 2021).
Nakamoto, S. (2008). *Bitcoin: A Peer-to-Peer Electronic Cash System.* Retrieved from: https://bitcoin.org/bitcoin.pdf (accessed 24 November 2021).
New Straits Times (2021). More messages linked to meat cartel leaked. New Straits Times. Retrieved from: www.nst.com.my/news/nation/2021/02/664309/more-messages-linked-meat-cartel-leaked (accessed 24 November 2021).
Pal, A. and Kant, K. (2019). Using blockchain for provenance and traceability in Internet of Things-integrated food logistics. *Computer,* 52(12), pp. 94–98.
Raikwar, M., Gligoroski, D., and Kralevska, K. (2019). SoK of used cryptography in blockchain. *IEEE Access,* 7, 148550–148575.
Razak, R. (2021). Come clean on companies behind "meat cartel" scandal, Lembah Pantai MP tells Putrajaya. *Malay Mail.* Retrieved from: https://bit.ly/3heIEOF (accessed 24 November 2021).
Rejeb, A. (2018). Halal meat supply chain traceability based on HACCP, blockchain and Internet of Things. *Acta Technica Jaurinensis,* 11(4), pp. 218–247.
Rozlin, I. and Ramli, M. A. (2020). Kartel tukar daging haram jadi halal. *Sinar Harian.* Retrieved from: www.sinarharian.com.my/article/112898/LAPORAN-KHAS/Kartel-tukar-daging-haram-jadi-halal (accessed 24 November 2021).
Scholten, H., Verdouw, C. N., Beulens, A., and van der Vorst, J. G. A. J. (2016). Defining and analyzing traceability systems in food supply chains. In M. Espiñeira and F. J. Santaclara (eds.), *Advances in Food Traceability Techniques and Technologies: Improving Quality Throughout the Food Chain.* London: Elsevier Ltd., pp. 9–33.
Seebacher, S. and Schüritz, R. (2017). Blockchain technology as an enabler of service systems: a structured literature review. *Lecture Notes in Business Information Processing,* 279, pp. 12–23.
Syaida, N. (2020). Kronologi isu kartel seludup daging sejuk beku tahun 2020. *Sinar Harian.* Retrieved from: https://m.sinarharian.com.my/mobile-article?articleid=139752 (accessed 24 November 2021).
Talib, M. S. A., Hamid, A. B. A. and Chin, T. A. (2015). Motivations and limitations in implementing Halal food certification: a Pareto analysis. *British Food Journal,* 117(11), pp. 2664–2705.
Tee, K. and Shahrizam, S. A. N. (2020). Backed by ex-IGP, Malay group demands reshuffle of Jakim over "meat cartel" scandal. *Malay Mail.* Retrieved from: https://bit.ly/36plZJz (accessed 24 November 2021).

Tieman, M. and Ghazali, M. C. (2014). Halal control activities and assurance activities in Halal food logistics. *Procedia – Social and Behavioral Sciences*, 121, pp. 44–57.

Zainul, E. (2019). Matrade targets 5% growth in halal exports for 2019. *The Edge Markets*. Retrieved from: www.theedgemarkets.com/article/matrade-%0Atargets-5-growth-halal-exports-2019 (accessed 24 November 2021).

Zulsyamini, M. and Suhaini, N. A. (2020). Avoid imported meat until trust issue resolved. *New Straits Times*. Retrieved from: https://bit.ly/3dADZ7F (accessed 24 November 2021).

11 Halal transportation adoption among SMEs in Malaysia

Abdul Hafaz Ngah, Serge Gabarre and Ramayah Thurasamy

Introduction

Islam is the world's fastest growing religion, with Muslims representing more than 25% of the world's population, with an expected 8.3 billion followers by 2030 (Pew Research Center, 2011). Due to growing concerns among Muslims regarding the quality of products they consume daily, many non-Muslim manufacturers have started producing Halal products and aligning their services with Halal requirements. Thus, the realm of Halal has expanded from foods to cosmetics, pharmaceuticals, logistics and banking services. The notion of Halal is not only limited to these, as several new products are expected to be introduced by world entrepreneurs to meet the demand for such products. Due to their hygienic and quality features, Halal products and services are not only popular among Muslims, but have started to attract non-Muslim consumers (Ngah et al., 2015). For these reasons, Halal products have a strong potential in the world market.

Small and medium-sized enterprises (SMEs) are the most common form of organization around the globe. In Malaysia, 98.5 % of business establishments are SMEs (SMECORP, 2021). Among these, 5.3% or 47,698 establishments are involved in the manufacturing industry. SMEs always play a crucial role not only as a major source of employment and economic growth for countries, but also as a source of technology adoption. SMEs are also commonly viewed as a source of innovation and product flexibility (Awa et al., 2015) which can enhance product resilience and diversification (Lorente-Martínez et al., 2020). Due to the importance of SMEs to the world economic activity, numerous studies have been conducted on the adoption of new technology among SMEs; however, there remains a lack of study addressing the use of Halal transportation services by SMEs.

The service of Halal transportation was initially introduced by Halal logistics providers in response to the demand from manufacturers of Halal products (Ngah et al., 2014a). All Halal products require Halal transportation services to ensure that the Halal quality is preserved throughout all stages of the transportation (Ngah et al., 2020a, 2020b). However, establishing Halal transportation is costly (Ngah et al., 2019a) since, Halal transportation is a special service which

DOI: 10.4324/9781003223719-15

requires specific tools and processes (Fathi et al., 2016; Zailani et al., 2019). Consequently, most Halal manufacturers remain hesitant in adopting the services of Halal transporters in their line of work (Ngah et al., 2021). Currently, Muslim consumers are looking beyond Halal ingredients and processes, and are seeking the implementation of Halal transportation in Halal manufacturers' commercial operation (Tieman et al., 2012). However, according to Ngah et al. (2019b), only 15% of Halal manufacturers have recourse to Halal transportation services. Thus, it is an obligation for scholars to search for obstacles and facilitators to the acceptance of Halal transportation services by Halal manufacturers.

Although the Halal supply chain has been well studied by Muslim and non-Muslim scholars, hardly any studies have been conducted to address the issues of Halal transportation acceptance by SMEs. The adoption of Halal transportation has only been the focus of a few studies (Ngah et al., 2019a; Ngah and Thurasamy, 2018) dealing with Halal pharmaceutical and cosmetics manufacturers (Ngah et al., 2020a, 2020b), the Halal supply chain among food manufacturers (Ngah et al., 2017, 2019b), the commitment to pay for Halal transportation (Azmi et al., 2019), Halal warehousing (Talib et al., 2017, 2020), Halal logistics (Rahman et al., 2018) and Halal air cargo. Hence, to address the gap in the literature, the authors employed the Technology–Organization–Environment (TOE) Framework to address the obstacles and facilitators to the adoption of Halal transportation by Halal SMEs in Malaysia.

The findings of the study are beneficial to providers in the Halal supply chain to prepare a meaningful marketing plan to enhance the acceptance of such services, especially for companies offering Halal transportation services. Moreover, the findings of the current study are also beneficial to government agencies related to Halal supply chain services, as it provides insightful information.

Literature review and hypothesis development

Technology–Organization–Environment Framework

The Technology–Organization–Environment (TOE) Framework is a prominent theory explaining the incorporation of technology in organizations. The authors used complexity and cost as factors to represent the technological dimension, organizational readiness to represent the organizational context, and competitive pressure and supplier availability to represent the environmental context.

Complexity

Complexity is defined as an innovation's level of difficulty to be understood and implemented by users or organizations. Complexity in new innovations is due to the lack of knowledge of the new elements in the technology. According to Dryden-Palmer et al. (2020), complexity emerges when an innovative procedure requires several steps and commitment from team members. Because Halal transportation is a novel approach based on new requirements introduced by JAKIM through Halal standards, it is quite complex for managers of SMEs to understand the requirements, the importance and the benefits for SMEs to adopt this service. Moreover, changing existing practice that team members are comfortable with contributes to the complexity of adopting an innovation. Most of the literature on technology adoption reports that complexity has a negative relationship with the intention to use new innovations. Complexity was identified as having a negative relationship with the intention to use blockchain among SMEs (Sun et al., 2021; Wong et al., 2020) and artificial intelligence adoption in China (Chen et al., 2021).

Even though adopting Halal transportation could provide a competitive advantage for Halal SMEs, the complexity of Halal transportation remains a hindrance. SMEs are burdened by the high cost of ensuring that their staff have sufficient knowledge and qualifications to ensure that their business operation adheres to Halal standards. Based on these premises, the authors propose that:

H1: *Complexity has a negative relationship with the decision to adopt Halal transportation among Halal SMEs*

H6: *Complexity has a positive relationship with the cost of adopting Halal transportation.*

Cost

Cost has always been considered a major factor in the top management's decision to implement a new technology in their company (Ngah et al., 2019c), especially for SMEs. Compared to big companies, SMEs are always concerned by the lack of resources to adopt new technologies. However, SMEs are still expected to have capabilities similar to those big organizations (Wong et al., 2020). Limited financial resources explain why cost is a major issue for SMEs to adopt new technology. Cost is referred to as a fee chargeable for using or implementing a new technology (Wong et al., 2020). The authors define cost as the potential payment required to adopt Halal transportation in Halal SMEs' business operations. To be certified as Halal service providers, logistics providers need to go through a critical process to fulfil specific requirements as Halal providers. This results in an increase in their operational cost (Iranmanesh et al., 2019). Consequently, the cost is transferred to Halal manufacturers (Ngah et al., 2020a, 2020b) which increases the cost of SMEs' business operations.

The decision to adopt new innovations is determined by the SMEs' perception of the value of the cost paid compared to the benefits gained (Wong et al., 2020). Previous studies revealed that cost has a negative relationship with the intention to adopt new technologies among SMEs in Malaysia (Ghobakhloo and Ching, 2019; Wong et al., 2020). Postulated to that, the authors propose that:

H2: *Cost has a negative relationship with the decision to adopt Halal transportation by Halal SMEs.*

Organization readiness

Readiness influences the ability of an organization to move forward in its business activity, especially when it is related to change in their business processes. Organization readiness has been defined (Zhang et al., 2020) as the characteristics of a business entity which are essential for its implementation and acceptance of a new method or technology in their activity. The authors define organizational readiness as the extent to which managers believe they have sufficient financial or human resources to use Halal transportation services to handle the movement of their Halal products.

As suggested by Sophonthummapharn (2009), organizational readiness can be measured by two dimensions: (1) financial readiness and (2) human resource readiness. Influenced by researchers (Alsaad et al., 2019; Rubbio et al., 2019) who measure organizational readiness as a higher order construct, the authors decided to treat organizational readiness as such in the present study.

Findings from previous studies revealed that organization readiness is positively related to the intention to employ Halal warehouses (Ngah et al., 2017) and other technology adoption among SMEs (Abed, 2020). Based on these, the authors propose that:

H3: Organizational readiness positively influences the adoption of Halal transportation services by Malaysian Halal SMEs.

Competitive pressure

Competitive pressure is referred to as the pressure created from a potential loss of competitiveness due to the failure to adopt new technologies which have been adopted by competitors in the same industry. Since SMEs are the most dominant players in the Halal industry, these notice which of their competitors adopt Halal transportation services. Previous studies report that competitive pressure has a positive influence on encouraging competitors to embrace the latest innovations. According to Wong et al. (2020), competitive pressure has a positive influence on the adoption of blockchain technology in the supply chain management of SMEs in Malaysia. Thus, the authors propose that:

H4: Competitive pressure positively influences the adoption of Halal transportation by Malaysian Halal SMEs.

Supplier availability

Suppliers play a crucial role in introducing new innovations to SMEs. As a provider or supplier of services, Halal transportation providers have a significant role in introducing their services to Halal SMEs. Without suppliers, it is impossible to adopt new services or innovations. Supplier availability is fundamental for services to be adopted. Findings from a previous study (Al-Qirim, 2007) revealed

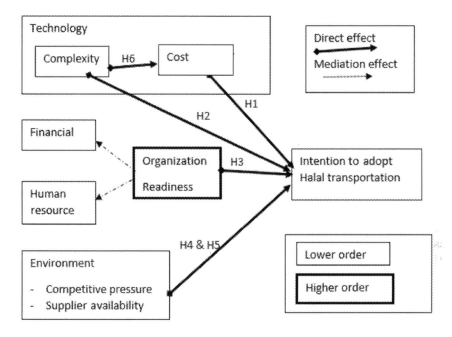

Figure 11.1 Framework of the research.

that supplier availability is positively related to the intention to adopt e-commerce (Figure 11.1). For these reasons, the authors propose that:

H5: *Supplier availability positively influences the adoption of Halal transportation by Malaysian Halal SMEs.*

Methodology

In the present study, the smallest unit of analysis is the organization. Thus, the top management or owners of Halal SMEs are considered valid respondents. To ensure the data were sufficient, the authors collected data from Halal SMEs who attended the Halal Festival (Halfest) and the Malaysia International Halal Showcase (MIHAS), which are annual events in Malaysia. Employing a purposeful sampling approach, all Halal SMEs were approached during both events and invited to participate in the study. From over 400 SMEs approached, the authors were able to recruit 327 participants. However, due to issues with the quality of the data such as straight line answers, only data from 306 respondents were considered valid and usable for further analysis.

As proposed by Hair et al. (2019), in studies where SmartPLS is employed for hypothesis testing, the minimum sample size is determined by the power of analysis which is based on the total number of predictors within the research framework. Gefen et al. (2011) set guidelines which were applied in the present study. Accordingly, with the power of 0.8, p = 0.05, a medium effect size, six predictors and an analysis using the G power software, results in a minimum sample size of 98 respondents for the current study. Thus, with 306 respondents, the sample size is not considered a methodological issue.

From 306 SMES, 71.9% are small, 19% are micro and 9.2% are medium. Exactly 71.6% are food manufacturers, 16% are cosmetics manufacturers, and 12.4% are pharmaceuticals manufacturers. Regarding the age of the SMEs, 34.3% had been established between three and six years, 28.1% had been in operation for more than nine years, 22.2% had been founded within the past three years, and 15.4% had started their business within the six to nine years range. The majority (46.7%) claimed to have more than seven Halal products, 22.2% had three or four Halal products, 18.6% had five Halal products and the rest produced one or two Halal products. From the 306 respondents, the majority were Muslims (87.9%), and women represented 51% of the total respondents. A total of 42.5% of the respondents claimed to have a Bachelor's degree as their minimum qualification. From the respondents, 16.3% were the owners of their business and the rest were part of the top management who handled the business operations in their respective companies.

As the number of publications on Halal transportation adoption is limited, the authors adopted measurement items from established literature in the context of supply chain studies. The intention to adopt was adopted from Chen et al. (2011), cost and complexity were adopted from Thiesse et al. (2011), and competitive pressure, organizational readiness and supplier availability from Sophonthummapharn (2009).

Analysis

The common method variance (CMV) is always a big concern for survey studies, especially when the data are collected from a single source, using the same method, and the independent and dependent variables are answered at the time (Ngah et al., 2018; MacKenzie and Podsakoff, 2012; Podsakoff et al., 2012). To remedy such an issue, it is necessary to apply the full collinearity testing statistical method as suggested by Kock (2015). A variance inflation factor (VIF) with a value that is greater than or equal to 3.3 suggests that the research is affected by a CMV issue. The findings from the current study reveal that all VIF values are lower than the threshold value of 3.3, thus confirming that CMV is not critical.

Smart Partial Least Square (PLS) is a structural equation modelling software which is suited to a study's predictive purpose (Ringle et al., 2015), hence the authors employed SmartPLS to test the hypothesis of the study. The analysis followed a two-step approach including (1) the measurement model and (2) the structural model. Both discriminant and convergent validities needed to be confirmed before transitioning to the second step, the structural model (Ngah et al., 2014b). To establish the measurement model for either lower order construct (LOC) or higher order construct (HOC), loading and average variance

Halal transportation adoption among SMEs 157

Table 11.1 Convergent validity

Construct		Item	Loading	CR	AVE
Lower order	Higher order				
Competitive pressure		Compe1	0.836	0.840	0.569
		Compe2	0.705		
		Compe3	0.694		
		Compe4	0.774		
Complexity		Compl1	0.907	0.926	0.807
		Compl2	0.908		
		Compl3	0.880		
Cost		Cost1	0.858	0.932	0.775
		Cost2	0.887		
		Cost3	0.886		
		Cost4	0.890		
Halal transport		HT1	0.889	0.936	0.831
		HT2	0.931		
		HT3	0.913		
Financial		Fin1	0.824	0.814	0.687
		Fin2	0.695		
Human resource		HR1	0.757	0.835	0.717
		HR2	0.814		
	Readiness	Financial	0.921	0.922	0.855
		Human resource	0.928		
Supplier		Supp1	0.810	0.910	0.717
		Supp2	0.880		
		Supp3	0.862		
		Supp4	0.833		

extracted (AVE) should be a value that is greater than or equal to 0.5, and composite reliability (CR) must be greater than or equal to 0.7 (Hair et al., 2013). Since the authors used type 1 of HOC to measure the organizational readiness, the repetitive indicator approach was applied to establish the convergent validity of the construct. Table 11.1 highlights results from the measurement model analysis. Regarding both LOCs and HOCs of the study, values for the loading, AVE and CR were higher than the values stated by Hair et al. (2013), which confirms that the convergent validity was confirmed for the present study. Figure 11.2 illustrates the measurement model of the study.

To establish the discriminant validity, as proposed by Franke and Sarstedt (2019), the authors relied on the heterotrait-monotrait ratio (HTMT). The discriminant validity is considered substantiated if each value is below or equal to the threshold set at 0.85 (Franke and Sarstedt, 2019). As can be seen in Table 11.2, each value for the HTMT ratios is smaller than 0.85, thus indicating that the discriminant validity has been confirmed in the current study.

Since the measurement model was established, the authors proceeded to the structural model to verify the study's hypotheses. A bootstrapping procedure

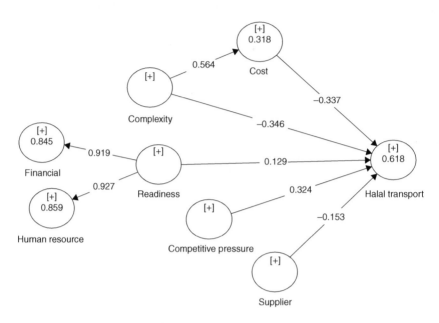

Figure 11.2 Measurement model.

Table 11.2 Discriminant validity

Construct	Competitive pressure	Complexity	Cost	Halal transport	Readiness	Supplier
Competitive pressure						
Complexity	0.261					
Cost	0.183	0.626				
Halal transport	0.334	0.656	0.728			
Readiness	0.194	0.044	0.124	0.195		
Supplier	0.336	0.314	0.203	0.256	0.193	

with a 5,000 resampling technique was used to verify the study's hypotheses. A hypothesis is considered supported when the t-value is greater than or equal to 1.645 for the direct hypothesis and 1.96 for the mediation analysis, the beta value is aligned with the direction of the hypothesis, the p-value is smaller than or equal to 0.05 and the confidence interval of both the lower level (LL) and upper level (UL) do not straddle 0 in between (Hair et al., 2019).

Prior to testing the hypothesis, it is fundamental to confirm that the study was free from multicollinearity issues. The analysis shows that all VIF values were smaller than 3.3 as suggested by the literature (Diamantopoulos and Siguaw, 2006), thus confirming that the results are free from multicollinearity issues. As can be seen in Table 11.3 for the analysis of the hypotheses testing for the direct effect

Table 11.3 Hypothesis testing

Hypothesis	Relationship	Beta	SE	T-value	P-value	LL	UL	VIF	F2
H1	Complexity → Halal transport	-0.346	0.051	6.821	0.001	-0.448	-0.275	1.558	0.222
H2	Cost → Halal transport	-0.337	0.055	6.150	0.001	-0.435	-0.246	1.605	0.195
H3	Readiness → Halal transport	0.129	0.042	3.038	0.001	0.064	0.190	1.040	0.039
H4	Competitive pressure → Halal transport	0.340	0.041	7.868	0.001	0.267	0.413	1.117	0.274
H5	Supplier → Halal Transport	-0.153	0.037	4.164	0.001	-0.203	-0.078	1.143	0.049
H6	Complexity → Cost	0.564	0.042	13.524	0.001	0.472	0.642	1.000	0.456

Table 11.4 PLS-predict

Item	RMSE	RMSE	PLS-LM	Q^2 predict
HT1	1.062	1.094	−0.032	0.499
HT2	0.97	1.02	−0.05	0.576
HT3	1.104	1.122	−0.018	0.533

of the study, competitive pressure, complexity, cost and organizational readiness have a significantly relation to the adoption of Halal transportation by Malaysian SME Halal manufacturers. Competitive pressure → Halal transport (β = 0.340, p-value ≤ 0.001), Complexity → Halal transport (β = -0.361, p-value ≤ 0.001), Cost → Halal transport (β = -0.343, p-value ≤ 0.001), and organizational readiness (β = 0.340, p-value ≤ 0.001), thus supporting H1, H2, H3 and H4 of the study. Conversely, for H5, supplier v Halal transportation, (β = −0.146, p-value ≤ 0.001), the hypothesis was not supported since the analysis revealed that the relationship was negatively related, although it was hypothesized as positively related.

For the last hypothesis related to the direct effect, the authors found that complexity has a positive relation to cost. With complexity → cost (β = 0.559, p-value ≤ 0.001), thus confirming that H6 of the study is supported.

The R^2 value is 0.318 for cost, and 0.618 for the intention to adopt Halal transportation proposing that complexity explains 31.8% of the variance in the cost. Also, complexity, cost, organizational readiness, competitive pressure and supplier explain 61.8% of Malaysian SMEs' intention to employ Halal transportation services. As noted above, the purpose of the study is predictive and the PLS-predict is the last method used to test the model's predictive power. As proposed by the literature (Shmueli et al., 2019), the PLS-predict measures the degree of error of the PLS model and the linear modelling (LM). A negative value for the result of the PLS RMSE – LM RMSE indicates that the PLS model has fewer errors than the LM model. Furthermore, all negative values for the result of the PLS RMSE – LM RMSE indicate that the model developed in the present study has a high predictive power. As can be seen in Table 11.4, all values for the PLS RMSE are smaller than the LM RMSE, thus indicating a high predictive power with the present model.

Discussion and conclusion

The results of the study reveal that variables for the technological factors have a significant relationship with the Malaysian SMEs' decision to employ Halal transportation services. The findings for complexity, which negatively influences the decision to employ Halal transportation, are supported by previous studies (Sun et al., 2021; Wong et al., 2020) related to SMEs' intention to employ blockchain technology. This confirms that complexity is an obstacle toward the use of Halal transportation by SMEs in Malaysia.

Cost represents the second variable representing the technological context, which was also found to have a negative influence on the decision of Halal SMEs in Malaysia to adopt Halal transportation. This confirms cost as a barrier toward the decision to adopt. The findings of the current study are in line with other studies (Ghobakhloo and Ching, 2019; Wong et al., 2020) where cost was also found to be negatively related to SMEs' intention to adopt new technologies in their respective contexts.

For the organizational factor, the authors discovered that organizational readiness positively influences Malaysian SMEs' decision to adopt Halal transportation. Such findings indicate that a high readiness results in a positive decision to adopt Halal transportation among Malaysian SMEs. These findings are aligned with Ngah et al.'s (2017) study, where it was discovered that organizational readiness has a positive relationship with the use of Halal warehouses. This suggests that readiness is an enabler toward Malaysian SMEs' decision to employ Halal transportation.

For the environmental context, competitive pressure was identified as having a positive influence on the intention to employ Halal transportation, thus prompting that competitive pressure is a facilitator toward the use of Halal transportation by SMEs in Malaysia. The findings are supported by Wong et al.'s (2020) publication where competitive pressure is identified as a facilitator to Malaysian SMEs' intention to employ blockchain technology.

Lastly, the authors also found that supplier availability has a significant but negative influence on the Malaysian SMEs' intention to use Halal transportation. This is justified by the location of SMEs, which are scattered throughout all states in Malaysia, whereas most Halal transportation providers only operate in the central region of Malaysia. This justifies why supplier availability has a negative influence on Malaysian SMEs' use of Halal transportation. It also implies that the intention to adopt is not an issue, but that the limited availability of suppliers in outlying areas suggests that the scarcity of suppliers is an obstacle to the use of Halal transportation by SMEs in Malaysia. To overcome this issue, Halal transportation providers in Malaysia should enhance their presence throughout all Malaysian states to ensure that Halal SMEs will adopt their services as part of their effort to ensure the condition of Halal products.

The present study is limited to five variables; however, several other variables could be tested to obtain a higher variance explaining the intention to use Halal transportation among SMEs. Future studies should explore other variables related to the owner's characteristics. Owners' innovativeness and openness to change could be good predictors explaining the intention to employ Halal transportation among SMEs.

The findings of the present study offer insightful information related to SMEs' intention to employ Halal transportation. Thus, Halal related agencies and providers of Halal logistics could make use of these findings as essential information for the purpose of crafting a better policy enhancing the use of Halal logistics services by Malaysian Halal manufacturers.

References

Abed, S. S. (2020). Social commerce adoption using TOE framework: an empirical investigation of Saudi Arabian SMEs. *International Journal of Information Management*, 53, 102118.

Al-Qirim, N. (2007). An empirical investigation of an e-commerce adoption-capability model in small businesses in New Zealand. *Electronic Markets*, 15(4), pp. 418–437.

Alsaad, A., Mohamad, R. and Ismail, N. A. (2019). The contingent role of dependency in predicting the intention to adopt B2B e-commerce. *Information Technology for Development*, 25(4), pp. 686–714.

Awa, H. O., Ojiabo, O. U. and Emecheta, B. C. (2015). Integrating TAM, TPB and TOE frameworks and expanding their characteristic constructs for e-commerce adoption by SMEs. *Journal of Science and Technology Policy Management*, 6(1), pp. 76–94.

Azmi, F. R., Abdullah, A., Musa, H. and Wan Mahmood, W. H. (2019). Perception of food manufacturers towards adoption of Halal food supply chain in Malaysia: exploratory factor analysis. *Journal of Islamic Marketing*, 11(3), pp. 571–589.

Chen, C. J. R., Gregoire, M. B., Arendt, S. and Shelley, M. C. (2011). College and university dining services administrators' intention to adopt sustainable practices: results from US institutions. *International Journal of Sustainability in Higher Education*, 12(2), pp. 145–162.

Chen, H., Li, L. and Chen, Y. (2021). Explore success factors that impact artificial intelligence adoption on telecom industry in China. *Journal of Management Analytics*, 8(1), pp. 36–68.

Diamantopoulos, A. and Siguaw, J. A. (2006). Formative versus reflective indicators in organizational measure development: a comparison and empirical illustration. *British Journal of Management*, 17(4), pp. 263–282.

Dryden-Palmer, K. D., Parshuram, C. S. and Berta, W. B. (2020). Context, complexity and process in the implementation of evidence-based innovation: a realist informed review. *BMC Health Services Research*, 20(81). https://doi.org/10.1186/s12913-020-4935-y

Fathi, E., Zailani, S., Iranmanesh, M., and Kanapathy, K. (2016). Drivers of consumers' willingness to pay for Halal logistics. *British Food Journal*, 118(2), pp. 464–479.

Franke, G. and Sarstedt, M. (2019). Heuristics versus statistics in discriminant validity testing: a comparison of four procedures. *Internet Research*, 29(3), pp. 431–447.

Gefen, D., Rigdon, E. E. and Straub, D. (2011). An update and extension to SEM guidelines for administrative and social science research. *MIS Quarterly*, 35(2), iii–A7.

Ghobakhloo, M. and Ching, N. T. (2019). Adoption of digital technologies of smart manufacturing in SMEs. *Journal of Industrial Information Integration*, 16, 100107.

Hair, J. F., Hult, G. T. M., Ringle, C. M., Sarstedt, M., Ringle, C. M., Sarstedt, M. and Ketchen, D. J. (2013). A primer on Partial Least Squares structural equation modeling. *Long Range Planning*, 46(1–2), pp. 184–185.

Hair, J. F., Risher, J. J., Sarstedt, M. and Ringle, C. M. (2019). When to use and how to report the results of PLS-SEM. *European Business Review*, 31(1), pp. 2–24.

Iranmanesh, M., Mirzaei, M., Hosseini, S. M. P. and Zailani, S. (2019). Muslims' willingness to pay for certified halal food: an extension of the theory of planned behaviour. *Journal of Islamic Marketing*, 11(1), pp. 14–30.

Kock, N. (2015). Common method bias in PLS-SEM. *International Journal of E-Collaboration*, 11(4), pp. 1–10.

Lorente-Martínez, J., Navío-Marco, J., and Rodrigo-Moya, B. (2020). Analysis of the adoption of customer facing InStore technologies in retail SMEs. *Journal of Retailing and Consumer Services*, 57, 102225.

MacKenzie, S. B. and Podsakoff, P. M. (2012). Common method bias in marketing: causes, mechanisms, and procedural remedies. *Journal of Retailing*, 88(4), pp. 542–555.

Ngah, A. H. and Thurasamy, R. (2018). Modelling the intention to adopt halal transportation among Halal pharmaceutical and cosmetic manufacturers in Malaysia. *Journal of Computational and Theoretical Nanoscience*, 24(1), pp. 205–207.

Ngah, A. H., Zainuddin, Y. and Thurasamy, R. (2014a). Obstacles and facilitators in adopting Halal transportation services: a study of Malaysian Halal manufacturers. *International Journal of Business and Management*, 2(2), pp. 49–70.

Ngah, A. H., Zainuddin, Y. and Thurasamy, R. (2014b). Contributing factors of Halal warehouse adoption. In F. L. Gaol, W. Mars and H. Saragih (Eds.), *Management and Technology in Knowledge, Service, Tourism and Hospitality*. Abingdon: Routledge, pp. 89–94.

Ngah, A. H., Zainuddin, Y. and Thurasamy, R. (2015). Obstacles and facilitators in adopting of Halal warehousing. *Journal of Islamic Marketing*, 6(3), pp. 354–376.

Ngah, A. H., Zainuddin, Y. and Thurasamy, R. (2017). Applying the TOE framework in the Halal warehouse adoption study. *Journal of Islamic Accounting and Business Research*, 8(2), pp. 161–181.

Ngah, A. H., Rahimi, A. H. M. and Norzalita, A. A. (2018). The influence of electronic word of mouth on theory of reasoned action and the visit intention to the world monument fund site. *Indian Journal of Public Health Research and Development*, 9(11), pp. 1277–1282.

Ngah, A. H., Ramayah, T., Ali, M. H. and Khan, M. I. (2019a). Halal transportation adoption among pharmaceuticals and cosmetics manufacturers. *Journal of Islamic Marketing*, 11(6), pp. 1619–1639.

Ngah, A. H., Thurasamy, R., Aziz, N. A., Ali, H. and Khan, M. I. (2019b). Modelling the adoption of Halal warehousing services among Halal pharmaceutical and cosmetic manufacturers. *Journal of Sustainability Science and Management*, 14(6), pp. 103–116.

Ngah, A. H., Kim, H. D., Hanafiah, R. M., Salleh, N. H. M., Jeevan, J. and Asri, N. M. (2019c). Willingness to pay for Halal transportation cost: the stimulus-organism-response model. *International Journal of E-Navigation and Maritime Economy*, 12, pp. 11–021.

Ngah, A. H., Hanafiah, R. M., Talib, M. S. A., Zulfakar, M. H. and Asri, N. M. (2020a). Mediating effects of attitude towards willingness to pay for Halal transportation. *Malaysian Journal of Consumer and Family Economics*, 24(S2).

Ngah, A. H., Gabarre, S., Eneizan, B. and Asri, N. (2020b). Mediated and moderated model of the willingness to pay for Halal transportation. *Journal of Islamic Marketing*. https://doi.org/10.1108/JIMA-10-2019-0199

Ngah, A. H., Ramayah, T., Mohd Salleh, N. H., Jeevan, J., Md. A. Hanapiah, R. and Eneizan, B. (2021). Halal transportation adoption among food manufacturers in Malaysia: the moderated model of Technology, Organization and Environment (TOE) Framework. *Journal of Islamic Marketing*, https://doi.org/10.1108/JIMA-03-2020-0079

Pew Research Center (2011). *The Future of the Global Muslim Population*. Retrieved from: www.pewforum.org/2011/01/27/the-future-of-the-global-muslim-population/ (accessed 24 November 2021).

Podsakoff, P. M., MacKenzie, S. B., and Podsakoff, N. (2012). Sources of method bias in social science research and recommendations on how to control it. *Annual Review of Psychology*, 63, pp. 539–569.

Rahman, N. A. A., Mohammad, M. F., Abdul Rahim, S. and Mohd Noh, H. (2018). Implementing air cargo Halal warehouse: insight from Malaysia. *Journal of Islamic Marketing*, 9(3), pp. 462–483.

Ringle, C. M., Wende, S. and Becker, J. M. (2015). *"Smart PLS 3." Boenningstedt: SmartPLS GmbH*. Retrieved from: www.smartpls.com (accessed 24 November 2021).

Rubbio, I., Bruccoleri, M., Pietrosi, A. and Ragonese, B. (2019). Digital health technology enhances resilient behaviour: evidence from the ward. *International Journal of Operations and Production Management*, 39(2), pp. 260–293.

Shmueli, G., Sarstedt, M., Hair, J. F., Cheah, J.-H., Ting, H., Vaithilingam, S. and Ringle, C. M. (2019). Predictive model assessment in PLS-SEM: guidelines for using PLSpredict. *European Journal of Marketing*, 53(11), pp. 2323–2347.

SMECORP (2021). *SMEs Are the Backbone of the Economy*. Retrieved from: www.smecorp.gov.my/index.php/en/policies/2020-02-11-08-01-24/sme-statistics (accessed 24 November 2021).

Sophonthummapharn, K. (2009). The adoption of techno-relationship innovations: a framework for electronic customer relationship management. *Marketing Intelligence and Planning*, 27(3), pp. 380–412.

Sun, W., Dedahanov, A. T., Shin, H. Y., and Li, W. P. (2021). Using extended complexity theory to test SMEs' adoption of blockchain-based loan system. *PLoS ONE*, 16(2). https://doi.org/10.1371/journal.pone.0245964

Talib, M. S. A., Rahim, M. A. R. A., Chin, T. A. and Hamid, A. B. A. (2017). Logistics service providers perceptions on Halal logistics certification. *International Journal of Logistics Economics and Globalisation*, 6(4), pp. 311–331.

Talib, M. S. A., Pang, L. L. and Ngah, A. H. (2020). The role of government in promoting Halal logistics: a systematic literature review. *Journal of Islamic Marketing*. https://doi.org/10.1108/JIMA-05-2020-0124

Thiesse, F., Staake, T., Schmitt, P. and Fleisch, E. (2011). The rise of the "next-generation bar code": an international RFID adoption study. *Supply Chain Management*, 16(5), pp. 328–345.

Tieman, M., van der Vorst, J. G. A. J. and Ghazali, M. C. (2012). Principles in Halal supply chain management. *Journal of Islamic Marketing*, 3(3), pp. 217–243.

Wong, L. W., Leong, L. Y., Hew, J. J., Tan, G. W. H. and Ooi, K. B. (2020). Time to seize the digital evolution: adoption of blockchain in operations and supply chain management among Malaysian SMEs. *International Journal of Information Management*, 52, 101997.

Zailani, S., Iranmanesh, M., Hyun, S. S. and Ali, M. H. (2019). Applying the theory of consumption values to explain drivers' willingness to pay for biofuels. *Sustainability*, 11(3), 668.

Zhang, Y., Sun, J., Yang, Z. and Wang, Y. (2020). Critical success factors of green innovation: technology, organization and environment readiness. *Journal of Cleaner Production*, 264. 121701.

12 Halal port development
Issues and challenges

Muna Norkhairunnisak Ustadi and Sharina Osman

Overview of Halal consumption

Generally, the demand for Halal food in the world market is escalated due to three main factors; the growth of the Muslim population, the increase of purchasing power among Muslim consumers and the awareness of Islamic rulings on Halal and Haram in society. Institutionally in Malaysia, the importance of Halal food was initiated by JAKIM and further developed and industrialized by the Halal Development Corporation (HDC). Furthermore, the Malaysian government is committed to developing the Halal industry to drive its economic growth – stating in RMK-11 its intention to globalize Malaysian Halal products (Roslan et al., 2016). Additionally, Malaysia was ranked first and second in 2018 and 2019, respectively, for the Halal food sector suggesting that its Halal ecosystem provides strong support for the development of the Islamic economy (Salam Gateway, 2018; Thomson Reuters, 2018). Thus, Malaysia is currently capable of internationalizing its Halal food products. Technically, Halal food should be prepared, processed and manufactured hygienically so it is safe to consume. This comprises the process of slaughtering, storing, displaying and preparing the food itself.

As a response to the growing understanding of the concept of Halal and Toyyiban among Muslim consumers in Malaysia, manufacturers and food operators gained Halal certification for their food and products (Khalek et al., 2017). However, there have been some issues of non-Halal consumption among Muslims, which need to be given serious attention, for example, consuming alcohol and its ingredients, dining in non-Halal food outlets and lack of awareness towards the Halal certification logo. Plus, the issues on understanding Muslim consumers' behaviour and manufacturers' behaviour should give attention. Then the Halal consumption culture can be established in this country. Henceforth, in developing Halal food consumption and the Halal industry in Malaysia, all aspects need to be analysed and further improved. This is important in ensuring that the Halal industry, especially the Halal food industry has developed holistically from the business, scientific and religious points of view. Halal trade is recognized as a benchmark not only to ensure the quality of products, but also including ports. The port plays a main role in maintaining the Halal condition of

DOI: 10.4324/9781003223719-16

goods in transit for export and import transactions. The question to be asked is, why a port should be considered to be a Halal port?

Understanding of port roles

Ports play a vital role as logistics platforms in the Halal supply chain. They act as a gateway in which the logistical handling of cargo is performed through four systems, which cover process of transfer, delivery or receipt, ship and storage (Slack, 2001). Hence, the establishment of Halal ports is of interest to the logistics service provider to ensure the integrity of Halal products and consequently enhance the Halal supply chain performance. Despite the growing interest in Halal logistics, the concept of the Halal port is relatively new and studies on this topic are still underresearched.

Traditionally, the main function of ports is to provide storage for cargo. In the second generation, the ports function includes cargo distribution, packing as well as processing for conventional and bulk cargo. Meanwhile, third-generation ports act as facilitators in cooperating and information-sharing activities among stakeholders. Consequently, the development of ports offers value-addition and facilitation services. Besides that, ports can transform into a knowledge-based global supply chain management centre (Lin and Tan, 2013).

Ports have several facilities and equipment inside the designated port area to support a series of cargo-handling activities from the wharf to the port gate or vice versa. Port investments to acquire those infrastructure facilities and equipment always involve a huge amount of money with a slow yield return and a long investment horizon. A port must optimize the utilization of its investments by attracting more cargo to handle; then it will have a shorter break event point and minimize the burden of loan interests. Some facilities in public ports are scarce and used to handle any cargo in high productivity to have the highest possible goods handled in a certain period. It might not be possible to have a dedicated area for a certain cargo in a port unless it is required by operation or safety standards; for example, refrigerated or dangerous goods. There is a possibility that damages, spoilage, breakage, contamination, theft and tampering occur to cargo handling in ports.

To maintain the integrity of a Halal product during transit at a port, simply providing a dedicated facility and handling methods that meet Halal standards is not enough. The port must be built and operated as a fully Halal facility from its facility design, equipment deployed, personnel, management system, Halal value commitment, investment financing and insurance protection. Additionally, all the handling processes and activities in the port that involve Halal products should be monitored and inspected by the Halal authority continuously.

The growth of Halal markets in Malaysia

As a leading country in the Halal industry, Malaysia has a good reputation, which is recognized around the world. The government of Malaysia has developed two organizations that under the control of the Islamic regulator, namely JAKIM (Jabatan Agama Kemajuan Islam, Malaysia) and the Halal Development Corporation (HDC). These two organizations are functioning in promoting Halal trade activities in various sectors such as logistics and supply chain, food and beverages, restaurants, tourism, banking, textile, medical devices and finance. The Malaysian government claims that one of the most imperative sectors to be looked into is Halal products. Moving to that mission, Malaysia's government has embraced the Halal industry since 1974. Nowadays, Malaysia is recognized as one of the global leaders of the Halal industry, and in 2021 it led the Global Islamic Economic Indicator for the fifth year (Dellyana and Sudrajad, 2021). In 2014, HDC reported that about 60% of Malaysians are Muslims. Malaysia's aim for the past few years has been to become a Halal hub among Muslim countries in the region (Dellyana and Sudrajad, 2021). Malaysia has taken many initiatives across regulation, trade and industry to further develop the Halal industry. One of the initiatives is to ensure the Halal compliance of each product and service, the Malaysian government collaborating with the Standard Department of Malaysia has developed Halal standards. In 2017, the total spending of the Halal economy reached USD 2.1 trillion and is expected to rise to USD 3 trillion in 2023. The positive reimbursement contributes to more countries across the world, both Muslim and non-Muslim. These have shown that both Muslim and non-Muslim countries are interested in the Halal industry (Shahara, 2019). This value may reflect to serve the significant upsurge in global demand for Halal products and services. Therefore, the buying power for Halal products is stronger and potentially competitive globally as well.

Figure 12.1 shows that the biggest contributing countries to Malaysia's export growth were Singapore (RM 4.9 billion) and China (RM 4.9 billion),

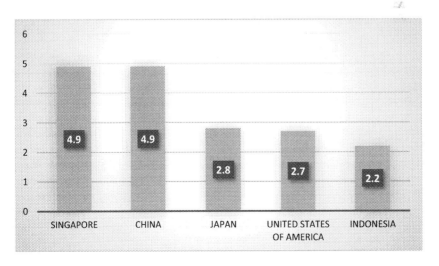

Figure 12.1 Malaysia's export destinations for Halal products in 2018 (RM billion).
Source: Zain et al., 2018.

followed by Japan (RM 2.8 billion), the USA (RM 2.7 billion) and Indonesia (RM 2.2 billion). China and Indonesia are among the top countries with the highest Muslim populations (Zain et al., 2018). These countries can accept Halal products because Malaysia has designed several initiatives that attract the following countries willing to import Halal products. One of the government initiatives in realizing the dream of establishing Malaysia as the centre of Halal food is to develop the Malaysian standard. The standard was developed by the National Industrial Standardization Committee related to Halal matters and is represented by multiple organizations including JAKIM, which acts as the chairman for the Technical Committee. The HDC has launched the Global Data Halal Pool (GDHP), the world's first Halal data pool, to connect Malaysia with the international Halal supply chain. GDHP will bring together and connect accredited Halal suppliers, manufacturers, product service providers, buyers and retailers in the global marketplace.

The initiatives taken by Malaysia's government make the growth of the Halal ecosystem more reliable in various sectors such as Halal certification systems, Islamic banking, Halal standards and regulations, infrastructure, logistics and human capital development. The reputable certification plays as a strong success factor and in line with work by the government that urges local businesses to utilize the country's advantage and enter the market globally, making Malaysia a leader in the Halal industry.

Nowadays, a new dimension of the supply chain needs to look at Halal transportation. Halal transportation is a subset of Halal logistics. Halal logistics is defined as the process of managing the procurement, movement, storage and handling of material parts, livestock, semi-products or finished products that must adhere to Shariah compliance (Zailani et al., 2018). Previously, Haleem and Khan (2017) described Halal logistics activities as similar to conventional logistics activities, comprising of planning, implementing and controlling the distribution and storage of Halal-certified products from the source to the point of consumption. This is a reason why Halal transportation services play a key role in protecting the Halal status of any given product along with the supply chain network until the product reaches its destination. There is no guarantee that the products are Halal at the point of consumption with the absence of the Halal services in between the factory to the end-users. This is because, without Halal transportation services, no one could confirm whether the Halal products are Halal at the point of consumption.

Halal transportation must comply with Shariah compliance to avoid cross-contamination during the transportation of Halal products from the place of manufacturer to the final destination. A manufacturer who produces Halal products should ensure that they use Halal transportation services to maintain the Halal integrity of their products. Several issues have been raised when the consumers question the Halal integrity of products along with the supply chain activities. Another issue arises when manufacturers who produce Halal foods or products do not follow the standard of Halal procedures proposed by JAKIM (Zailani et al., 2018). The hygienic practices and Halal certification issues also are questioned by consumers. Due to these considerations, this study will focus on Halal logistics capabilities by narrowing in on Halal transportation among manufacturers that produce Halal products.

From the perspective of transportation handling, Halal products need to use separate containers from non-Halal products during the carrying and loading processes. The reason for this segregation is to prevent Halal and non-Halal products from mixing and thus to avoid cross-contamination. These practices are suitable for implementation in warehousing processes. The situation is faced differently in non-Muslim countries, where Halal and non-Halal products may be combined, or put on the same pallet and mixed vertically (Hong et al., 2019). The refrigerated shipments should not be mixed in the same container, and Halal products must not be stored with non-Halal products such as pork. Manufacturers should be alert to this matter when selecting modes of transport and choosing the transport companies who must apply Halal practices before these Halal products are put on load carrier or pallet used to protect the Halal transportation along the supply chain.

Several logistics companies realize and understand that to maintain the integrity of Halal products, the company must be certified with JAKIM to react as Halal transportation service providers (Ab Talib et al., 2017). Containerization is the most suitable transportation to use for carrying goods, whether Halal or non-Halal products. The reason for choosing containerization is because it is flexible for the loading and unloading process either at the port of origin/destination or warehouse. It has dominated due to inbound and outbound logistics providers. Normal practices that are applied in containerization involve the providers reusing containers after they have been used to transport non-Halal products. In this scenario, only the logistics providers can identify the next usage for reusing containers that will carry Halal products or not based on the information given by their clients. These logistics providers can notify the information data stated for Halal products. Containers that have been used to transport non-Halal products must undergo the ritual cleansing processor known as the Sertu process before they can be used for the transportation of Halal products. After the Sertu process, the containers must not be exposed to any contaminants so that they can preserve the purity of the Halal products. The Halal container must be used only for transporting Halal products. This study focuses on containerization as the mode of transportation. This is vital to ensure end-to-end Halal supply chain process. This will help to alleviate any doubts among Muslim consumers regarding the use of the Halal products available in the market if their services are utilized.

Halal transportation perspective

Ekwall and Lantz (2019) defined transportation activities as the movement of goods from the starting point to the described destination that includes time and place utilities, that is, in the context of logistics activities, the movement of goods from the manufacturers until it reaches the customers. The relationships between good transportation systems in logistics and supply chain management are interconnected and create not only efficient and effective logistics systems but also can cut down operation costs and upgrade the service quality for overall logistics performance.

From an Islamic perspective, manufacturers who have produced Halal products use Halal transportation in their supply chain activities to maintain the Halal integrity of their products, also known as Halal from farm to fork (Ngah et al., 2020). Halal transportation is a new dimension of the supply chain in which Halal products are handled separately from non-Halal products according to Shariah compliance. The purpose of following Shariah compliance is to avoid cross-contamination in order to maintain their Halal integrity (Noorsiah and Shariff, 2016). On the other hand, Tieman and Ghazali (2014) mentioned the one thing that differentiates between conventional transportation and Halal transportation is the need to comply with Shariah principles as the fundamental guidelines of Halal standards in logistics activities. Since the government of Malaysia and related authority bodies have introduced Halal standards, those who are involved in the business, especially the industry players, have to act accordingly and are bound by the regulations when they offer their services to the customers.

A past study from Ustadi et al. (2020) revealed that Halal integrity, knowledge of Halal practices and perceived usefulness have a strong relationship with the intention to use Halal transport. The results also suggest that the intention to use Halal transport will ultimately influence the behaviour to use Halal transportation. The findings of this study will primarily be beneficial to manufacturers and businesses, such as Halal transportation providers, as this information can be the reference point for them to plan further initiatives to adopt Halal transportation services. By using the results of this study, Halal service providers can work together with government authorities, such as JAKIM and HDC, to determine the area of focus that is important to address if they were to implement Halal logistic management as a whole.

Conclusion

The transformations that ports have undergone have redefined their significance in the Halal supply chain. To develop the Halal port, the governments and port authorities need to designate their facilities, types of equipment, management, inspections and regulations in handling the Halal products. Plus, several arrangements must be conducted to prevent the mixing of Halal and non-Halal cargo. The Halal control and assurance activities conducted at transport, warehouse and terminal should be examined in terms of preserving the Halal status of the goods. The management must ensure that the mode of transport is cleaned before use according to hygienic standards. Similar to transportation, the management must ensure that there is physical segregation of Halal products from non-Halal products during the warehouse and terminal processes to avoid contamination. This chapter extends our understanding of the Halal supply chain, specifically the role of Halal ports in Halal logistics. This includes Halal control and assurance activities in logistics processes such as having dedicated Halal transport or through containerization at a lower level. Although the ports' daily activities include both Halal and non-Halal products, Halal supply chain integrity could potentially provide a reliable platform for delivering the Halal products to the end consumers based on the Islamic rules.

References

Ab Talib, M. S., Ai Chin, T. and Fischer, J. (2017). Linking Halal food certification and business performance. *British Food Journal*, 119(7), pp. 1606–1618.

Dellyana, D. and Sudrajad, O. Y. (2021). Capturing the velocity of Sharia economy through an Islamic boarding school's (Pesantren) B2B e-commerce. In M. N. Almunawar, M. A. Ali and S. A. Lim (Eds.), *Handbook of Research on Innovation and Development of E-Commerce and E-Business in ASEAN*. Hershey, PA: IGI Global, pp. 457–484.

Ekwall, D. and Lantz, B. (2019). The moderating role of transport chain location in cargo theft risk. *The TQM Journal*, 32(5), pp. 1003–1019.

Haleem, A. and Khan, M. I. (2017). Towards successful adoption of halal logistics and its implications for the stakeholders. *British Food Journal*, 119(7), pp. 1592–1605.

Hong, M., Sun, S., Beg, A. R. and Zhou, Z. (2019). Determinants of Halal purchasing behaviour: evidences from China. *Journal of Islamic Marketing*, 10(9).

Khalek, A. A., Ismail, S. H. S. and Ibrahim, H. M. (2017). A study on the factors influencing young Muslims' behavioral intention in consuming Halal food in Malaysia. *Jurnal Syariah*, 23(1), pp. 79–102.

Lin, R. and Tan, J. (2013). Evaluation of port development based on the theory of the driving force and the law of entropy weight. *Procedia-Social and Behavioral Sciences*, 96, pp. 1774–1783.

Ngah, A. H., Jeevan, J., Salleh, N. H. M. and Lee, T. T. H. (2020). Willingness to pay for Halal transportation cost: the moderating effect of knowledge on the Theory of Planned Behavior. *Journal of Environmental Treatment Techniques*, 8(1), pp. 13–22.

Noorsiah, A. and Shariff, S. M. (2016). Supply chain management: Sertu cleansing for Halal logistics integrity. *Procedia Economics and Finance*, 37, pp. 418–425.

Roslan, N. F., Rahman, F. A., Ahmad, F. and Ngadiman, N. I. (2016). Halal logistics certificate in Malaysia: challenges and practices. *International Journal of Supply Chain Management*, 5(3), pp. 142–146.

Salam Gateway (2018). *Report: State of the Global Islamic Economy 2018/19*. Retrieved from: www.salaamgateway.com/en/story/report_state_of_the_global_islamic_economy_201819-SALAA M06092018061914 (accessed 24 November 2021).

Shahara, W. S. S. (2019). *Halal Economic: Challenges and Merging Opportunities in Malaysia*. Doctoral dissertation. Selangor: Kolej Universiti Islam Antarabangsa Selangor.

Slack, B. (2001). *Globalisation in Maritime Transportation: Competition, Uncertainty and Implications for Port Development Strategy*. Retrieved from: https://ssrn.com/abstract=272131 (accessed 24 November 2021).

Thomson Reuters (2018). *States of the Global Islamic Economy Report 2018/19*. Retrieved from: www.slideshare.net/EzzedineGHLAMALLAH/state-of-the-global-islamic-economy-report-201819 (accessed 24 November 2021).

Tieman, M. and Ghazali, M. C. (2014). Halal control activities and assurance activities in Halal food logistics. *Procedia – Social and Behavioral Sciences*, 121, pp. 44–57.

Ustadi, M. N., Osman, S. and Rasi, R. Z. (2020). Perception of non-Muslim manufacturers towards Halal food supply chain in Malaysia. *International Journal of Innovation, Creativity and Change*, 10(11).

Zailani, S., Jafarzadeh, S., Iranmanesh, M., Nikbin, D. and Selim, N. I. I. (2018). Halal logistics service quality: conceptual model and empirical evidence. *British Food Journal*, 120(11), pp. 2599–2614.

Zain, N. F. B. M., Jaafar, H. S. and Ibrahim, I. B. (2018). Modelling Halal supply chain: strategy for industrial parks in Malaysia. *Advances in Transportation and Logistics Research*, 1, pp. 540–551.

Part IV
Halal logistics review, certification and regulatory frameworks

13 Halal logistics, supply chain and quality control in Malaysia

Muna Norkhairunnisak Ustadi, Sharina Osman and Raja Zuraidah Raja Mohd Rasi

Definition of Halal concept

Halal is an Arabic term that means an act or product that is lawful and permitted (Al-Qaradawi, 2007). Linguistically, the word "Halal" is derived from the verb "Halla", which means "to be or become lawful, legal, licit, legitimate, permissible, permitted, allowable, allowed, admissible, un-prohibited, and unforbidden". In the Quran, several Surah explain Halal rules on food and guide Muslims in their customary practices. These Surah repeat the recommendations for Muslims to eat only wholesome things which are lawful. All the contents or ingredients of the food must comply with Islamic dietary law. The word Halal comes from Arabic words: "Halla", "Yahillu", "Hillan" and "Wahalalan", which means allowed or permitted in the Shariah law (Al-Qaradawi, 2013; Baharuddin et al., 2015). The meaning also can be extended to mean "to untie, unfasten, unbind, undo, unravel, loosen, unloose, unfix, unwind, unscrew, untangle, disengage, and free" (JAKIM, 2015, 2018).

The definition of Halal has been discussed from various perspectives. Farag (2020) elaborates that Halal covers preparation, slaughtering, storage, display, hygiene and sanitation. Halal is a quality benchmark since the products have been handled with a high level of hygiene, produced in a clean environment and meet a standard of safety and nutrition. Based on the definition that has been discussed, it is concluded as Halal is something permissible by Allah (SWT) and dictated to be the way of life in matters covering food, consumerism, "Muamalah" affairs, and other aspects.

In the supply chain context, the Halal concept applies from the farm to the table. It also requires specific items to be prepared from permissible ingredients that must be clean and hygienic. Table 13.1 lists the selected Halal definitions. These definitions are selected mainly due to comprehensiveness and cover most of the scholars in Halal study.

Al-Qaradawi (2013) stated 11 aspects about Halal and Haram that can be the guidelines for Muslim as follows: the origin of something that would be permissible (Mubah),the determination of Halal would be the absolute right of Allah (SWT), making forbidden something Halal and vice versa would be deviant to Allah (SWT), something Haram will create evil, hazard and negativity, everything

DOI: 10.4324/9781003223719-18

Table 13.1 Definition of Halal

Authors	Definition
Al-Qaradawi (2013)	Halal is something allowed in Islam, a forbidden tie that is cut off and allowed in Shariah to do it.
Baharuddin et al. (2015)	The word Halal comes from Arabic words: Halla, Yahillu, Hillan, and Wahalalan, which means allowed or permitted in the Shariah Law.
JAKIM (2015)	Halal is to untie, unfasten, unbind, undo, unravel, loosen, unloose, unfix, unwind, unscrew, untangle, disengage, and accessible.
Farag (2019)	Halal principles cover the aspects of preparation, slaughtering, storage, display, hygiene, and sanitation.

Source: Compiled by author, 2021.

Halal does not require anything Haram, its mediator would also regard as Haram, investigating anything that is Haram is Haram, good intention does not make flexible the Haram, steer clear of Syubhah so it will not be turning into Haram, something that is Haram happens to all, and emergencies will enable something forbidden.

Mainly on the Quran and Hadiths source, Islam has specified broad legal rules to categorize an organization's input, process and output covering activities, products and services into generally lawful (Halal) and obligated (Haram). The Islamic legal rulings on what is lawful (Halal), represented by obligatory (Wajib) and permissible (recommended, permissible, disliked). In the context of Halal products, production should monitor that all ingredients must be free from anything harmful and the finished product must be prepared based on Shariah compliance. Noorliza (2020), stated that Halal is a universal term that applies to all facets of life and can be applied to food products, meat products, cosmetics, personal care products, food ingredients, pharmaceuticals and food contact materials. Thus, it covers activities of daily life, from consumption to business practices. Based on the understanding of the requirement of Halal products, Halal product providers' emphasize this status to capture the market. Since the Halal product is in great demand, specifically by Muslims around the world, food providers tend to create an image of Halal, including the use of words related to the Islamic dietary code such as "Muslim", "Islamic" and "Halal" as part of the brand name.

Halal supply chain management system

Supply chain management is a network of companies ranging from manufacturers until the end of the customer. Zainuddin et al. (2020) view a supply chain as the flow of products and services from raw materials manufacturers or raw material suppliers, to the component or intermediate suppliers (manufacturers), then to the final product manufacturers. Next, these final product manufacturers supply

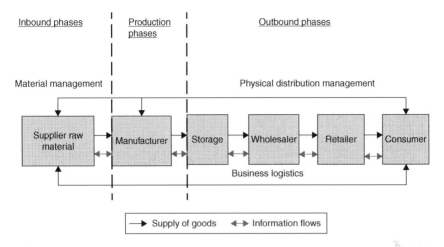

Figure 13.1 The flows of a conventional supply chain.
Source: Rasi et al., 2017.

the products or services to wholesalers, distributors and last to retailers. Also, the supply chain process is connected by transportation and storage activities. It is controlled through integrated information to plan the process activities.

This supply chain management concept requires consideration of the planning and management of component and services sourcing, procurement, conversion and logistics management. Additionally, this concept needs to fulfil customer requests and coordinate production, inventory, facility of location and transportation among all parties. As shown in Figure 13.1, there are three phases of the conventional supply chain: inbound phases, production phases and outbound phases. During an inbound phase, organizations deal with material procurement and management. It involves transportation, storage and delivery of the supplies coming into the plants or businesses.

The Halal supply chain ensures proper segregation between Halal and non-Halal food during distribution in storage, handling, transportation and retailing. Conventional supply chains focus on maximizing profits while fulfilling consumer demands. In contrast, Halal supply chains' primary objective is to extend Halal integrity following Shariah law from source to the point of consumer purchase (Jaafar et al., 2017). Hence, the Halal product is not only for Muslims, non-Muslims also buy and consume Halal products.

The disciplines of Halal logistics and supply chain were introduced at the beginning of the 1980s and 1990s, respectively (Jaafar et al., 2017). One of the objectives in Islamic law, known as Maqasid Shariah, refers to the avoidance of contamination with Haram and hazardous products throughout the supply chain process, which covers sourcing, handling, production, transportation and storage. At each stage, segregation and dedication must be practised (Jaafar et al., 2017).

For the Halal food industry, as an example, the handling the food along the supply chain process is significant. Manufacturers should take care of cleanliness and Halal integrity all along the delivery process from the supply source to the final customers. The Halal status for the food can be achieved when all possible contamination caused by Haram and hazardous products is avoided along the supply chain process. The status of Halal is not only focusing on production. There is some issues raised when manufacturers use third-party logistics providers (3PL) to plan and control transportation and distribution activities from manufacturers. The majority of 3PL companies aim to reduce the total cost of logistics activities. For standard practices in current logistics activities, the providers or manufacturers will mix Halal products and non-Halal products. Therefore, these companies need to segregate Halal products and non-Halal products according to the type of products, such as wet and dry products, with the specific temperature control. This will increase the total cost of logistics activities.

Table 13.2 discusses the differences between conventional and Halal supply chains. There are four elements necessary for manufacturers or logistics service providers to stress or look up in handling Halal and non-Halal products.

Table 13.2 Differences between conventional and Halal supply chains

Elements	Conventional supply chain	Halal supply chain
Definition	Involves the coordination of production, inventory, location, and transportation between the participants in the supply chain, intending to achieve the best responsiveness and efficiency in the market presented	Covers everything from the preparation and enforcement of Halal ingredients to be manufactured and delivered the final product to the customer, according to Shariah law.
Objective	Minimize cost, maximize profit	Preserves the integrity of the Halal product and ensure the product is Halal and Toyyiban.
Cross-contamination occurrence	Possibilities of cross-contamination exist	Avoids direct contact with Haram goods, manages the risk of cross-contamination between Halal and Haram goods, ensures supply chain management is in line with Muslim consumers' perceptions (Tieman, 2020).
Segregation needs	Mixing of Halal and non-Halal cargo	Segregation of Halal products from non-Halal products; requires dedicated Halal facilities.

Source: Adapted from Hussein et al., 2017; Ustadi et al., 2020.

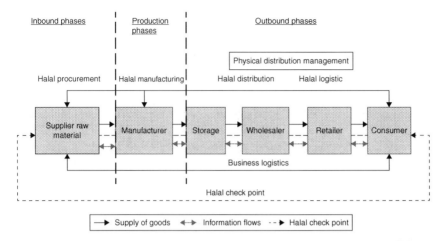

Figure 13.2 Conceptual model of Halal supply chain management.
Source: Rasi et al., 2017.

According to Rasi et al. (2017), Figure 13.2 shows the conceptual model of Halal supply chain management flow. This figure also shows activities of Halal checkpoints throughout the supply chain. A Halal supply chain is a formulation and implementation of Halal business policies and actions that simultaneously uphold market positions and generate profits. During each stage, it is crucial to ensure that organizations always consider and plan for Halal quality (Rahman et al., 2016). Meanwhile, the Halal supply chain is the interconnectivity of value-added activities that includes clear separation at the source of procurement and during storage, transportation, manufacturing, handling and distribution. Managing supply chain flow needs extra attention to ensure the integrity of Halal products.

Today, several logistic companies in the industry understand how to play their part in maintaining the Halal integrity of products; hence they rely on the logistics service capabilities needed in Halal transportation service providers (Dewi and Trihardani, 2017). A previous study suggested that all stakeholders in Halal transportation providers urged to bear this responsibility can practise using a Halal quality assurance system in the organization (Jaafar et al., 2011). Despite the need for Halal logistics management, the responsibility to ensure Halal integrity in transportation handling is still questionable.

The reason why products cannot simply be put together in the same distribution system is due to the necessity of maintaining a product's Halal status. The right person must handle the product using the proper process to maintain the Halal integrity of the products. Halal companies need to look at their production and extend Halal to the entire supply chain to ensure that transportation, storage and handling comply with Shariah practice to meet the requirements of the Muslim market.

Halal logistics perspective

Halal logistics can be defined as a fundamental principle to ensure the segregation of Halal cargo from non-Halal cargo. This segregation process is to avoid cross-contamination and ensure that the logistics system is aligned to the expectations of Muslim consumers, so Halal integrity is thus protected along the whole supply chain (Aziz and Zailani, 2016). Tieman (2020) claimed that the basic principle of Halal logistics is to ensure the segregation of Halal products from non-Halal products. The segregation purposely avoids cross-contamination and ensures that the logistics system is aligned to the expectations of Muslim consumers. Therefore, consumer interests change towards food safety, animal welfare and convenience in preparing Halal food. Halal logistics is more concerned about the movement of goods, services, and related information from suppliers based on the end-user that must comply with the general principles of Shariah law (Nordin, 2018). Hussein et al. (2017) describe Halal logistics as conventional logistics activities, comprising of planning, implementation and controlling the distribution and storage of Halal-certified products from the sources to the point of consumption. Several definitions about Halal logistics are shown in Table 13.3.

The logistics roles are to act as part of the supply chain activities that involve warehousing and storage, transportation process, handling and packaging. This supports various products according to their size, weight, volume, quality and safety. For example, one of the standards is to segregate between Halal and non-Halal products for contamination avoidance to protect the Halal status. This issue has created new services in the company to accommodate step by step in managing the integrity of a Halal product (Ngah et al., 2020).

Table 13.3 Definitions of Halal logistics

Authors	Definitions
Tieman (2020)	The basic principle of Halal logistics is to ensure the segregation of Halal products from non-Halal products. This is to avoid cross-contamination and ensure that the logistics system is aligned to the expectations of Muslim consumers.
Nordin (2018)	Halal logistics is concerned about the movement of goods, services, and related information from suppliers based on the end-user that must comply with the general principles of Shariah law.
Hussein et al. (2017)	Halal logistics comprises planning, implementation and controlling the distribution and storage of Halal-certified products from the sources to the point of consumption.
Aziz and Zailani (2016)	The logistic activities adhere clearly to the Halal standards to avoid the issue of doubtfulness and, even worse, cross-contamination.

Source: Compiled by author, 2020.

Nowadays, consumers are demanding transparency that the ingredients of the products and the packaging, handling and transportation processes comply with Shariah law or the Halal standard (Tieman et al., 2019). In order to ensure the integrity of Halal products and services, preventive actions should take place as early as possible, starting with the sourcing process. The consumer for Halal products and services is willing to pay more for the Halal products to avoid doubtfulness and ensure the services do not risk the contamination of the products. This is true because even though a product is made from all fresh and safe Halal ingredients, cross-contamination may occur during transportation, during packaging and from the environment in which it is stored.

Halal quality control in Malaysia Standard 2018

Every organization needs to identify, control and ensure the overall sources are clean and Halal. These organizations must ensure the documentation aligns and complies with requirements in the MS2400 series on the Halalan-Toyyiban assurance pipeline standard. If the organizations incorporate the documentation of the Halal management system in an existing management system, their relationship shall be clearly described in the existing management system documentation (Department of Standards Malaysia, 2018). Requirements and specifications for Halal logistics include processing, handling, distribution, packaging and labelling the products as stated in MS2400:2010.

These guidelines also proposed the general requirements for premises, infrastructure, facilities and personnel either in manufacturing or handling Halal goods. Figure 13.3 shows the application of Halal standards designed by the Department of Standards Malaysia (2018). Referring to these figures suggests producers or manufacturers able to follow the Halal product standards. Meanwhile, Halal supply chain standards are suitable for organizations involved in warehousing, retailing and transportation activities.

The demand for Halal products that mainly focus on Halal food increases every year (Dewi and Trihardani, 2017). The market increases because Muslim

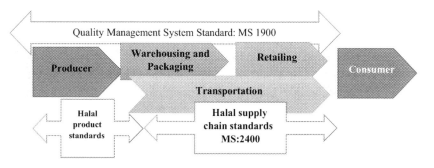

Figure 13.3 Application of Halal standards.
Source: Department of Standards Malaysia, 2018.

Table 13.4 The MS2400 series on Halal supply chains

Malaysian Standards (MS)	Description
MS 2400_1: Halalan Toyyiban Assurance – Pipe – Management of transportation service systems/freight chain services	This standard proposed to organize the transportation requirement of Halal products, goods, or cargo. The integrity of goods or cargo while handling the shipment through the various modes of transportation is secured.
M.S. 2400_2: Halalan Toyyiban Assurance – Pipe – Management of warehousing services systems and related activities	A standard of the management system that focuses on warehousing services system and related activities
M.S. 2400_3: Halalan Toyyiban Assurance – Retail management systems requirement	This standard of management system focuses on retailing requirements towards Halal products, goods, and cargo for assurance of the Halalan-Toyyiban integrity.

Source: Department of Standards Malaysia, 2018.

consumers have become more knowledgeable and aware of their religious obligations for Halal products. Consumers also realize that the Halal status covers materials and includes all machines and tools under one roof, logistics management (Rasi et al., 2017). The processes start from dealing with raw materials or sub-components suppliers right up until the products reach the consumers. All parties involved in the supply chain process must take proactive actions to ensure the element of Halal integrity is applied (Ngah et al., 2020). The ultimate success of the Halal industry will depend on the management's ability to combine the elements of the supply chain.

Table 13.4 outlines the Malaysian Standards requirements for assurance in transportation service systems or freight chain services perspectives, warehousing services systems and assurance towards products or goods at the retailing stage (Department of Standards Malaysia, 2018). In Malaysian Standards, the MS2400 series on the Halal supply chain is divided into three categories: management of transportation service systems/freight chain services, management of warehousing services systems and retail management systems requirement. The management of transportation service systems category prescribes the requirements to assure the integrity of goods or cargo being handled through the various modes of transportation. Management of warehousing management systems prescribes the requirements made of warehousing systems, including handling equipment used in warehousing activities stated under the second category. The third category, retail management systems, includes the requirements for assurance of the Halalan-Toyyiban integrity of products and goods at the retailing stage.

Therefore, organizations must establish documented procedures and a Halal risk management plan to ensure consistency and compliance with the requirements of the JAKIM standard and the organizations' stated policy and objective of Halal principles. These organizations should take into consideration all current issues and developments to the Halal principles. Industry players involved in the supply chain process and activities such as the manufacturers or suppliers, transportation providers, warehouse companies, third- or fourth-party logistics and customers collaborate to complete the supply chain.

Implications and recommendations for practice

A major issue highlighted in the Halal industry is a shortage of qualified and knowledgeable workforce that understands the Halal and Shariah law requirements on Halal food production (Ustadi et al., 2020). These studies mentioned that while anyone may have the right understanding, it has been a challenge to apply the theoretical knowledge into the actual day-to-day industry operating practice. These studies claimed that the current workforce in the Halal industry of both the skilled and the semi-skilled workers, who work in the front line of the supply chain, do not have proper training in terms of maintaining the integrity of Halal products (Ustadi et al., 2020). Therefore, a shortage of qualified and well-trained workforce in the Halal industry may affect or compromise the Halal status or Halal integrity as the food products move along the supply chain.

However, due to the rapid growth of the industry, there is a shortage of competent workers at every level of operations and management. People who are working in the Halal industry must be able to demonstrate comprehensive knowledge and understanding of both theoretical and practical Halal principles and practices. The workforce in the Halal food industry extends beyond the people performing the slaughtering process. The rest of the workforce in the daily production line operations, including the management, should also be given the necessary awareness and education to prevent unnecessary action that might compromise the Halal status of the product.

Conclusion

In conclusion, manufacturers should be concerned with quality assurance, for instance, the Halal logo and the Halal certification. Manufacturers need to make sure that the modes of transportation in use are appropriate to the type of Halal food. Referring to Rasi et al. (2017), Halal integrity has a positive influence on the product adaptation strategy for Halal products for catering to local and international demands. This is because only manufacturers can identify the origin of the materials of the product, as well as the preparation of transportation to carry products from the beginning of the production process until the end consumers. Therefore, it is the manufacturers' responsibility to ensure the protection of Halal integrity in the transportation handling, so as not to be questioned by the consumers on the Halal status.

Manufacturers need to know how to fulfil the existing standard requirements, and must also understand the Shariah law to ensure the implementation of Halal logistics meets the requirements as provided by the certification bodies, especially in the context of Malaysia. In this line of thought, manufacturers can determine the status of the product (whether it is Halal or not) at every stage of the supply chain until it is delivered to the consumers. In other words, manufacturers can guarantee that in the process of producing and delivering the products, they undergo Shariah-compliant processes and procedures. Hence, it is evident that manufacturers would have the intention to use Halal transportation services when they have an understanding of the correct method of the entire production process of Halal food.

References

Al-Qaradawi, Y. (2007). *The Lawful and the Prohibited in Islam*. Kuala Lumpur: Islamic Book Trust.

Al-Qaradawi, Y. (2013). *The Lawful and the Prohibited in Islam*:الحلال او الحرام في الاسلام. New York, NY: The Other Press.

Aziz, A. A. and Zailani, S. (2016). Halal logistics: the role of ports, issues and challenges. In D. S. Mutum, M. M. Butt and M. Rashid, M. (Eds.), *Advances in Islamic Finance, Marketing, and Management*. Bingley: Emerald Group Publishing Limited, pp. 309–321.

Baharuddin, K., Kassim, N. A., Nordin, S. K. and Buyong, S. Z. (2015). Understanding the Halal concept and the importance of information on Halal food business needed by potential Malaysian entrepreneurs. *International Journal of Academic Research in Business and Social Sciences*, 5(2), pp. 170–180.

Department of Standards Malaysia (2018). *Shariah-Based Quality Management Systems – Requirements with Guidance (2nd Revision), MS 1900:2018*. Kuala Lumpur: Department of Standards Malaysia.

Dewi, O. A. C. and Trihardani, L. (2017). How Halal transportation system impact the location routing problem. *Journal of Engineering and Management in Industrial System*, 5(1), pp. 8–19.

Farag, M. D. E. D. H. (2019). Halal food in Egypt. In Y. R. Al-Teinaz, S. Spear and I. H. A. A. El-Rahim (Eds), The Halal Food Handbook. Hoboken, NJ: John Wiley & Sons, Inc., pp. 369–392.

Hussein, M. Z., Husny, Z. J. and Shima, N. (2017). Delay as a challenge in prosecuting non-compliance in the Halal Industry. *International Journal of Supply Chain Management*, 6(1), pp. 141–145.

Jaafar, H. S., Endut, I. R., Intan, R., Faisol, N. and Omar, E. N. (2011). Innovation in logistics services: Halal logistics. *Proceedings of the 16th International Symposium on Logistics (ISL)*, Berlin, 10–13 July, pp. 844–851.

Jaafar, H. S., Faisol, N., Rahman, F. A. and Muhammad, A. (2017). Halal logistics versus Halal supply chain: a preliminary insight. In S. Ab Manan, F. Abd Rahman and M. Sahri (Eds.), *Contemporary Issues and Development in the Global Halal Industry*. Singapore: Springer, pp. 579–588.

JAKIM. (2015). *Manual Procedure for Malaysia Halal Certification (Third Revision 2014)*. Putrajaya: Jabatan Kemajuan Islam Malaysia (JAKIM).

JAKIM. (2018). *Manual Procedure for Malaysia Halal Certification (Fourth Revision 2018)*. Putrajaya: Jabatan Kemajuan Islam Malaysia (JAKIM).

Ngah, A. H., Jeevan, J., Salleh, N. H. M. and Lee, T. T. H. (2020). Willingness to pay for Halal transportation cost: the moderating effect of knowledge on the Theory of Planned Behavior. *Journal of Environmental Treatment Techniques*, 8(1), pp. 13–22.

Noorliza, K. (2020). Resource-capability of Halal logistics services, its extent and impact on performance. *Journal of Islamic Marketing*, 12(4), pp. 813–829.

Nordin, N. A. N. B. (2018). *The Development of Halal Hub Malaysia from Halal Industry Development Corporation (HDC) Perspective: The Qualitative Approach in Refining its Implications and Challenges*. Retrieved from: https://ir.uitm.edu.my/id/eprint/23377/1/PPb_NOR%20AMIRA%20NAJWA%20NORDIN%20ACI%20B%2018_5.pdf (accessed 24 November 2021).

Rahman, F. A., Jaafar, H. S., Idha, S. and Muhammad, A. (2016). Ethics of food handlers throughout the supply chain in the Halal food industry: Halal perspective. In S. Ab Manan, F. Abd Rahman and M. Sahri (Eds.), *Contemporary Issues and Development in the Global Halal Industry*. Singapore: Springer, pp. 483–498.

Rasi, R. Z., Masrom, N. R., Omar, S. S., Ahmad, M. F. and Sham, R. (2017). Designing Halal supply chain: Malaysia's halal industry scenarios. In *MATEC Web of Conferences*, Vol. 135. EDP Sciences.

Tieman, M. (2020). Measuring corporate Halal reputation: a corporate Halal reputation index and research propositions. *Journal of Islamic Marketing*, 11(3), pp. 591–601.

Tieman, M., Darun, M. R., Fernando, Y. and Ngah, A. B. (2019). Utilizing blockchain technology to enhance Halal integrity: the perspectives of Halal certification bodies. In Y. Xia and L. J. Zhang (Eds.), *Services – SERVICES 2019. SERVICES 2019. Lecture Notes in Computer Science*, Vol. 11517. Cham, Springer, pp. 119–128.

Ustadi, M. N., Osman, S. and Rasi, R. Z. (2020). Perception of non-Muslim manufacturers towards Halal food supply chain in Malaysia. *International Journal of Innovation, Creativity and Change*, 10(11).

Zainuddin, A., Ridzwan, S. I. and Ridzwan, S. B. (2020). The role of Halalan-Toyyiban supply chain practices as significant predictors towards excellent customer service management. *Advances in Business Research International Journal*, 6(1), pp. 1–10.

14 Development of the Halal industry in South Korea

Pilot project of Halal logistics

James (Jang Suh) Noh

Introduction

As of 2019, the number of Muslim residents in Korea was estimated to be about 200,000. The majority of Muslims living in Korea are migrant workers, and the number of international students is increasing. As the world's Muslim population is estimated at about 1.8 billion, the proportion of Muslims living in Korea is very small. Compared to Korea's total population of 51.71 million in 2019, the proportion of Muslims residing in Korea is only 0.4%. Therefore, for Korean companies, the Halal market means overseas export markets. This chapter examines how the Halal industry has developed in Korea under the guidance of the Korean government, which has recognized the importance of the global Halal market. In particular, it describes a series of journeys for the application of Halal logistics in Korea, which were carried out in stages from 2017 to 2019. As a leader at the centre of this journey, I hope that this record can contribute to the development of the global Halal industry.

The status of Halal certification in South Korea

In South Korea, there are four Halal certification bodies. The first Halal certification body is KMF. Founded in 1967 with permission as a religious foundation, KMF began Halal certification services in 1994 and is now recognized by JAKIM in Malaysia and MUIS in Singapore. The second Halal certification body is the Korea Halal Association (KOHAS). KOHAS received permission to establish a non-profit corporation from the Ministry of Agriculture, Food and Rural Affairs (MAFRA) in 2013. KOHAS has been working on Halal certification since 2017 and has been recognized by IFANCA in the United States. The third Halal certification body is the Korea Halal Authority (KHA). Established in 2015, it was recognized by JAKIM in 2020. The fourth Halal certification body is the International Halal Certification Centre (IHCC). Established in 2018, IHCC was registered as a Halal certification body with Emirates Authority for Standardization and Metrology (ESMA) of the UAE through the accreditation of the Philippine Accreditation Bureau (PAB) in 2019. In addition to domestic Halal certification bodies, Korean companies also acquire Halal certification from

DOI: 10.4324/9781003223719-19

overseas Halal certification bodies such as Malaysia's JAKIM, Indonesia's MUI, Singapore's WAREES and the USA's IFANCA. In the case of MUI, there are two MUI designated agents that mediate the Halal certification process for Korean companies. So far, no Halal certification body in Korea has been recognized by MUI.

Meanwhile, in Korea, there is an accreditation body that carries out accreditation of Halal certification bodies. This accreditation body is the Korea Accreditation Board (KAB). The institution started accreditation of Halal certification bodies in 2019. KAB is a private accreditation body established in 1995 to do accreditation business based on the ISO management system. KAB established the Halal certification body requirements and Halal certification scheme requirements in 2019. In the same year, to secure international recognition, it signed an MoU with ESMA of the United Arab Emirates and became an accreditation body recognized by ESMA. KAB joined the International Halal Accreditation Forum (IHAF), a global Halal unifying platform. Through these processes, KAB has laid the groundwork for Korean Halal certification organizations to be internationally recognized. According to a survey report of the Korea Food Research Institute (KFRI), the number of Halal certificates issuance in Korea is 531 and the largest organization issuing Halal certificates is KMF (KFRI, 2019, p. 11). As for the items certified, food is the most, followed by cosmetics. Southeast Asia is the region to which Korean Halal certified companies export the most, followed by the Middle East (KFRI, 2019, p. 20).

Development of the Halal industry in Korea

It was in the 2010s that companies' interest in Halal certification began to grow in Korea. In 2010, KOTRA and Samsung Economic Research Institute each published a report on the prospects of the Halal market. In 2011, the Korea Agro-Fisheries & Food Trade Corporation published a similar report. In October 2011, Malaysia's Halal Development Corporation's (HDC) experts were invited to present in a seminar on Malaysian Halal Certification for the first time in Korea. In 2012, a seminar on Halal certification in Singapore was held inviting experts from WAREES. In 2013, KOHAS, an organization of companies exporting Halal food, was established with the permission of MAFRA. In the same year, *Halal Economics*, a book that empirically analyses the demand for Halal meat in Korea, was published. In 2014, the Korea Institute of Halal Industry (KIHI), a non-profit Halal research institute approved by MAFRA, was established.

In 2015, the Korean government signed an MoU on Halal food cooperation with the UAE during the president's visit to the Middle East in March. Recognizing the promotion of the Halal food industry as a major export increase strategy for domestic agrifood, MAFRA announced a plan to promote the Halal food industry in June of the same year (MAFRA, 2015). With this opportunity, the Korea Food Research Institute (KFRI) was selected as an agency to support the government's Halal food industry support project. The main countermeasures that emerged at this time were the installation of a control centre within MAFRA, which would conduct an in-depth information survey on the Halal market and Halal certification and a Halal professional manpower development project, expand investment in R&D for Halal food development and strengthen the foundation for domestic Halal certification and Halal domestic agrifood. This includes strengthening market awareness and activating domestic Halal food distribution. In 2015, for the first time in Korea, the Halal Trade Expo Korea was held, and the government held the Korea International Halal Certification Body Conference, inviting representatives of renowned overseas Halal organizations. In the field of Halal education, KIHI held five Halal internal auditor training sessions with INHART of International Islamic University Malaysia and received a great response from Korean food industry.

The Korean government's Halal industry promotion initiative continued in 2016. At the 10th Trade and Investment Promotion Conference in July 2016, the Korean government announced measures to revitalize investment focusing on fostering new industries. In order to promote domestic investment, the Korean government announced the Halal/Kosher industry, pet industry, real estate service, promotion of private investment in the sports industry and the virtual reality industry as five new industries that need to be fostered. What stands out is that it has revealed intensive measures to foster not only food but also cosmetics in the Halal field. The main tasks announced at this time were promotion of participation in the International Halal Accreditation Forum, installation of Halal laboratories and the support of Korean Halal foods entering overseas online shopping malls (MOEF, 2016).

Regarding the Halal cosmetics promotion business, the Ministry of Food, Drug and Safety (MFDS) has begun a Halal certification consulting project for cosmetics companies, a Halal certification education support project, and an international Halal cosmetics seminar. KIHI has been selected as implementing agency from 2016 up to now and has been carrying out these projects every year. Hundreds of Korean cosmetics companies, including representative cosmetics companies such as Amore Pacific and LG Household & Health Care, participated in the projects. In 2020, when COVID-19 had a major impact, Halal certification training and international seminars were held online. Next, the Halal laboratory support project was also launched by MFDS. Korea's first Halal laboratory is currently installed at the Korea Food Research Institute. KFRI cooperates with Halal certification bodies to support Haram testing for products seeking Halal certification. The Halal laboratory of the Korea Food Research Institute opened its doors in 2019 with the attendance of JAKIM officials, and is also focusing on international standardization, such as obtaining ISO 17025 certification.

The Halal professional education support project has also started, and private qualifications such as Halal consultant, Halal certification expert and Halal trade expert have been registered to the Korea Research Institute for Vocational Education and Training under the Prime Minister's Office. Halal trade expert training has been supported by the government, and more than 100 people have obtained qualifications. Korea's Halal industry education has continued to develop, and in 2017, Korea's first online Halal education site, EduHalal.kr, was born, and Halal basic education has been offered free of charge from November 2017 to the present. The continuous efforts of the Korean government in 2015 and 2016 contributed greatly to the widespread awareness that the Halal industry is a very important export industry. In particular, such government-led initiatives stimulated Korea's Halal industry, which has a relatively unimpressive history, to follow international Halal issues. In this process, the recognition that it is necessary to improve the reliability of the product was formed in order to expand the export of Korean Halal food, and finally, interest in Halal logistics grew.

Halal logistics industry in-depth research (2017)

Recognizing the importance of Halal logistics to enhance the reliability of Korean Halal food, KFRI announced a plan to conduct in-depth research on the Halal logistics industry in 2017. At the time, there was little information on Halal logistics, so the research project focused on overseas case studies. Among Islamic countries, Malaysia was selected as the subject of case study, while in non-Islamic countries, the Netherlands and Belgium were selected as the subject of case study. The consortium of KIHI and Sejung Shipping was selected as the research agency. The research period took about five months from June to November 2017. The overseas case studies were conducted through interviews with experts and representatives of Halal logistics companies in each country to be surveyed, and visits to the Halal logistics operation sites. The survey subjects in Malaysia were JAKIM, LBB International, A-Transglobal, Nippon Express Malaysia, MITRANS, Northport and HDC. The survey subjects in the Netherlands were Halal Audit Company and Eurofrigo, while the subjects in Belgium were Halal Balancing, HFCE, Zeebrugge Port Authority and Zeebrugge Food Logistics. KIHI and Sejung Shipping Consortium submitted a 232-pages research report to KFRI (KFRI, 2017), and the table of contents is shown in Table 14.1.

Halal product production and distribution status and Halal logistics demand research (2018)

In 2018, KFRI announced a new plan to conduct research on Halal product production and distribution status and Halal logistics demand as a follow-up project to the 2017 Halal logistics industry in-depth research project. The new research is characterized by a very broad range. The research scope includes domestic Halal production status, domestic Halal logistics status, domestic Halal logistics demand survey, domestic Halal food distribution status, domestic Muslim Halal food consumption status and Halal food distribution status at overseas distribution stores. In other words, the new research was a project for the entire Halal food supply chain (production–logistics–distribution–consumption). The consortium of KIHI and Sejung Shipping was once again selected as research agency. The purpose of this survey was to properly understand the production and distribution of Halal food in Korea, as well as the scale of Halal food consumption by Muslim residents in Korea, and further diagnose the possibility of

Table 14.1 Table of contents – research report to KFRI

PART I	International trade and global Halal logistics trends 1. International trade trends 2. Halal product trade trend 3. Halal logistics trend and prospect 4. Implication
PART II	Production and distribution of Halal products and the need for Halal logistics 1. Halal food and Halal integrity guarantee 2. Halal management activities and Halal guarantee activities in Halal logistics 3. Halal logistics standards and requirements
PART III	Status of Halal logistics in Malaysia 1. Country overview 2. Malaysia's Halal logistics policy and direction 3. Malaysia's Halal logistics standard 4. Malaysia's Halal supply chain management and logistics industry 5. implication
PART IV	Status of Halal logistics in Europe 1. Muslim and Halal industries in Europe 2. Halal logistics in the Netherlands 3. Halal logistics in Belgium 4. Comparison of Halal logistics between the Netherlands and Belgium 5. implication
PART V	Implications and application plan 1. Implications of the findings 2. Evaluation of readiness for application of Halal logistics in Korea 3. Application plan

Source: KFRI, 2017.

introducing Halal logistics in Korea by checking Halal food producers' demand on Halal logistics.

The survey was conducted for about three months from July to October 2018. Among the 569 Korean companies that acquired Halal certification, 111 responded to the survey on the production status of Halal products in Korea (KFRI, 2018, p. 8). For the distribution of Halal products in Korea, 22 large supermarkets, ten small-sized supermarkets and ten convenience stores were investigated, along with and 13 foreign marts located in major cities of Incheon, Daejeon, Daegu, Busan, Gimhae and Gwangju (KFRI, 2018, pp. 74–101). A survey on food consumption was conducted for 165 Muslim consumers residing in South Korea (KFRI, 2018, pp. 104–135). In addition to these domestic surveys, overseas surveys were made. Indonesian retail store investigation was conducted on four large supermarket stores and two convenience stores in Jakarta. Malaysian distribution store survey was also conducted on five hypermarkets and two convenience stores in Kuala Lumpur and surrounding cities. And UAE's retail store survey was made on four supermarkets, three convenience stores and two Korean mart stores in Dubai (KFRI, 2018, pp. 138–185).

Summarizing the results of the survey on the status of logistics for Halal products in Korea, the percentage of use of dry containers was found to be 75.9% for the types of containers used to transport Halal products. On the other hand, the proportion of refrigerated containers used was 13.0% (KFRI, 2018, pp. 45–46). It was found that many of the companies responding to the survey mainly export dry foods or products that do not require special temperature control. In the survey on whether they checked if the container is contaminated with Haram elements before loading Halal cargo, 33% of respondents answered that they checked whether the container was cleansed or the history of shipping non-Halal products. The remaining 67% answered that they did not check or did not know well. As for the reason for not checking the container for contamination before loading Halal products, 47.4% answered that buyers did not require Halal logistics, 18.4% answered that Halal logistics is not needed yet and 10.5% said that Halal logistics is not yet required in the Halal market (KFRI, 2018, pp. 47–53).

Through the domestic distribution network survey, few products bearing the Halal logo were found in Korean foods, but many products bearing the Halal logo were found in imported foods (KFRI, 2018, pp. 97–101). In contrast to the fact that Korean Halal processed foods are actively distributed in overseas Halal markets (KFRI, 2018, pp. 138–185), the reality that Korean Halal foods are rarely distributed in the Korean distribution network was an unexpected result. Meanwhile, in the food consumption survey for Muslims in Korea, it was found that they spend about 752 billion won per year on food consumption in Korea (KFRI, 2018, p. 135). However, in the domestic food distribution network, most Korean processed foods do not bear the Halal logo, so it was found that Muslim consumers residing in Korea are having considerable difficulty in purchasing Korean Halal foods.

Halal logistics transportation pilot project (2019)

In 2019, Sejung Shipping conducted a Halal logistics pilot project by establishing a Halal transportation system with funding from KFRI. The pilot project was implemented under the advice of KIHI, and the overall project outline is as shown in Figure 14.1.

First of all, environment building is the stage of preparing physical tools for the implementation of the project. Sejung Shipping purchased a vehicle for Halal transportation. Sejung Shipping imported Halal-certified detergent from Malaysia for Sertu cleaning, and prepared the equipment necessary for cleansing, such as a high-pressure washer. In addition, Sejung Shipping has prepared a "Halal Supply Chain" sticker, which is a sign attached to the cargo, to protect Halal cargo in the Halal supply chain.

The second step is the establishment of a Halal guarantee system. In accordance with the advice of KIHI, Sejung Shipping has established a Halal logistics assurance

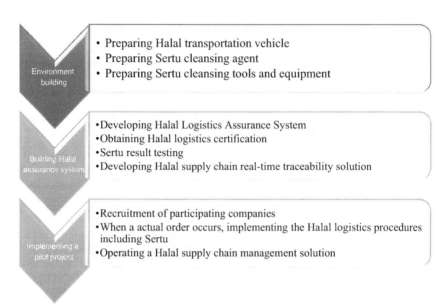

Figure 14.1 Overall outline of Sejung Shipping's Halal logistics pilot project.

system (HLAS) consisting of a Halal committee, a Halal logistics assurance system manual, a Halal cargo transportation procedure, a Halal vehicle Sertu procedure and a process flow diagram. Sejung Shipping's Halal logistics assurance system was established by referring to Malaysia's Halal standards documents such as MS 2400-1:2010 (P): Halalan-Toyyiban Assurance Pipeline. – Part 1: Management System Requirements for Transportation Of Goods and/or Cargo Chain Services (DSM, 2010), the Guidelines for Halal Assurance Management System (JAKIM, 2012) of Malaysia Halal certification, and the Manual Procedure for Malaysia Halal Certification (JAKIM, 2015), as there was no standard for reference in Korea. Based on this, Sejung Shipping acquired Korea's first Halal logistics (transport) certification from KMF. During the on-site inspection of KMF, Sertu cleansing was demonstrated. The wastewater generated during the demonstration was sent to the Korea Testing Laboratory for the issuance of a test report showing no detection of porcine ingredients. In addition, Sejung Shipping developed and piloted a Halal transportation management solution, software that can check the monitoring results of each Halal critical point, vehicle location and temperature in real time during the Halal transportation process. During the pilot project, Sejung Shipping carried out a procedure to write a statement on the bill of lading (B/L) confirming that the cargo was transported according to the Halal logistics assurance system.

Based on the above preparations, Sejung Shipping carried out the final stage, the Halal logistics (transport) pilot project. Three Halal certified food export companies participated in the pilot project. When a participating company applies for Halal transportation to Sejung Shipping for products produced according to actual orders of overseas buyers, Sejung Shipping performed Halal transportation in accordance with the Halal logistics assurance system that has already been established. At the same time, the Halal transportation management solution was activated so that the Halal critical point (HCP) monitoring result of the transportation process, cargo location information and temperature information could be shared in real time with producers, Sejung Shipping, and buyers. After the pilot project was finished, Sejung Shipping produced various promotional materials to promote its Halal logistics business. In particular, Sejung Shipping released a video on YouTube that recorded the Sertu cleansing process and the test process for wastewater generated after the Sertu cleansing. On September 20, 2019, Sejung Shipping signed an MoU with MAS Kargo in Malaysia for Halal logistics between the two countries. This deserves evaluation as a very important agreement in terms of establishing an international Halal logistics pipeline.

Implications from the first Halal transportation pilot project in Korea

Depending on the nature of the cargo to be transported, the level of risk at which Halal products can be contaminated is different. Because the level of contamination risk varies by type of cargo, International Halal Integrity Alliance (IHIA) standards classify Halal transportation procedures into four categories: bulk shipment, refrigerated shipment, non-refrigerated shipment and livestock (IHIA, 2010, pp. 13–14). There are two main sources of contamination that can cause cross-contamination during transport of Halal products. One source is when the container transporting Halal products has been contaminated with Haram in the past and the pollutant remains. Another source is when the container is contaminated due to leakage of damaged contents of the non-Halal product while the Halal product and the non-Halal product are transported together. Even in the case of mixed transportation in one container, it is recognized that there is a difference in the risk of contamination when Halal products are placed above and below non-Halal products. Also, there is a difference between the risk of Halal products being transported by full container load (FCL) and transport by less than container load (LCL).

In order to ensure the integrity of Halal products during the transportation process, major Halal transportation standards and guidelines suggest the principle of Sertu cleansing of containers prior to transportation and the prohibition of mixed transportation of Halal and Haram products (JAKIM, 2015, p. 42). Pre-transport Sertu cleansing is required to be performed in cases where past transport information is unclear, in addition to cases of explicit contamination with major Najis (IHIA, 2010, pp. 13–14). In the case of FCL, the risk of contamination of Halal products is not a big issue if the container is cleansed well before shipment. The problem is LCL shipping. Halal products from many small and medium-sized enterprises (SMEs) have to be transported by LCL because the containers are not fully filled. LCL is a transportation method that presupposes mixed transportation. In order to fundamentally prevent contamination of Halal products, non-Halal cargo with low risk to Halal products is loaded and transported in a container that has been subjected to Sertu cleansing. However, it will not be easy to check the risks of other products one by one to determine whether mixed transportation is possible. Clearly, the ideal situation would be collect only other Halal cargo and transport it together. However, it is naive to believe that a container can be filled with a variety of Halal products in a timely manner in a non-Islamic country. Therefore, mixed transportation of Halal and non-Halal products is often unavoidable.

According to KFRI's survey results, there is almost no meat among Korean Halal foods exported to major Islamic countries. All Halal foods exported are packaged processed foods, except for fresh foods such as apples, pears and strawberries. Noodles such as ramen, snacks such as confectionery, seasoned laver, beverages, pickled foods such as kimchi, sauces such as red pepper paste, and packaged processed foods such as beverages like aloe juice are the main export items of South Korea (KFRI, 2018, pp. 138–185). Well-packaged processed foods can be evaluated as relatively safe products as long as there is no damage to the packaging, even if they are transported mixed with other products by the LCL method. In particular, 75.9% of Korean Halal products are transported in dry containers rather than cold containers. Even for refrigerated and frozen Halal foods, most of them are completely sealed products, so the risk of packaging damage is low (Chaudry et al., 2000).

In the case of shipping containers used in international trade, it is difficult to obtain accurate information on what products were transported in the past, so if the requirements of major Halal transportation standards are followed, unconditional Sertu cleaning procedures should be implemented. Sertu cleaning in Korea costs a lot of money due to strict environmental regulations. In addition to the cost of rental use of a licensed washing station, it takes a lot of time to wash and dry, which may cause a setback in the timely input of containers. It is also not easy to pass on the cost of Sertu to the shipper. There are still not many requests for Halal transportation from overseas buyers. Therefore, Halal product exporters are not interested in Halal transportation. Halal products made in South Korea are rarely distributed in domestic retail stores, so it is difficult to find demand for Halal transportation in domestic Halal product distribution. In order to activate Halal transportation and secure the Halal integrity of South Korean Halal products, a plan that can dramatically lower the cost should be created.

In South Korea, as an alternative to the unconditional Sertu washing, which is mandatory when the past transport information of a container is unclear, a method to directly test whether a container is contaminated with severe Najis is being discussed. Samples are to be collected from the inside of the container to be used for the transportation of Halal products and immediately checked for contamination on site. For this, there should be a standard for sampling the inside of a container and a diagnostic device that can determine whether the sample is contaminated in the field within a short time. The key is to secure an accurate and reliable diagnostic technology and a low-cost diagnostic system that can be widely distributed. Currently, in Korea, point-of-care (POC) diagnostic test device manufacturers are engaged in R&D in this field.

References

Chaudry, M. M., Jackson, M. A. and Riaz, M. N. (2000). *Halal Industry Production Standards*. Illinois, IL: J&M Food Products Company.

Department of Standard Malaysia (2010). *MS 2400-1:2010 (P): Halalan-Toyyiban Assurance Pipeline – Part 1: Management System Requirements for Transportation of Goods and/or Cargo Chain Services*. Retrieved from: www.khidi.or.kr (accessed 24 November 2021).

International Halal Integrity Alliance (IHIA). (2010). *Halal Standard- Logistics. IHIAS 0100*. Kuala Lumpur: IHIA.

JAKIM (2012). *The Guidelines for Halal Assurance Management System*. Retrieved from: www.halal.gov.my/v4/images/pdf/halalassurancesystem.pdf (accessed 24 November 2021).

JAKIM (2015). *Manual Procedure for Malaysia Halal Certification*. Retrieved from: www.halal.gov.my/v4/images/pdf/MPPHM2014BI.pdf (accessed 24 November 2021).

Korea Food Research Institute (KFRI) (2017). *Halal Logistics Industry In-Depth Research*. Wanjugun: Korea Food Research Institute.

Korea Food Research Institute (KFRI) (2018). *Halal Product Production and Distribution Status and Halal Logistics Demand Survey*. Wanjugun: Korea Food Research Institute.

Korea Food Research Institute (KFRI) (2019). *Survey on Halal and Kosher Food Producers*. Wanjugun: Korea Food Research Institute.

Ministry of Agriculture, Food and Rural Affairs (MAFRA) (2015). *Halal Food Industry Development and Export Revitalization Measures*. Retrieved from www.mafra.go.kr/bbs/mafra/68/312426/artclView (accessed 24 November 2021).

Ministry of Economy and Finance (MOEF) (2016). *Investment Revitalization Measures – Focus on New Industry*. Retrieved from: www.korea.kr/news/pressReleaseView.do?newsId=156140977 (accessed 24 November 2021).

15 Halal logistics certification and regulations in Japan

Nurul Faezawaty Jamaludin and Kosei Sugawara

Introduction

Today's commerce environment is facing a massive challenge due to the effects of the global coronavirus pandemic. This has made a huge impact on various supply chains, including business to consumer (B2C), business to business (B2B) and maybe even customer to customer (C2C). In coping with government lockdown restrictions and the near-complete halt of worldwide aviation, numerous businesses and manufacturing operations have been severely constrained in their activities, or even forced to close down. But despite these challenges, the logistics industry has attempted to continue business as usual, albeit with additional safety measures, to ensure that essential goods might be delivered across borders. To safeguard the sustainability of the post-COVID trading world, it is time for a huge digital transformation throughout the whole logistics system.

The logistics industry is the backbone of international and domestic trade, permitting entrepreneurial exchange by providing transport, storage and delivery of goods. Logistics companies execute cargo transportation services by land, air and water. In 2018, the global logistics market reached over USD 6.67 trillion (Wunsch, 2020), and in 2019, the global Halal logistics market size was valued at approximately USD 286.96 billion and is expected to develop at a compound annual growth rate of 8.4% from 2020 to 2027 to reach USD 525.09 billion by 2027. Transporting the two giant pandas Xing Xing and Liang Liang from China to Malaysia, and transporting organs for life-saving transplant or even ensuring salted snacks reach shelves nationwide, the logistics industry plays a crucial role in delivery and transport to almost anywhere on the world. This shows the diversity of the logistics industry encompassing every element from air freight to container shipping, and domestic courier companies to international port operators. With the new norm of post-COVID, the logistics industry has dramatically evolved in response to market trends. People are encouraged to remain at home and take care of their shopping needs online by utilizing courier companies, meaning that the logistics industry is providing an essential service.

DOI: 10.4324/9781003223719-20

Logistic industry market overview

The world's population is growing and is predicted to reach in nine billion people in 2050. Accompanying that population growth has been an increase in the amount of people in emerging markets who are now able to access global markets. The amount of smartphone subscriptions is predicted to almost double to four billion by 2025, with nearly all of that growth coming from emerging markets. With a growing global bourgeoisie and expanded internet access, increased demand for e-commerce would require logistics providers to deliver to remote locations in emerging economies for the first time – especially in Asia where many rural communities are not connected to the rail network (World Economic Forum, 2016). The analysis shows that there is USD 1.5 trillion at stake for logistics players and an extra USD 2.4 trillion worth of societal benefits as a result of the digital transformation of the industry up until 2025. In other words, industry stakeholders need to be aware of and to prioritize advanced changes in digital transformation initiatives given the potential for a significantly higher value to be created (World Economic Forum, 2016).

The internet revolution has infiltrated and changed our daily lives over the past 20 years. With email eclipsing "snail mail" and digital downloads replacing physical products, this could have dealt a devastating blow to the logistics industry – but, remarkably, more packages than ever before are now being shipped. On any single day, a staggering 85 million packages and documents are delivered around the world. Looking at this scenario, the logistics business has no time to honeymoon and luxuriate in the golden moment in shipments. Logistics nowadays has introduced digital innovations at a slower pace than other industries. This slower digital adoption rate may lead to risks for even big multinational companies if no action is being taken.

The logistics market in Japan after the COVID-19 crisis

One of Nippon Express's subsidiaries, Nittsu Research Institute and Consulting, Inc. (NRIC) has published an extensive report on a logistics component, called *Japan's Economic and Freight Outlook* for the years 2020 and 2021 (NRIC, 2020a). From an economic perspective, although the worldwide economy was anticipated to shrink by 4.4% in 2020 basically due to the COVID-19 pandemic, it was anticipated to grow by 5.2% in 2021. The Japanese economy has been intensely harmed by the consumption tax hike in October 2019 as well as the COVID-19 crisis. The real growth rate in 2020 is estimated to be a 5.3% decrease. For 2021, it is expected to turn positive with a 3.5% increase but, in any case, strong development is needed (NRIC, 2020a, 2020b).

Domestic freight transport of Japan

In the first half of 2020, in addition to the COVID-19 crisis, the consumption tax climb of the previous year also had an effect and freight volume of all commodities

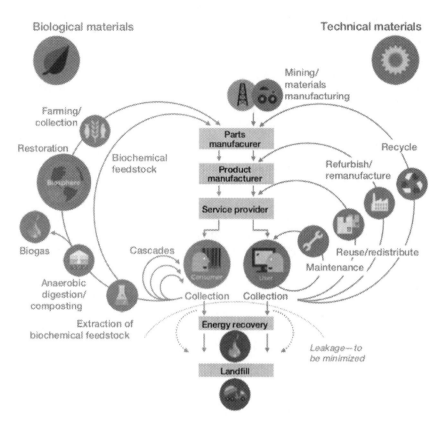

Figure 15.1 The circular economy in the logistics landscape.
Source: World Economic Forum, 2016.

declined significantly. Even though the negative edge was anticipated to recoil to some degree in the second half of the year, slow development will proceed, centred on production-related freight, stagnant capital investment and industrial production. For the 2020 as a whole, the forecast was a decrease of 7.0%, which is worse than that of 2009 (6.0% decrease) after the Lehman Brothers crisis. In 2021, it was predicted to turn positive for the first time in four years, but the increment is 1.7%. Due to the response to sharp decline within the past year, consumption-related freight will increase by 3%. Production-related freight is expected to grow by only about 4%, well below the level in 2019. Although public works spending is expected to increase, construction-related freight will continue to decline by about 2%, as large-scale civil engineering work is not expected to be executed (NRIC, 2020a, 2020b).

Rail freight

The freight volume by Japan Railway (JR) containers was projected to decrease by 7.3% in 2020 since the volume of most commodities fell beneath the previous year's level due to the economic downturn caused by the COVID-19 crisis. As modern ways of life such as remote work have become common, the negative range of paper and pulp has expanded. Eco-related supplies (such as the construction surplus soil of the Linear Chuo Shinkansen) have experienced positive growth. Automobile parts are expected to recover after the start of the year. Although the freight volume by JR containers was expected to rise by 5.6% in 2021, this would still not return to the level of 2019. Rail freight transport other than JR was anticipated to decrease by 9.9% in 2020 and increase by 4.9% in 2021 primarily due to transport of oil, cement and limestone (NRIC, 2020a, 2020b).

Motor freight

Commercial motor freight was forecast to decline by 7.0% in 2020 as a result of the COVID-19 crisis, where all commodities decreased significantly. Specifically, due to stagnant industrial production and capital investment, production-related freight was forecast to decline by about 10%, significantly pushing down the motor freight volume. It was expected to increase by 2.5% in 2021 with the reaction taken from experience in the previous year (NRIC, 2020a, 2020b).

Coastal shipping freight

Freight transport by coastal shipping was expected to decrease by 10.2% in 2020 and increase by 3.9% in 2021. In 2020, production-related freight and construction-related freight were forecast to fall sharply. However, in 2021, production was expected to pick up and forecast to increase by 3.9%, the first increase in eight years. This is mainly due to a rise in petroleum products, steel, chemical industry products, etc. (NRIC, 2020a, 2020b).

Domestic air freight

In 2020, domestic air freight was expected to decrease sharply by 33.3%, owing to low demand and a decline in the supply capacity of aircraft caused by self-restraint from going out during the COVID-19 crisis. In 2021, it was projected to increase by 27.2%, for the first time in eight years, with a positive reversal from the past year. Whereas a huge rise in demand cannot be expected, it would return about half of the decrease in the previous year at most (NRIC, 2020a, 2020b).

Logistics companies in Japan

Japan has a total land area of about 378,000 square kilometres, with a population of 125.28 million of which 0.1% was Muslim in 2021 (United Nations, 2021). In comparison, although it has a similar land area, Malaysia's population is 32.78 million of which 62% are Muslim. Japan is an archipelago country within the Pacific Ocean, on the eastern Asia continent. The land comprises four main islands, Honshu, Hokkaido, Kyushu and Shikoku, together with nearly 4,000 smaller islands. The four major islands account for 90% of Japan's land area.

Tokyo, Osaka and Kyoto are situated at Honshu. As for the neighbouring region, the nearest mainland on the north is the Siberian region of Russia and Korea, and on the far south is China. Almost four-fifths of Japan is covered with mountains.

The Japanese are famous for their willingness to work very hard and their commitment. Punctuality is a must. Those factors make Japan the third-largest economy in the world. Japan is also famous for its high-tech industry especially in electronic products and vehicles. That has indirectly contributed to the logistics industry in Japan. There are hundreds of logistics companies in Japan, with some of the biggest names being Nippon Express Group, Yusen Logistics, Kintetsu World Express NNR Global Logistic, HAVI and Hitachi Transport System. These and many more offer high-quality third-party logistics (3PL) services, as Japan is one of the biggest hubs in the 3PL industry. Thus, companies offer an international business approach especially for multinational companies and also approaches tailored to small and medium-sized enterprises (SMEs), which depend on services that are reliable, flexible and user friendly with worldwide reach. The services offered by the logistics companies together with their supporting partner in the dedicated platform cover the full spectrum of services. With global digital facilitated shipping platforms, individual sellers are connected with thousands of potential buyers. All the red tape such as customs, international packaging and import payment can be resolved and minimized. All the necessary demands in the supply chain can be consolidated.

Previously, dedicated global integrated companies seem to monopolize the contracts in delivering global shipments, but with the cross-border opening approach, the logistics platform can now break down the end-to-end delivery process into delicate steps independently. This implies SMEs can compete alongside the big players.

Figures 15.2 and 15.3 shows the importance and current practice of logistic industry in Japan that involve integrated halal logistics players in Japan.

Global Halal market

The global Muslim population is approaching 1.6 billion people. Muslims are expected to account for 30% of the world's population by 2025. It is estimated that there are 1.5 billion Halal consumers, which means that one in four people are Halal consumers. The global Halal market value for trade in food and beverages is estimated at USD 547 billion a year and this demonstrates promising potential to food manufacturers across the world. Apart from the global Halal market, the Halal logistics market has shown a gradual increase from 2016 to 2027 as per Figure 15.4.

Halal in Japan

Malaysia is the first and only country in the world to have a government institution providing Halal certification. This shows the commitment of Malaysia's government in handling matters related to Halal certification. Malaysia's Halal

Halal logistics certification in Japan 201

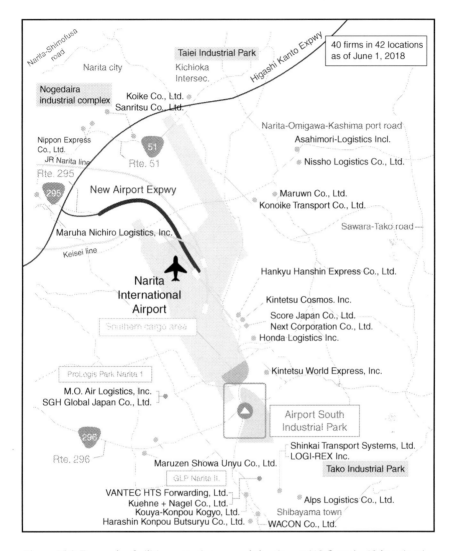

Figure 15.2 Forwarder facilities emerging around the airport (40 firms in 42 locations).
Source: Narita International Airport, 2021.

certification body has rapidly evolved to serve Halal globally. Strategic committee members have been involved in constructing and developing the Halal Malaysian Standard (MS Halal) by the Department of Standards Malaysia (DSM) together with the Halal Hub Division in the Department of Islamic Development Malaysia (JAKIM). By ensuring the integrity of Halal, the Malaysia Standard is the most stringent Halal standard in the world. Japan generally represents a non-Muslim

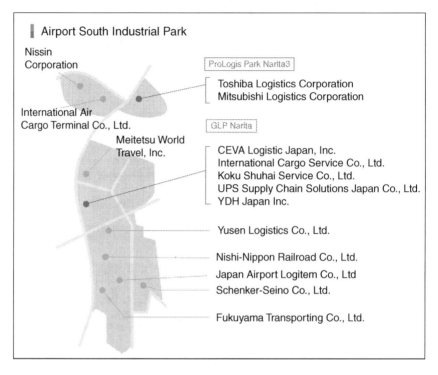

Figure 15.3 Airport South Industrial Park.
Source: Narita International Airport, 2021.

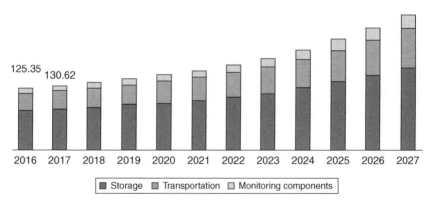

Figure 15.4 Asia Pacific Halal logistics market size by component.
Source: Grandview Research, 2021.

country with significant Halal industry development. Be that as it may, the Halal concept is mushrooming nowadays. Halal is getting to be a modern trending subject, and it covers not only food and beverages but is more broadly connected to other products, such as cosmetics, pharmaceuticals and even hotels and tourism. Japan is aiming to invest in huge amount in the Halal sector and to be among the top five exporters globally.

According to Masayuki (2015) and Kawabata (2015), two factors have influenced the Halal boom in Japan, known as "inbound" and "outbound". These two factors are the reason that Halal is growing exponentially compared to previous years. Japan's food industry is encouraged to raise its profits by exporting products to Islamic countries. From this fact, it is obvious that Japan's motivation for spreading Halal in Japan is strongly related to economic factors. The most challenging part for Japanese industries when they want to export their products to Islamic countries is Halal certification. Japanese companies have to obtain the Halal mark in different countries where they want to export their products, as Halal certification in Japan only applies to local consumption and is not for consumption abroad. In other words, to sell their products to the Islamic world, Japanese companies have to obtain Halal certification from various countries. Obtaining Halal certification is not easy, because the requirements that need to be fulfilled by the companies are very strict and complicated. Therefore, it can be concluded that the problem with Halal certification is one of the big challenges to Japan penetrating the Muslim market.

Halal certification bodies in Japan

Halal certification bodies play their role in certifying products and ensuring that every product submitted for Halal inspection fulfils the requirement of Halal to be consumed by Muslims and meets the Halal standard. Halal certification refers to the assessment of raw materials, ingredients usage and food processing from preparation, slaughtering, cleaning and process handling up to storage and transportation to retailers and consumers. Nowadays, Halal certification is globally accessible in more than 60 countries by a variety of Islamic centres and organizations along with government institutions, issuing different types of Halal certificates (Bon and Hussain, 2010).

As of February 2020, there are 84 foreign Halal certification bodies (FHCBs) in 46 countries certified and recognized by JAKIM. Japan has seven FHCBs certified by JAKIM, with its own Halal certificates and Halal logo. Besides these, Keigo Nakagawa, a researcher and consultant for the Tokyo-based Japan Halal Business Association, with 152 member companies, says there are 22 Halal certifying entities in Japan. Despite this, Japan's Muslims are still yet to completely implement Halal due to confusion on several complex issues like logistics. For this particular issue, the Japanese Halal certification body will get more information from other Halal authorities in other countries, especially Malaysia. Malaysia is the preferred referral point for Halal matters for Japan. The numbers of Halal certification bodies can be divided into three categories: non-profit organizations, religious corporations and other organization forms (Sasaki, 2014). The first certification for Halal food in Japan was established in 1986 and administered by the Japan Muslim Association (Jp. Shūkyō Hōjin Nihon Musurimu Kyōkai). This association is a religious corporation that plays the main function of voluntarily assisting the community (Kawabata, 2015). Among the other Halal certification bodies, some well-known names are: the Japan Muslim Association in Tokyo, established in 1953 as the first Muslim organization; the Japan Halal Association, a non-profit organization in Osaka; the Japan Halal Unit Association; the Japan Islamic Trust at Masjid Otsuka founded in 1978; the Muslim Professional Japan Association started by Malaysian citizen Akmal Abu Hassan; Malaysia Halal Corporation founded in 2010; the Nippon Asia Halal Association in the city of Chiba; the Japan Halal Foundation; the Islamic Centre Japan; the Malaysia Halal Corporation; the Kyoto Halal Kyōgikai; the Halal Business Association; the Asia Halal Association; and the Halal Development Foundation Japan. These Halal certification bodies were established between 1986 and 2012. According to Masayuki (2015), certification bodies with a long history of certification experience tend to have stricter Halal standards compared to those that are newly established.

Different standards and certification

The emergence of Halal certification bodies in Japan triggered the rise of the Halal market. Japanese companies have seen the importance of obtaining Halal certification to penetrate the Muslim market. The lack of a single and unified global Halal standard is a pressing issue within the Halal industry. Most of the Halal certification bodies in Japan adopt the Halal certification procedure from other Islamic countries. Currently, there is no specific regulation agency that controls these different Halal standards in Japan, which leads to confusion among Muslims (Yasuda, 2014). Halal certification issued by the local body is valid within Japan's domestic market and "inbound" demand only and the Halal logo is not well accepted yet in other countries in the world. Recently, there has been an effort from Japanese entrepreneurs with support from the Japanese government to get Halal certification from an established body like JAKIM by implementing the MS standard. With this effort, a Japanese wagyu beef entrepreneur has entered the world meat market, which means entering the "outbound" world Halal market. This is an indicator of how serious the Japanese are about the Halal market demand. Despite all this, it is too soon to predict whether Japan will have a Halal organization initiated by the government authorities.

Halal logistics in Japan

Several countries are attempting to capture a slice of Japan's USD 800 billion in the food and beverage market. Malaysia in particular, using the Tokyo Olympics 2021 as a launch-pad, has been managing an account on the Games to trade its Halal goods and services worth up to USD 300 million (Halal in Japan, 2020).

Halal logistics is another sector of the global Halal market that shows significant potential for enormous growth. Halal logistics refers to an approach to avoid contamination of perishable products, raw materials, food and consumer goods during transportation or distribution activities. It is also to avoid products missing information and to ensure that Muslim consumers will receive and consume only Halalan Toyyiban products. The Halal logistics framework refers to operations such as fleet management, storage/warehousing, and materials handling according to the principles of Shariah law in ensuring the integrity of the Halal products at the point of consumption. The most feasible terminology for Halal logistics is the application of Shariah law to the logistics process. Starting from the beginning of the logistics process until the final consumers, Shariah law must be followed. This is to ensure the Halal product must also follow Halal logistics and in ensuring the Halal logistics, the Halal integrity among the channel members must be applied. This will include proper segregation and a proper logistics system of the products throughout the logistics process (Jaafar et al., 2013). Figure 15.1 illustrates the circular economy in the logistics landscape.

Nippon Express Co. Ltd.

Nippon Express, which carries out such logistics services, is a Japanese company that was established in the year 1937 (Nippon Express, 2021). The group's turnover is 2,138.5 billion yen, and the company has built a worldwide network that incorporates 725 bases situated in 311 cities in 48 countries. Nippon Express utilizes this global network to supply proficient logistics to numerous distinctive industries such as the automobile industry, precision equipment industry, fashion industry, pharmaceutical industry and food industry. One of the largest logistics companies in Japan, Nippon Express has been swiftly working on the development of "Halal logistics" so that the Halal nature of the products is not ruined in the process of transporting goods. For Muslims in Japan, Nippon Express is working to develop a transportation environment for Halal products exported from Malaysia and Indonesia to Japan that can be used with peace of mind. In December 2014, Nippon Express became the very first Japanese company to received Halal logistics certification, MS2400-1 (Transportation) by the JAKIM, famously known for its stringent Halal certification procedure. Since then, the full-scale operation of the transportation of Halal products began in Malaysia. After obtaining its first Halal certification for warehousing in Japan in January 2016; certification issued by the Japan Halal Association was acquired by Tokyo Marine Shipping Branch (Warehouse). A month after, in February 2016, it obtained Halal certification issued by the same association in the sector of transportation by container trolley. Since then, the company introduced Halal-only roll boxes for consolidated transport of small lot cargo amounting to less than a full truckload as well as Halal-only rail containers for large-lot cargo into its warehouse-based transport services as it expanded its handling of Halal products. Less than a year later, in March 2017, Nippon Express created another victory by

206 *Jamaludin and Sugawara*

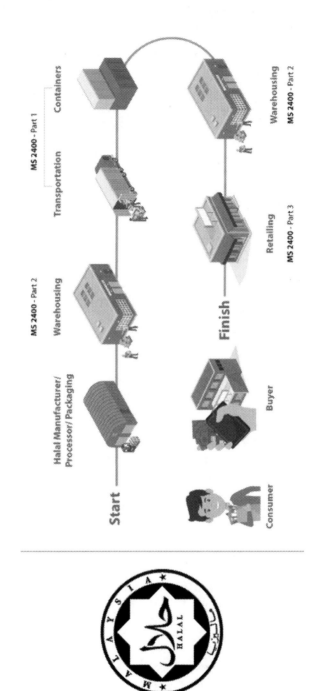

Figure 15.5 Halal supply chain ecosystem.
Source: A-Transglobal Logistics, n.d.

receiving certification issued by the Japan Halal Association acquired by Fukuoka Marine Shipping Branch (warehouses and transportation by container trolley).

In October 2016, JAKIM supported the in-house "Sertu" process. Nippon Express received the Halal certification MS2400-2 (Warehouse) in May 2017. In Indonesia, the company also obtained certification issued by LPPOM-MUI, acquired by Nippon Express Indonesia, Nittsu Lemo Indonesia Logistik and NEX Logistics Indonesia, in April, June and July 2018 respectively. The recent certification received by Nippon Express is expanding its domestic Halal logistics services in Japan with the start of a new Halal-certified domestic air cargo transport service on 8 March 2021. With interest in Halal products growing in Japan, Nippon Express has been constructing a Halal logistics service network to support customers' supply chains and provide safety and peace of mind to Muslim customers and others as visualized in Figure 15.6. It is offering a complete supply chain from farm to fork. The services offered by Nippon Express are air freight services, ocean freight services, container trolley services, warehouse storage at dedicated temperature (room, refrigerated and frozen), and special freight insurance for the transportation of Halal produce (Nippon Express, 2021).

Yusen Logistics

Yusen Logistics is one of the biggest transport companies that has also taken a step toward growing it is business in Southeast Asia by gaining certification for shipping goods in compliance with Islamic law. TASCO Berhad, a Yusen Logistics subsidiary in Malaysia, has acquired Halal certification issued in April 2015 by JAKIM. The two certifications, MS2400-1, required for transportation, and MS2400-2, required for warehousing, were acquired simultaneously – a first for a Japanese logistics company. The MS2400-1 Halal certification applies to 25 vehicles located at TASCO's main operating facilities, based in Penang, Malacca, Selangor and Johor. MS2400-2 applies to the Penang Prai Logistics Centre, allowing for Halal handling in a space measuring approximately 9,000m^2. Yusen Logistics sees Halal certification in Southeast Asia as something that will help them win shipping orders from food producers in Australia, Brazil and other countries that export to the region (Yusen Logistics, 2015).

Sumitomo Corporation Kyushu

Sumitomo Corporation Kyushu has entered the Halal logistic market on the export of Halal food products produced in Japan and certified by the Japan Halal Unit Association (JHUA), having its head office in Fukuoka City that serves as the export liaison. Food products certified by JHUA can be exported to Malaysia with full confidence to the consumer that the products have been stringently audited by JHUA according to a Halal certification process recognized by JAKIM. Sumitomo Corporation Kyushu will be exporting JHUA certified products and to potential sales destinations. Export of Japan's high-quality food products worldwide is expected to accelerate. With JHUA suitably certifying Japanese

Figure 15.6 Nippon Express Halal logistics system.
Source: Nippon Express, 2021.

food products and logistics as Halal, Japan Halal Standards providing consulting and educational services, and Sumitomo Corporation Kyushu supporting export operations and overseas sales of Halal foods processed by Islamic law, Japanese products should make even greater inroads into the global Halal food market (Sumitomo Corporation, 2017).

Conclusion

With a growing global middle class and expanded internet access, increased demand for e-commerce will require logistics providers to deliver to remote locations in emerging economies for the first time – especially in Asia where many rural communities are not connected to the rail network. The analysis shows that there is USD 1.5 trillion of value at stake for logistics players and a further USD 2.4 trillion worth of societal benefits as a result of digital transformation of the industry up to 2025. In other words, industry stakeholders ought come together to prioritize advances changes in digital transformation initiatives given the potential for significantly higher value to be created. Technology adoption or application in the Halal logistics is vital to uphold the integrity of the Halal product along the supply chain process. With the current and future development of technology and digitalisation, the control of the Halal product in term of tracking and tracing could be successfully implement and secure Halal end-to-end value chain. Future scholars in Halal logistics and supply chain are also called to explore this issue in their future research especially from non-Muslim Halal country practice perspective.

References

A-Transglobal Logistics (n.d.). *Halal Supply Chain Ecosystem*. Retrieved from: https://atransglobal.com/V2/halalservices-2/ (accessed 24 November 2021).

Bon, M. and Hussain, M. (2010). Halal food and tourism: prospect and challenges. In N. Scott and J. Jafari (Eds.), *Tourism in the Muslim World: Bridging Tourism Theory and Practice*. Bingley: Emerald Group Publishing, pp. 47–59.

Grandview Research (2021). *Halal Logistics Market Size*. Retrieved from: www.randviewreserach.com (accessed 24 November 2021).

Halal in Japan (2020). *Halal Market Expansion in Japan*. Retrieved from: www.halalinjapan.com/blog/halal-market-expansion-in-japan (accessed 24 November 2021).

Jaafar, H. S., Omar, E. N., Omar, E. N. and Faisol, N. (2013). The concept of Halal logistics – an insight. *The 5th International Conference on Transport and Logistics (ICLT 2013)*. Kyoto: Doshisha University.

Kawabata, T. (2015). "Harāru bijinesu" no būmuka to kadai: masumedia no ronchō kara yomitoku. *Chūtō Kenkyū*, 523, pp. 62–74.

Masayuki, N. (2015). *A Religious Sociological Study of Halal Boom in Japan: Intercultural Understandings Brought by the Religious Taboo*. Osaka: Otemon Gakuin University.

Narita International Airport (2021). *Global Mega Logistic City*. Retrieved from: www.narita-airport.jp (accessed 24 November 2021).

Nippon Express (2021). *Japan's Economic and Freight Outlook and Short-term Survey of Freight Movement in Japan (Nittsu Soken Tan-kan)*. Retrieved from: www.nipponexpress.com/press/report/10-Feb-21.html (accessed 24 November 2021).

Nittsu Research Institute and Consulting, Inc. (NRIC) (2020a). *Japan's Economic and Freight Outlook*. Retrieved from: www.nittsu-soken.co.jp/wp-content/uploads/2020/12/report-20201225.pdf (accessed 24 November 2021).

Nittsu Research Institute and Consulting, Inc. (NRIC) (2020b). *Short-term Survey of Freight Movement in Japan (Nittsu Soken Tan-kan)*. Retrieved from: www.nittsu-soken.co.jp/wp-content/uploads/2021/01/tankan2020-12.pdf (accessed 24 November 2021).

United Nations (UN) (2021). *Population by Religion, Sex and Urban/Rural Residence*. Retrieve from http://data.un.org (accessed 24 November 2021).

Sasaki, Y. (2014). *Harāru Māketo Saizensen*. Tokyo: Jitsugyounonihonsha.

Sumitomo Corporation (2017). *Halal Certification of Domestically-Produced Food Products and Export Support*. Retrieved from: www.sumitomocorp.com/en/easia/news/release/2017/group/20170203 (accessed 24 November 2021).

Wunsch, N-G. (2020). Global Halal market – statistics and facts. *Statistica*. Retrieved from: https://bit.ly/3qWLcV1 (accessed 24 November 2021).

World Economic Forum (WEF) (2016). *Digital Transformation Industries: Logistics Industry*. Retrieve from: https://bit.ly/3qWLcV1 (accessed 24 November 2021).

Yasuda, S. (2014). Nihon ni Okeru Musurimu Kankōkyaku – Kankō ni okeru harāru ninshōseido no juyō o meguru genjō to kadai. *Chūtō Kenkyū*, pp. 49–55.

Yusen Logistics (2015). *Yusen Logistics Group Certified Halal-compliant in Malaysia*. Retrieved from: www.yusen-logistics.com/en/resources/press-and-media/1815 (accessed 24 November 2021).

16 Halal market opportunities and logistics in Spain

Fernando Mayor-Vitoria

Introduction

Muslims today understand the term Halal as a lifestyle, a global and comprehensive concept that influences and affects everyday issues such as food, hygiene, health, economy, fashion, trade and tourism. It is a term that includes everything that is allowed, and therefore, everything that is beneficial and healthy for the human being, leading to an improvement in the quality of life and the reduction of health risks. It could be translated as authorized, recommended, healthy, ethical or non-abusive.

On the other hand, Haram is the term that refers to everything that is prohibited, not allowed, harmful or abusive. Things that are considered Haram, according to Islamic regulations, include the meat of the animal found dead, the meat of pork and wild boar, animals slaughtered without the invocation of the name of God, alcohol, alcoholic beverages, noxious or poisonous substances and toxic plants or drinks. Finally, there is a third concept, which is "Masbouh". This is a concept that refers to things for which their origin cannot be clearly determined or where there are differences in valuation in the different Koranic traditions, in which case each Muslim decides their own personal position.

Religious commitment plays a categorical role in the lives of many communities by shaping their beliefs, knowledge and daily attitudes (Jamal, 2003) and influencing people's feelings and attitudes towards consumption (Hackett et al., 2019). Today, Islam is the fastest growing religion in the world, which justifies the recent prominence of the Halal concept and its engagement in Muslim consumption. This growth makes Halal certification more important. The Halal certificate is a document issued by the Muslim authority of the exporting country certifying that a particular food or pharmaceutical product meets the requirements of Islamic law for consumption by the Muslim population. In the case of foods, beverages, products or services to be considered Halal, they must comply with the Islamic regulations contained in the Koran, in the traditions of the Prophet and in the teachings of Islamic jurists, as well as with the current regulations of the country of destination.

The procedure for obtaining certification includes audits of the companies, documentary evaluation of the quality and production systems of the companies

DOI: 10.4324/9781003223719-21

as well as evaluation of tests of samples taken in the factory and of the final products. In addition, the personnel involved in the various steps of production, such as slaughterers, butchers, cutting operators, processing and distribution are also evaluated. According to the Halal Institute (2021), in Spain, the following companies offer Halal certification services: Instituto Halal de Junta Islámica, Halal Consulting and Halal Food & Quality. The interested operator should contact them in order to learn, in detail, the services offered, such as products, conditions, countries in which their certifications are recognized and so on.

This certificate is especially important in countries like Spain because it is one of the European countries with more historical and artistic heritage of Arab origin. The Muslim presence in the Iberian Peninsula for almost eight centuries has left an indelible mark, tangible and intangible, in buildings, names and customs, such as the Mosque-Cathedral of Cordoba together with its historic centre and the caliphate city of Medina Azahara, the Alhambra, the Generalife and the Albaicin in Granada, and the Cathedral Giralda and the Alcazar in Seville, all of them declared World Heritage Sites by the United Nations Educational, Scientific and Cultural Organization (UNESCO). The routes of the Andalusi Legacy (recognized by the Council of Europe in 1997 as European cultural routes) are another example of this (UNESCO, 2021). This rich cultural heritage makes Spain a destination with a clear potential to attract Muslim tourists. Thus, websites, blogs and forums dedicated to Halal tourism recommend (among others) visits to these places, which are representatives of the Arab and Muslim legacy present in the history and heritage of Spain.

According to FoodNavigator (2020), there are many Spanish cities with a high percentage of Muslim residents who could be potential customers of Halal products if there were companies that provide them, since the Muslim population represents 4% of the population of Spain with a total of 1,190,000 people. More than a quarter of these Muslims live in Catalonia (515,000), followed by Andalusia (310,000), Madrid (283,000) and the Valencian Community (205,000). The Spanish provinces with the largest number of Muslim residents are Barcelona (Catalonia, 328,000), Madrid (Community of Madrid, 286,000), Murcia (Region of Murcia, 102,000), Almeria (Andalusia, 94,000), Alicante (Valencian Community, 94,000), Malaga (Andalusia, 91,000), Girona (Catalonia, 86,000), Valencia (Valencian Community, 75,000), Balearic Islands (54,000) and Las Palmas (Canary Islands, 53,000).

However, Halal products are no longer only marketed in neighbourhoods or areas with a high percentage of immigrants, but some supermarkets are beginning to sell this type of certified products. Some Carrefour or Eroski supermarkets in Spain sell meat with the Halal label; and although in Spain this Halal sale in supermarkets is not yet widespread, in other countries such as France it is very common to enter a supermarket and find these products.

Opportunities for the Halal market

The Halal market has been a sector in full discovery, which is configured as a commercial field in full evolution. In other words, it is a market that transcends

Table 16.1 SWOT analysis

Strengths	Weaknesses
• Growing global awareness of the potential of the Halal market by governments, corporations and financial institutions • Halal foods are playing a more prominent role in global sporting events, for example, the Olympics • New business opportunity for start-ups • Recognition of Halal as a potential for economic growth • Synergy between various sub-sectors (e.g., food and travel)	• Confusion as to the interpretation of the rules • Obvious fraud and rumours that undermine the integrity of the market • Lack of financing for start-ups and SMEs • Insufficient awareness among financial institutions • Lack of Halal training and capacity building for human resources
Opportunities	**Threats**
• Financing and other alternative investment platforms • Investment opportunities in niche markets of food and personal care • Provision of accurate and properly researched market data • Ethical values-based marketing • Increased use of effective social media campaigns • Vertical integration to ensure a Halal-compliant supply chain • More focused scientific research on the benefits of Halal foods	• War, violence and social unrest in the Middle East • Acts of terrorism fuelling Islamophobia in the West • Opposition from dissenting animal welfare groups, especially against live animal exports and slaughter • Prohibition of slaughter without stunning, for example, in Denmark • Fake Halal logos on non-Halal products • Opposition by non-Muslim customers to unlabelled Halal food

geographical, cultural and religious boundaries and with which 1.6 billion consumers around the world are identified. Despite the current popularity of the term Halal, it is true that this type of product has been marketed and consumed in the world for more than 1,400 years. However, the first officially recognized Halal standard did not materialize until 2004.

Prior to analysis of the three most important sectors in the Halal market at the international level, it is necessary to provide analysis of the global environment affecting the market in general. For this purpose, the different strengths, weaknesses, opportunities and threats of the Halal market at the international level have been studied. The different strengths, weaknesses, opportunities and threats of the Halal market at world level are summarized in Table 16.1 and they serve as a presentation of the subsequent analysis of the agrifood, cosmetics and tourism sectors.

Agrifood sector

According to the International Trade Centre (2015), one of the most dynamic sectors in the Halal market is the agrifood sector and Halal products currently account for 16% of global food and beverage consumption, contributing more than €40 billion to the European Union economy. It is important to consider that fruit and vegetable products, cereals, nuts, oils and pulses do not require Halal certification, as these types of natural products are, by definition, Halal. In recent years, with the recognition of Halal product traceability, special attention must be paid to the treatment of these Halal products, avoiding cross-contamination as a result of the use of additives and micro-ingredients derived from Haram products. Spain is a leading country in the agrifood sector. Agrifood exports have reached a value of €38 billion euros, which represents 16.2% of total exports at national level. Spain is therefore the eighth largest exporter of agrifood products in the world. Its strategic location between Europe and Africa, its excellent relations with the Gulf countries and the rapid growth of the European Halal industry have made Spain a key player in the global Halal markets.

Recently, as per Flanders Investment & Trade (2019), Halal food and beverage exports also manifested significant growth, increasing by more than 82%, rising from 11,200 tons in 2017 to 20,500 tons in 2019. Exports of beef increased by 90% between 2017 and 2019, rising from 2,931 tons to over 5,500 tons in 2019. Those of other products, such as chicken, sheep and goats also increased significantly. In addition, to meet this growing demand for Spanish Halal food and beverages abroad, the number of exporting companies certified by the Halal Institute increased from 33 in 2017 to 80 in 2019, while the number of countries to which they export increased from 31 in 2017 to 53 in 2019. Algeria was the main destination for Halal products exported by certified companies in 2019, with 52% of the total exported, while Morocco, with 10% of the share, ranked as the second largest trading partner. In the period 2017–2019, Algeria increased the purchase of our products by 32%. Morocco went from buying 724 tons in 2012 to more than 2,400 tons in 2014; Kuwait, from 25 tons in 2017 to more than 976 tons in 2014 and Saudi Arabia, from 46 tons in 2012 to 1,496 tons in 2019. Among the European markets, two stand out: France, which accounts for 8.5% of Halal exports, and the United Kingdom, with 4%. While it is true that this growth of the Halal industry is reflected in a higher market share and its origin in a gradual increase of the Muslim population and their consumption habits, the main reason for this booming phenomenon is hidden in aspects such as quality, hygiene and food safety, among other factors. The desire and need of Muslim societies to have access to quality Halal products, with full assurance that they meet their dietary requirements, is pushing consumers to be more demanding, as well as the agencies of importing countries, which are establishing regulatory measures and more control mechanisms to ensure the traceability of the Halal food chain.

Tourism sector

According to Halal International Tourism (2019), two million international tourists from Muslim-majority countries visited Spain, with Algeria (220,000), Turkey (215,000) and Morocco (200,000) as the main issuing countries. In addition, tourists from countries such as Saudi Arabia (40,780), the United Arab

Emirates (39,053) and Indonesia (37,272) are increasingly numerous. In relative terms, it is also worth mentioning the increase in the number of tourists from Jordan (90%), Turkey (88%), Kazakhstan (87%) and Indonesia (18%) (National Statistics Institute, 2007). Along these lines, recent data from the Global Muslim Travel Index (MasterCard, 2019), during 2018 and the first nine months of 2019, show that the number of tourists from Asia and Africa is progressively increasing, with Morocco (675,000) as the main issuing country. The economic impact for the destination of this type of tourists is particularly notable, with an average expenditure per person of €1,500 and an average stay of nine days, higher than the other tourist segments. Among the Muslims who spent the most (per purchase) were those from the United Arab Emirates (€600), Kazakhstan (€486) and Qatar (€440) (Han et al., 2019). The Institute of Tourism Studies of Spain, with data corresponding to 2019, has determined the countries with the highest average expenditure per person: Saudi Arabia (€4,521), the United Arab Emirates (€2,988), Tunisia (€1,762), Turkey, (€1,510) and Morocco (€1,094). It should be noted that in Spain, tourist spending by Muslims reaches only about 1% of total tourist spend, indicating the growth potential of Halal tourism (Junaidi, 2020).

In 2019, the Global Muslim Travel Index (MasterCard, 2019) also reflected the remarkable growth potential of this tourism segment for Spain (see also Rehman and Shabbir, 2010), considered the third most attractive European destination, behind only the United Kingdom and France, while ranking ninth among non-Organization of Islamic Cooperation (OIC) countries and first among inbound destinations for Muslims (in non-OIC countries). In addition, this study noted that the Muslim travel market will continue to be one of the fastest growing segments in the global travel industry. Specifically, in 2018 there were an estimated 140 million international Muslim travellers, with the expectation of reaching 230 million by 2026 and with their travel spending skyrocketing to USD 180 billion for online travel purchases. Clearly, this is related to the growth of the Muslim population, which is expected to account for one in three people by 2050 (UCIDE, 2020).

Another indicator of the volume and attractiveness that the domestic tourism market of the Muslim population can reach is the increase in the resident Muslim population in Spain. According to the latest demographic study from the World Travel and Tourism Council (WTTC, 2019) involving the Union of Islamic Communities of Spain, the Muslim population in Spain is estimated at more than two million, specifically 2,091,656 on that date, while five years earlier it was 1,858,409, with an increase of 135,266 people (7%) in a context of a slight decrease in the total resident population in Spain. This means that Muslims now represent just over 4% of the total population, and 42% of them have Spanish nationality (five years earlier, that figure was only 38%). Among the foreign-born, Moroccans are the most numerous (two-thirds of the total). By region, the majority of Muslims are concentrated in Catalonia (27%), Andalusia (16%), Madrid (14%) and Valencia (11%).

In addition, the number of Muslims residing in the main countries of origin of tourists to Spain (France, Germany, the United Kingdom) is notable. It is a significant population derived, mainly, from the descendants of immigrants from Africa. In 2019, the Institut Montaigne (a Paris-based non-profit organization) published a report entitled "A French Islam is Possible", concluding that the majority of French Muslims originate from North Africa: 38% are of Algerian origin, 25% Moroccan, 8% Turkish and 9% are from sub-Saharan countries. Muslims who are foreigners are also from North Africa, sub-Saharan Africa or Turkey. These regions account for more than 88% of people without French citizenship. Another study conducted in 2019, entitled "Growth of Muslim Populations in Europe", estimates that the Muslim population in France is 5.72 million, being the European Union country with the largest number of Muslims (UCIDE, 2020).

According to the Pew Research Center (2017), the country in the European Union with the second largest number of Muslims is Germany, with 4.95 million. Specifically, according to the German Federal Statistical Office (Destatis, 2020), an estimated 1.5 million people were from Turkey in 2018. As for the UK, according to 2018 data (ONS, 2020), it has an immigrant population from very diverse OIC member states, such as Pakistan (194,000), Nigeria (94,000), Bangladesh (83,000), Turkey (62,000), Iraq (40,000), Afghanistan (39,000), Malaysia (34,000), Iran (32,000), Saudi Arabia (13,000), etc. In addition, according to a survey of the religion of the population of England and Wales conducted by the UK Office for National Statistics in 2011, a total of 2.7 million people identified as Muslims (4.8% of the population), positioning Islam as the most predominant minority religion. London stands out as the city with the highest proportion of Muslim population, at 12.4%. More recent estimates place the United Kingdom as the third largest European country in terms of Muslim population, with 4.13 million (UCIDE, 2020).

Cosmetics sector

The cosmetics sector is the one that has generated the least turnover so far in relation to other sectors such as food or tourism, but despite this it enjoys significant growth potential, estimated to generate almost €190 billion by 2020, according to the newspaper *El País*. The Halal Institute recognizes textually for the case of cosmetics and perfumery that a series of requirements must be met:

- Cosmetics and perfumery products shall be produced using Halal raw materials.
- Production may be carried out manually, industrially or artificially, provided they do not contain any prohibited materials.
- All processing steps, storage of raw materials, internal transport, handling and any steps affecting the production process shall be done in such way to ensure that there is no cross-contamination with other products and that traceability of the process is maintained.
- Products will have to undergo an analysis for DNA detection of Haram elements before being launched on the market.

- Packages shall be provided with a label, authorized by the Halal Institute, which shall be affixed at the place of production, prior to dispatch and in a manner that does not allow a second use.

The products must be clearly identified with the Halal guarantee mark and a legend on the product, the company's registration number assigned by the Halal Institute and the Halal consumer service telephone number. Such is the importance of the sanitary requirements in this sector that it is recognized that there is an obligation to submit the product to an analysis of DNA detection of Haram elements, before being launched on the market. For a Halal cosmetic product to be offered to the market, it must follow a series of procedures. Unlike what happens in the agrifood sector, where the food to be offered has to be controlled from the moment of its production, cosmetic and pharmaceutical products are controlled once they have been produced. That is to say, once they have been produced, an analysis of their composition is carried out to ensure the absence of Haram products. As for the certification for cosmetic products, the entity in managing and granting the Halal guarantee mark is also the Halal Institute, which applies to cosmetic products offered to people of Islamic faith in Spain and abroad. Cosmetics for Muslims are composed of natural ingredients such as plant extracts and minerals without alcohol or animal products, apart from having Halal accreditation. If any product does not have the certification, Muslims will not buy the product, which is why it is of vital importance to comply with these requirements.

According to the International Council of Certification (2020), cosmetic products that wish to be certified are subjected to some tests to verify that they meet the requirements that deserve the accreditation: first, screening for the presence of pork and pork by-products, with a detection limit of 0.0005%. Second, test for the existence of alcohol, must contain less than 0.05%. Finally, once these investigations are successfully approved, certification is granted. Since 2018 the expenditure on Halal cosmetics has increased considerably in Spain. With Islamic laws, it was difficult for Muslims in the country to buy, for example, a face cream, shampoo or lipstick that complies with the principles of the law. However, today there are companies in Spain that market Halal-accredited products, such as Halal Food & Quality, and recently the Parisian company Advanced Halal Cosmetics arrived in Spain with its brand Mademoiselle Saint Cloud, which uses ingredients such as stem cells and retinol.

An example in the Spanish cosmetic sector is Laboratorio Cosmético Válquer of Toledo, which has obtained Halal certification, which distinguishes products suitable for use by Muslims, guaranteeing that they have been produced in compliance with the Quran. Válquer thus became the first manufacturer in the Spanish cosmetics sector to receive this seal. Obtaining the Halal certificate guarantees that neither raw materials of animal origin nor ethanol, nor any other Haram component are used in the manufacturing and/or handling processes of Halal products. It also ensures that there is no cross-contamination with other products, that the traceability of the process is maintained at all times and that the personnel involved have received Halal training. This allows the Spanish company to sell its cosmetics to the Muslim population in Spain and Europe, and also to other Muslim countries.

Halal logistics in Spain

In recent years, exports of Halal products have grown and have become a differentiating component, mainly for agrifood exporting companies, which want to increase their presence in both Muslim and traditional European markets. According to data from the Halal Institute (2020), there are more than 300 Halal-certified companies in Spain, not only in the food sector but also in tourism, banking, pharmaceuticals, fashion and cosmetics. In the field of logistics, there are a number of sensitive products such as food, beverages, cosmetics or health products whose logistics can be managed by ensuring Halal traceability, so that they reach the final consumer, guaranteeing not only their origin but also their proper handling, storage, transport and distribution. Logistics resulting from the requirements imposed on the production, storage and transport of Halal products leads experts to believe that innovations for logistics processes will be forthcoming in the future. In fact, it is already stressed that trust, assurance and traceability of the supply chain, from farm to fork, are much more demanding for these products. There is, therefore, a closer collaboration with logistics operators to increase reliability and therefore consumer confidence in both the producing companies and the agents in the transport chain. Thus, in terms of logistics processes, Halal products and their distribution processes from producers to consumers are already undergoing an evolution from the mere reservation of space in transport and warehouses to what could be called a dedicated logistics chain, perhaps also with exclusive logistics platforms.

The transport company Tiba was the first Spanish operator to obtain this certification, which guarantees that its logistics processes comply with the rules of the Islamic culture. The "Halal Food & Quality" certificate guarantees compliance with the laws of the Muslim world in food matters, and confirms that the approved food, products and services meet the requirements. This certification is the guarantee for exporters and importers that the company knows the rules and particularities of this culture and that they work to provide solutions and pay special attention to ensure that the logistics processes are within the permitted limits, avoiding any health risks. In this sense, Tiba places special emphasis on preventing products from being contaminated when they come into contact with those that are not permitted by Islam, protecting the goods throughout the logistics chain. Thus, the company offers physical separation in Friopuerto's warehouses, which provide this service and have specific isolated locations for Halal products. For this purpose, they have trained and specialized personnel, which allows them to guarantee their customers the transport of orders by air, sea and land, both in full container and in groupage.

In addition, in the documentation delivered to the shipping company, airline or land transport operator, it will be indicated that they are Halal products and instructions will be given so that the goods are handled according to procedure. Tiba also has a customs team that ensures that these types of controls are carried out without contaminating the shipment, and that there are a network of agents at the destination ready to receive the goods. Another important company in the logistics sector is Algetransit. Currently, this freight forwarder strengthens its offer for the transport of perishable goods from the port of Bahia de Algeciras, which is the main port of Andalusia in the transit of this kind of product. The forwarding company is planning to reinforce its business in Andalusia guaranteeing its logistics to operate products in the Halal market.

The company has accredited its foreign trade advisory services, customs management and freight forwarding with the Halal conformity certificate issued by the Halal Institute, an entity in charge of guaranteeing goods and services suitable for Muslim consumption. With the certification, Algetransit strengthens its offer for the transport of perishable goods from the port of Algeciras Bay. In fact, the freight forwarder is a reference specialist in the Andalusian location for the dispatch of perishable goods, as well as in the physical inspections of goods at the border inspection post, which helps optimize time and improve economic and financial processes, as it has a good approach to customs procedures. Algetransit operates in all kinds of perishable products, including fishery, fruit and vegetables, meat, processed and dairy products. The company highlights the role of Algeciras, a port that has become the main platform for managing Halal exports from Andalusia, including olive oil flows that increased by 178% during 2020 to Indonesia, Malaysia, Thailand, the UAE, Saudi Arabia, Turkey and Morocco (Algetransit, 2020).

The Halal market is currently growing very fast, with a huge value for Spanish exports. In this sense, from the port of Algeciras it is explained that being accredited with the certificate that guarantees the traceability of the product throughout the logistics chain is a determining and differentiating factor to access a world market that integrates more than 1,700 million people and 57 Muslim countries (International Trade Centre, 2015). Similarly, the port of Valencia also wants to position itself as a reference within the logistics of Halal products. The Port Authority of Valencia is preparing to respond to this new logistics challenge that can play a strategic differentiating role in the introduction of products not only in Muslim markets but also in Europe. On the European continent alone, these products have a potential consumer market of more than 44 million people. And it is not just the major ports in Spain that have obtained the Halal certification, the Port of Huelva has received the Halal Certificate, which certifies to the Muslim community that it has the appropriate infrastructures, facilities, services and operating procedures to guarantee the conditions required by each of these religious communities in the handling of products during their passage through the port service area, both for export and import. Huelva is one of the first ports in Spain to have this certification, which is an important boost both for imports and exports to countries such as the United States or Morocco.

Conclusion

Logistics has always been associated with business activity, since the transfer of goods from one place to another has always been necessary for the production and sale of products. The importance of logistics in companies today lies in the fact of being able to supply raw materials and products in a short period of time, so that the final product can be available to the consumer as soon as possible. In the case of Halal logistics, it is the process through which the movement and storage of raw materials is carried out, so that companies and consumers can always be supplied with the products they need. Nowadays, the supply of companies is essential to increase their competitiveness in a market where there are more and more competing companies and where customer demands are increasing. Also, from the government's point of view, more development projects and more public support must be provided to make available to companies the infrastructures that will allow them to develop this niche market, which is vital for their future development and to compete not only in Spain but also internationally.

Moreover, in the case of Spain, the growth of the resident Muslim population, as well as the increase in international arrivals from Muslim-majority countries, indicate Spain's growing interest in this community worldwide and, therefore, the significant potential for developing a Halal or Muslim-friendly tourism offer as a business opportunity, if it is conveniently adapted to the requirements of Muslim tourists, which are not always homogeneous due to the existence of different interpretations of Islam and levels of religiosity. It should be noted that the current areas of Halal tourism research are mainly focused on obtaining knowledge about the profiles, perceptions and behaviours of Halal tourists, along with the correct implementation of this type of offer in the different tourism subsectors (accommodation establishments, restaurants). In this sense, the authentication of Halal or Muslim-friendly services is a key factor. The opportunity, although not without difficulties, is right in front of us, and it is up to us to bet on it and manage it to create appealing tourism experiences for this market segment, as other countries are doing. Are we ready and willing to do so?

References

Algetransit (2020). *About Us*. Retrieved from: www.algetransit.es/ (accessed 24 November 2021).
Destatis (2020). *Home*. Retrieved from: www.destatis.de/ (accessed 24 November 2021).
Flanders Investment & Trade (2019). *About Us*. Retrieved from: www.flandersinvestmentandtrade.com/ (accessed 24 November 2021).
FoodNavigator (2020). *News*. Retrieved from: www.foodnavigator.com/ (accessed November 2021).
Hackett, C., Stonawski, M., Potančoková, M., Connor, P., Shi, A. F., Kramer, S. and Marshall, J. (2019). Projections of Europe's growing Muslim population under three migration scenarios, *Journal of Religion and Demography*, 6(1), pp. 87–122.
Halal Institute (2020). *About Us*. Retrieved from: www.institutohalal.com (accessed 24 November 2021).
Halal Institute (2021). *Certification*. Retrieved from: www.institutohalal.com/acreditaciones/(accessed 24 November 2021).
Halal International Tourism (2019). *Home*. Retrieved from: www.halalinternationaltourism.org/ (accessed 24 November 2021).

Han, H., Al-Ansi, A., Koseoglu, M. A., Lin, P. M. C., Park, J., Yu, J. and Kim, W. (2019). Halal tourism: travel motivators and customer retention. *Journal of Travel & Tourism Marketing*, 36(9), pp. 1012–1024.

International Council of Certification (2020). *Our certificates*. Retrieved from: https://icc-iso.org/ (accessed 24 November 2021).

International Trade Centre (2015). *Home*. Retrieved from: www.intracen.org/ (accessed 24 November 2021).

Jamal, A. (2003). Marketing in a multicultural world: the interplay of marketing, ethnicity and consumption. *European Journal of Marketing*, 37(11/12), pp. 1599–1620.

Junaidi, J. (2020). Halal-friendly tourism and factors influencing Halal tourism. *Management Science Letters*, 10(8), pp. 1755–1762.

MasterCard (2019). *Global Muslim Travel Index 2019*. Retrieved from: www.crescentrating.com/reports/global-muslim-travel-index-2019.html (accessed 24 November 2021).

National Statistics Institute (2007). *Tourism Expenditure Survey: Egatur*. Madrid: INE.

Office for National Statistics (ONS) (2020). *Population of the UK by Country of Birth and Nationality*. Retrieved from: https://bit.ly/2SI5ZyP (accessed 24 November 2021).

Pew Research Center (2017). *Religion*. Retrieved from: www.pewforum.org/ (accessed 24 November 2021).

Rehman, A. and Shabbir, M. S. (2010). The relationship between religiosity and new product adoption. *Journal of Islamic Marketing* 1(1), pp. 63–69.

Union of Islamic Communities of Spain (UCIDE) (2020). *Informes Anuales, el Islam en España, Observatorio Andalusí*. Madrid: UCIDE.

United Nations Educational, Scientific and Cultural Organization (UNESCO) (2021). *Spain*. Retrieved from: https://whc.unesco.org/en/statesparties/es (accessed 24 November 2021).

World Travel and Tourism Council (WTTC) (2019). *The Tourism Sector Is Growing Again*. London: WTTC.

17 Halal logistics certification

A Middle East perspective

Nor Aida Abdul Rahman and Zainab Al Balushi

Introduction to the worldwide Halal market and the need for Halal certification

The global Halal food market is valued at USD 700 billion and is estimated to increase to USD 1,060 billion by the year 2025. The Halal market is not limited to Halal food only, but features other products and services such as pharmaceutical products, cosmetics, medical devices, clothing, Halal leather, tourism, cleaning and logistics (Rahman et al., 2020a, 2020b). Globally, the word Halal is used to refer to goods or services that are safe to consume, conform to quality, assure wholesomeness and align with Islamic law or Shariah principles. It is also known as "Halal Toyyiban". The term Halal has gained increasing acceptance from many countries, not only Muslim majority countries, but also in the Western context (Tieman, 2020; Fuseini et al., 2021). Halal products are known as safe, reliable, high quality and permissible, and with the use of Halal logos and Halal certification, customer trust towards the usage of Halal products will increase. In fact, it could also reduce the uncertainty of the consumer regarding whether the Halal product have certified by Halal certification bodies and, at the same time, will establish Halal branding in the customers' mind (Wilson 2018; Rahman et al., 2020a; 2020b).

In the Middle East perspective, the concept of "Kullu Halal" refers to the situation where people believe that all goods offered or sold in Muslim countries are Halal, thus foods are permissible to eat and strictly prepared according to Islamic law. The growing demand and awareness of Halal products and services have witnessed a significant increase every year. Halal products refer to any item, beverage or food that has been strictly produced or prepared according to Islamic Shariah law (Rahman et al., 2018; Khairuddin et al., 2018). Hence, it is vital to explore issues related to Halal practices and monitoring. A study from Perdana and Altunişik (2017) has called for research scholars to explore Halal certification issues in the Middle East. From the business point of view, Halal certification has proven to increase profit for Halal players since there is high demand for Halal products and services not only from Muslim countries, but also non-Muslim countries. Those Halal businesses with Halal certification will give

DOI: 10.4324/9781003223719-22

additional value-added to Halal organizations to expand their business in both local and international markets. As highlighted by Perdana and Altunişik (2017), there is high demand regarding the issuance of Halal certification in Turkey. This is also supported by Liow (2012) who argues that Halal certification helps Halal business players to expand their businesses more successfully.

In general, Neiburg (2013) states that there is no jurisdiction for a Halal certification practices in the Islamic countries in Middle East region such as Bahrain, Oman, Jordan, Syria, Kuwait, Lebanon, Yemen, the United Arab Emirates and others. There is high demand on Halal products, supply and consumption from all over the world. Hence it is also important for all parties involved in Halal supply networks from the point of origin to point of consumption to maintain their Halal integrity status. Halal integrity here refers to the situation whereby Halal products' status is maintained Halal throughout the whole supply chain network until it is consumed by the end user (Majid et al., 2019; Talib et al., 2020). The main task of every Halal player is to ensure the legitimacy of the Halal products' status. It is also important to note that the process of Halal certification, evaluation and monitoring activities related to Halal product is in place.

Despite the increasing demand of Halal products worldwide, certification plays a vital role in elevating customer trust towards the use of Halal product consumption and services. It is important for Halal players to gain customer trust and certification helps with this. In fact, certification not only increases trust from the user but it is also a good sign for many Halal businesses to attract their market and expand their business beyond Muslim countries. It is also used as a marketing tool in branding the Halal products (Wilson, 2018).

Having this background, this chapter aims to explore Halal certification development in Middle East countries, referring to Halal certification bodies in Malaysia as a principal reference. The next section will discuss global Halal key manufacturers worldwide.

Global key Halal manufacturers for the Halal meat market in the East, West and Middle East

It is acknowledged that the Halal industry now has further developed from Halal food to Halal restaurants, banking, clothing, pharmaceuticals, medical devices and many more. In term of the Halal meat market and Halal food products, this remains the top demand of all. The popularity of Halal food products is not only among Muslim people but is also recognized by non-Muslims. This is due to the fact that Halal products are safe to be consumed, of high quality, nutritious and clean. Globally, there are several key players of Halal food, frozen food and meat providers. They are Nestlé, Carrefour, Barra Manssa, Tahira Foods, Tariq Halal, Al Islami, Tesco, Halal-ash and many more. Figure 17.1 represents the leading global Halal players for the food and meat market.

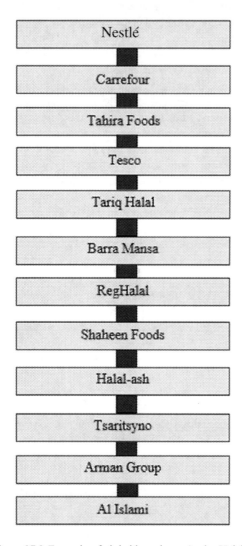

Figure 17.1 Example of global key players in the Halal market.

Halal certification body: history, role and Malaysia as a main reference

According to Aziz and Chok (2013), Halal certification is a process of getting an official recognition of the orderly process of preparing, handling and cleaning of Halal products according to Islamic law as guided by relevant Halal management practices by the established body such as Islamic authorities in any country. Halal certification bodies (HCBs) play a significant role in evaluating and certifying

Halal logistics certification: Middle East 225

any Halal product and service. In the context of consumer research, Halal logos or Halal certificates produced by Islamic authorities or HCBs are used as a main instrument to promote Halal products and services. This certificate or Halal logo is required to show the acceptance of the Halal product and service as assurance that product is approved by Islamic Shariah law. It is also aligning with Islamic principles. As highlighted by Fuseini et al. (2021), obtaining Halal certification helps organizations to always abide to the Islamic rules and maintain the procedures for monitoring Halal related activities.

Malaysia has been known as a leading country in Halal industry worldwide since the 1990s. The role of Malaysia in the Halal industry has led to its recognition as the key reference for many countries across the region. Obtaining Halal certification is essential for many businesses to market their products. Halal certificates also assure consumers that both products and services are thoroughly checked in accordance with Islamic Shariah principles. Since the buyer or consumer are looking at the sign and certification logo before buying any Halal item, getting Halal certification is vital for every Halal product and service provider. Besides that, businesses obtain other benefits if they have Halal certificates for their products and services, as shown in Figure 17.2.

In Malaysia, Halal certification is led by the Department of Islamic Development Malaysia (JAKIM), as well as Majlis Agama Islam Negeri-negeri (MAIN). JAKIM is the agency responsible for Islamic affairs including Halal certification in Malaysia. Therefore, JAKIM plays a very important role in protecting Muslim consumers in Malaysia and it has always been JAKIM's responsibility to assure consumers to seek Halal products as urged by Shariah. For the purpose of Halal certification, JAKIM has to ascertain the Halal status of the product at

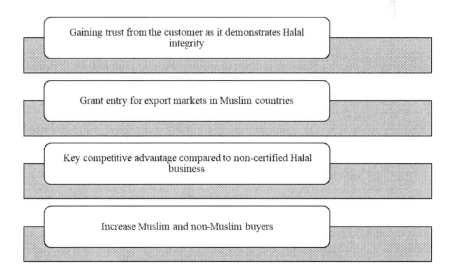

Figure 17.2 Key benefits of having Halal certification for Halal goods and service providers.

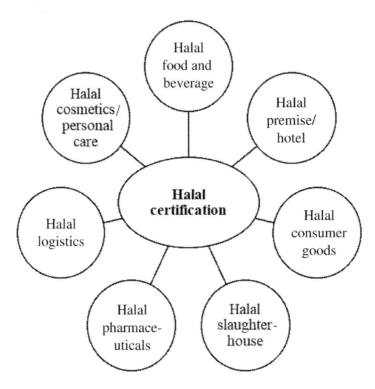

Figure 17.3 Halal logistics certification in Malaysia.

every stage and at every process involved. This is accomplished by carrying out an official site inspection on the plants purposely to examine how the Halal status of the raw material is maintained and consistently monitored.

In the process of Halal certification, evaluation is performed covering all products and consumables, food premises, slaughterhouses that supply meat, and others. However, the Malaysia Halal certification is voluntary, the applicant participating in this certification is subject to the terms and conditions set by the department. In Malaysia, the Halal certification body cover seven sets of Halal schemes which cover both goods and services. The seven categories for Halal certification are food and beverage, hotel (food premise), consumer goods, cosmetics and personal care, pharmaceuticals, slaughterhouses and logistics (see Figure 17.3).

Halal certification bodies in the Middle East and Halal logistics certification opportunities

It was recognized that from a global perspective, the key leading roles in Halal certification are spearheaded by Malaysia, Australia and Pakistan (Neo, 2019).

Figure 17.4 Halal and Made in Oman logos.

As highlighted in this chapter, Malaysia has taken the lead as regards HCBs and being a reference for many countries including in the Middle East. From a Middle Eastern perspective, Oman is also known as a popular country for international standards, referred to as world class Islamic tradition in the Arabic language. In Muscat and Salalah, there is an increasing demand for the certification since it was a mandate from regulatory bodies in food manufacturing and cosmetics to have Halal certification for their products. For instance, products produced in Oman carry a logo as seen in Figure 17.4, written in Arabic and English. Similarly the Halal logo is being used in the UAE.

At present, most of the Halal products that get certified for Halal in Middle East region are coming from Halal food products and beverages, pharmaceuticals, cosmetics and meat. Halal logistics is recognized as a new opportunity for the logistics provider, especially those handling transportation and warehousing activities for Halal related products.

There are certain issues highlighted by previous studies related to the challenges facing Halal logistics implementation in Islamic countries. One of the key factors highlighted by Zailani et al. (2017) and Talib et al. (2013) is related to the limited number of international Halal certification bodies that focus on Halal logistics which include Halal transportation, Halal warehousing and Halal retailing (Rahman et al., 2020a, 2020b). There is a significant need to have more Halal logistics certification bodies in order to increase the number of logistics service providers to get Halal logistics certified.

Information on Halal logistics certification that relates to its management system of transportation, warehousing and retailing activity should have proper communication and information flow to the end consumer or a business entity. There should be one-stop centre that gathers all information on how to implement Halal logistics so as to fulfil Halal logistics market demand (Roslan et al., 2016; Rahman et al., 2018). In fact, a proper channel network is also needed to convey the correct and sufficient information that guides the related party to get Halal logistics certification.

On the other hand, Sapry et al. (2020) argue that even though Halal logistics is an opportunity for global Halal players to widen their network and market, they also need to invest in Halal related facilities in order to successfully implement Halal logistics. This is because of the cost that may incur during Halal logistics handling, especially on special investment in pallets, storage, a Halal dedicated area at the warehouse, specific Halal handling equipment for Sertu activity, and also for Halal staff training. To implement Halal logistics, it is also important for staff to send for Halal training to increase their knowledge on Halal handling and to ensure that the status of any Halal product is still Halal until it reaches consumption point.

It is very interesting to see the development of Halal logistics activities in the Eastern region such as Malaysia, Indonesia and Thailand. In the Western context, such as in the United Kingdom, there is also an increasing awareness on the importance of Halal logistics and increased demand by logistics providers to get certified for their Halal logistics activity. Therefore, in the Middle East perspective also, even though there is a "Kullu Halal" concept for Halal products in Middle Eastern countries, still the integrity of the Halal status need to be maintained and secured, to avoid cross-contamination happening and affecting the status of Halal products.

Conclusion and future research recommendations

To conclude, there is a significant opportunity for both scholars and practitioners to explore the prospect of implementing Halal logistics and certifying logistics service providers. To maintain the status of Halal products in local and international markets, the status of Halal should be maintained and secured with proper handling. The current status of Halal logistics implementation should be changed from voluntary to compulsory to all Halal providers to ensure the integrity of the Halal products is secured throughout the supply chain activity. As highlighted by Talib et al. (2015, 2020), Zailani et al. (2017) and Rahman et al. (2020a), future Halal logistics study could look in detail at the developments and challenges of implementing Halal transportation, Halal warehousing and Halal retailing. The focus of research in the area of Halal training and Halal monitoring system would also contribute to Halal logistics theories.

References

Aziz, Y. A. and Chok, N. V. (2013). The role of Halal awareness, Halal certification, and marketing components in determining Halal Purchase intention among non-Muslims in Malaysia: a structural equation modeling approach. *Journal of International Food & Agribusiness Marketing*, 25(1), pp. 1–23.

Fuseini, A., Hadley, P. and Knowles, T. (2021). Halal food marketing: an evaluation of UK Halal standards, *Journal of Islamic Marketing*, 12(5), pp. 977–991.

Khairuddin, M. M., Rahman, N. A. A., Mohammad, M. F., Majid, Z. A. and Ahmad, M. F. (2018). Regulator perspective on Halal air cargo warehouse compliance, *International Journal of Supply Chain Management*, 7(3), pp. 202–207.

Liow, R. J. (2012). *Marketing Halal, Creating New Economy, New Wealth*. Petaling Jaya: MPH Group Publishing.

Majid, Z. A., Shamsudin, M. F., Rahman, N. A. A., Jaafar, H. S., Mohammad, M. F. and Khairuddin, M. M. (2019). Innovation in logistics from 1PL toward 10PL: counting the numbers. *Advances in Transportation and Logistics Research*, 2, pp. 440–447.

Neiburg, O. (2013). *Catering to the Middle East: Halal certification and alcohol-free labeling with Mondelez*. Retrieved from: www.confectionerynews.com/Article/2013/01/28/Halal-chocolate-and-alcoholfree-confectionery-with-Mondelez (accessed 24 November 2021).

Neo, P. (2019). *Halal Food Leaders: Malaysia, Australia and Pakistan Retain Top APAC Spots in Global Islamic Economy Report's Top 10 List*. Retrieved from: www.foodnavigator-asia.com/Article/2019/12/18/Halal-food-leaders-Malaysia-Australia-and-Pakistan-retain-top-APAC-spots-in-Global-Islamic-Economy-report-s-Top-10-list (accessed 24 November 2021).

Perdana, F. F. P. and Altunişik, R. (2017). A study on the saliency of the Halal certification towards food products in Turkey. *Journal of Halal Life Style*, 1(1).

Rahman, N. A. A., Mohammad, M. F., Rahim, S. A. and Noh, H. M. (2018). Implementing air cargo Halal warehouse: insight from Malaysia. *Journal of Islamic Marketing*, 9(3), pp. 462–483.

Rahman, N. A. A., Majid, Z. A., Mohammad, M. F., Ahmad, M. F., Rahim, S. A. and Mokhtar, A. Z. (2020a). The development of Halal logistics standards in South-East Asia: Halal supply chain standards (MS2400) as a principal reference in Halal logistics and supply chain management in Southeast Asia. In N. A. A. Rahman, A. Hassan and M. F. Mohammad (Eds.), *Halal Logistics and Supply Chain in South East Asia: Development and Challenges*. Singapore: Routledge, pp. 149–160.

Rahman, N. A. A., Rahim, S. A., Ahmad, M. F. and Hafizuddin-Syah, B. A. M. (2020b). Exploring COVID-19 pandemic: its impact to global aviation industry and the key strategy. *International Journal of Advanced Science and Technology*, 29(6), pp. 1829–1836.

Roslan, N. F., Rahman, F. A., Ahmad, F. and Ngadiman, N. I. (2016). Halal logistics certificate in Malaysia: challenges and practices. *International Journal of Supply Chain Management*, 5(3), pp. 142–146.

Sapry, H. R. M., Takiudin, N. S. M. and Ahmad, A. R. (2020). Challenges faced by non-Muslim transporter in adopting Halal logistics certificate. *Journal of Critical Reviews*, 7(8), pp. 141–146.

Talib, M. S. A., Rubin, L. and Zhengyi, V. K. (2013). Qualitative research on critical issues in Halal logistics. *Journal of Emerging Economies and Islamic Research*, 1(2), pp. 1–20.

Talib, M. S. A., Hamid, A. B. A., Zulfakar, M. H. and Chin, T. A. (2015). Barriers to halal logistics operation: views from Malaysian logistics experts. *International Journal of Logistics Systems and Management*, 22(2), pp. 193–209.

Talib, M. S. A., Pang, L. L. and Ngah, A. H. (2020). The role of government in promoting Halal logistics: a systematic literature review. *Journal of Islamic Marketing*. https://doi.org/10.1108/JIMA-05-2020-0124

Tieman, M. (2020). *Halal Business Management: A Guide to Achieving Halal Excellence*. New York: Routledge.

Wilson, J. A. J. (2018). *Halal Branding*. Swansea: Claritas Books.

Zailani, S., Iranmanesh, M., Aziz, A. A. and Kanapathy, K. (2017). Halal logistics opportunities and challenges. *Journal of Islamic Marketing*, 8(1), pp. 127–139.

18 Halal logistics and supply chain management research

Recent COVID-19 effects and future development

Muhammad Munzir Khairuddin, Fathien Azuien Yusriza, Nor Aida Abdul Rahman, Abdul Manan Dos Mohamed, Suzari Abdul Rahim and Md Fauzi Ahmad

Introduction

The Halal economy is recognized as one of the fastest growing economies worldwide and the market for Halal products and services is continuously increasing year by year. The increase in Halal product production and Halal service offerings mainly shows the stability of the industry, which is seen as the engine of economic growth for many countries, not only Islamic countries but also non-Islamic countries. The demand for Halal product is everywhere and it is coming from both Muslim and non-Muslim customers. "Halal" is an Arabic term that carries the meaning of permissible and Toyyiban. Permissible here refers to the situation where any Halal product or services are produced and managed according to Islamic Shariah principles. While "Toyyiban" or cleanliness refers to Halal product characteristics which are safe to consume, safe to use, of high quality and wholesome (Rahman et al., 2018, 2020a; Khairuddin and Rahman, 2020; Khairuddin et al., 2018;).

The demand for Halal product is expected to continuously increase as the Muslim population increases. As reported by NST (2018), the Islamic community spreads to over 200 countries, including both Islamic and non-Islamic countries. It is also published that the Muslim population is around two billion at present, and is expected to grow to 2.2 billion by the year 2030. This shows the Halal economy is developing and growing well in many countries across the globe. The awareness and importance of the Halal industry in every country seems to be accepted and recognizes its characteristics of being safe, of high quality and clean to use and be consumed. With this, the Halal ecosystem consisting of the local and global Halal players, the ministries, business stakeholders and agencies should strategically collaborate to ensure the steady growth of the Halal market is preserved.

DOI: 10.4324/9781003223719-23

Recently, starting in December 2019, the global COVID-19 pandemic has caused economic decline across the world due to disruptions in the supply and demand chain in markets. The Halal industry is among the affected industries. As highlighted by Laila et al. (2017), this pandemic has affected the Halal industry via Halal tourism activity, the economy and cargo from travellers are decreasing due to the travel ban, and in terms of Halal in medical logistics and supply chains, related to the distribution of vaccines. This effect was experience by many Islamic countries. In the next section, the authors will provide more elaboration on the COVID-19 pandemic and the global Halal industry.

Introduction to the COVID-19 pandemic and its major effects

COVID-19 or coronavirus is a new pandemic disease caused by the SARS-CoV-2 virus, which transmits or spreads to people in various ways. It was first detected in Wuhan, China and has spread around the globe with current cases globally exceeding 175 million. This killer disease has harmful affected not only people, but also business entities and environmental factors. According to recent articles published by Rahman et al. (2020b), Fonseca and Azevedo (2020) and Jaiyeoba (2021), it is important to discuss the issue of the COVID-19 pandemic, how it has affected business entities and economies, and how long the harmful effects of the pandemic may last. It is vital to find solutions to each challenge to ensure the sustainability and continued existence of the businesses in the industry. Almost all sectors have been affected by this pandemic, such as the air travel industry, transportation industry, food manufacturing, retail, automotive industry, tourism activity, logistics sector, marine, oil and gas, healthcare industry, as well as the Halal sector. It has caused supply chain disruption especially on the movement of the products and workers in both service and product sectors. Many organizations got hits by the pandemic, which then led to business failure in the industries. Table 18.1 shows various industries affected by the worldwide COVID-19 pandemic.

Table 18.1 Various industries affected by the COVID-19 pandemic

No	Industry affected due to COVID-19	Key references
1	Aviation industry	Rahman et al., 2020a, 2020b
2	Halal industry	Jaiyeoba, 2021
3	Pharmaceutical	Di Tella et al., 2020
4	Transportation	Kim, 2021
5	Tourism	Uğur and Akbiyik, 2020
6	Food industry	Espitia et al., 2020
7	Education	Miani et al., 2021
8	Automotive	Kanapathipillai, 2020
9	Agriculture	Siche, 2020

Additionally, as mentioned by Craighead and Ketchen (2021), the impact of the pandemic could lead to bigger crises, such as bigger disruption on demand and supply, safety problems and others. However, from all these dark sides of the COVID-19 pandemic, there is one positive insight that can be related to Halal food consumption and supply chain. It was recognized that COVID-19 pandemic virus was origin and accelerated by bat (Schild et al., 2020). In Halal food consumption, it is already stated to eat only good, quality, safe and permissible products. With Halal food consumption, perhaps it may be possible to avoid and reduce the possibility of another such serious disease.

The pandemic and how COVID-19 is affecting global industry and businesses including Halal

The effects of the pandemic have spread not only to medical and health contexts, but also to other major business and industry players such as manufacturing, transportation, logistics and tourism, as well as the Halal industry. The uncertain spillover effect from this pandemic has alerted the affected industry and businesses to find the appropriate and actionable solutions to improve their business performance and to avoid supply chain disruption from happening.

As reported by Ozili and Arun (2020), the pandemic created a major shock in demand and supply, as well as the logistics of the affected product. From the perspective of Halal demand and Halal logistics, these were affected due to travel bans announced by many countries and the closure of tourism activity in many cities and countries. As highlighted by Jaiyeoba (2021), 2020 saw a $314 billion drop on travel industry revenue, representing a 55% decline in the industry.

From a logistics and supply chain perspective, the pandemic has caused Halal product supply chain disruption. The recognition of the Halal product is increased as it is safe and clean to consume, and in fact the increased demand for the products affects the Halal manufacturing operation. The increased demand and higher number of demand compared to the Halal product supply lead to supply chain disruption of the Halal product.

The effect of this pandemic on the transport and logistics sector has been large. It has resulted in a decrease in travel by all transportation modes such as rail, air, sea and ground. In the transportation sector, the aviation industry was the hardest hit by the pandemic. In responding to this challenging situation, logistics companies as well as transportation companies have had to take precautions to sustain their local and international mobility. This sudden change has also affected other sectors including airlines, tourism, oil and gas, healthcare industry, automotive, pharmaceuticals, e-commerce, retail and many more.

In a global outlook, for example, even cargo organization is categorized under one of the essential services, however, it is also badly affected especially for small size logistics player. A number of cargo handling companies had to shut down their businesses during the outbreak, even ports are operating under restrictions. All this, of course, leads to supply chain disruption of the related products or services. This also aligns with Fetzer et al. (2020). The risk of damage to cargo or Halal cargo is higher at this time due to COVID-19 restrictions on operation. There is also delays and disruption on machineries and maintenance. This could worsen the industry operation and impact business performance. It has been noticed that supply of products and services was also disrupted during this challenging time.

The impact of the COVID-19 pandemic has been felt by almost every country, including Islamic countries such as Malaysia, Indonesia, Brunei, Bahrain, Pakistan, Jordan, Oman, Qatar, Turkey and many others. This has resulted in significant impacts to the whole economies of the affected countries. The lockdowns, movement restrictions, travel bans, supply and demand fluctuations and supply chain disruptions are among the key challenges for every business player, including Halal businesses.

The COVID-19 pandemic and supply chain disruption: what are countries doing to ensure Halal trade keeps moving?

As highlighted above, the COVID-19 pandemic really hit global and local economies and left its footprint on most industries in the world. It is important to note that the establishment of proper business plans, operational plans and business strategies are vital to ensure industries, including the Halal industry, keep moving. Proper plans and strategic recovery strategies are significant to all industries and all business players in order to help them understand and respond to each impact of the pandemic they are experiencing (Fidrmuc and Korhonen, 2010; Rahman et al., 2020b; Musson and Rousselière, 2019). As recommended by Jaiyeoba (2021), fast decision-making and support from the government are among the most critical factors to support all affected business to grow again in the market. It is acknowledged that the pandemic has triggered a big recession for many countries including Malaysia, however the fast respond from the government, especially on business grants, business moratoriums, revised policies and others, has helped companies to rebuild and improve their performance.

In terms of the Halal industry, once the situation improves with the vaccination programme organized by governments, travellers may travel again since the countries' borders will reopen and allow tourism activity to take place again. The end of travel restrictions will enable travellers to travel again and it is expected that the increase of inbound or outbound travellers will also lead to an increase in demand for Halal products and services, including Halal logistics, which merely refers to the transportation and storage of cargo. At the same time, as suggested in recent study by Jaiyeoba (2021), any Halal companies must have a quick response in adapting to the new norms in business due to this pandemic. To lessen the impact of pandemic, Halal industry players should be able to transform, rethink and strategize their strategies in adapting to the new business environment, as now it is expected that COVID-19 will be with us for the long term. In fact, the exploration of technology adoption to make contactless logistics activities, for instance, may help to reduce the impact of COVID-19 to logistics employees that handle transportation and warehousing activities. At the same time, the Islamic regulatory body of every country may make the decision to ask all Halal related players to get Halal certificates, as we know Halal status of any product or services is about cleanliness and hygiene in handling anything. At the same time, the Halal players may also look into technology adoption or transformation to help with screening and detecting any issues, as well as improving the smoothness of the logistics operation for both import and export activities.

Conclusion, recommendations and future research

It is important for every Halal player to understand the effects of the COVID-19 pandemic and how it has affected business operations. A proper strategy needs to be undertaken to avoid disruption in Halal business operations including Halal logistics and disruption in the Halal supply chain. A detailed discussion among the Halal industry players, the regulators and the certification bodies may help to find a solution on how to be more prepared during this uncertain pandemic and be more prepared with managing the crisis. This is vital to ensure every Halal business player is ready and aware of what the external possibilities are that can affect their business and operation so that they could sustain in the industry for the long term. There is also an opportunity for future Halal scholars to further explore the impact of the pandemic on specific issues such as in Halal transportation and Halal warehousing. They may offer different interesting findings from different modes of investigation with regards to Halal transportation. The process, factors and impact may differ a bit and create new theories on the issues discussed. Future researchers may also investigate the issue with providing more solid discussion and linked it with the appropriate theories in exploring Halal performance during the pandemic crisis.

References

Craighead, D. J. and Ketchen, C. W. (2021). Toward a theory of supply chain entrepreneurial embeddedness in disrupted and normal states. *Journal of Supply Chain Management*, 57(1), pp. 50–57.

Di Tella, M., Romeo, A., Benfante, A. and Castelli, L. (2020). Mental health of healthcare workers during the COVID-19 pandemic in Italy. *Journal of Evaluation in Clinical Practice*, 26(6), pp. 1583–1587.

Espitia, A., Rocha, N. and Ruta, M. (2020). *COVID-19 and Food Protectionism: The Impact of the Pandemic and Export Restrictions on World Food Markets*. Washington, DC: World Bank Group.

Fetzer, T., Hensel, L., Hermle, J. and Roth, C. (2020). Coronavirus perceptions and economic anxiety. *The Review of Economics and Statistics*, pp. 1–60.

Fidrmuc, J. and Korhonen, I. (2010). The impact of the global financial crisis on business cycles in Asian emerging economies. *Journal of Asian Economics*, 21(3), pp. 293–303.

Fonseca, L. and Azevedo A. (2020). COVID-19: outcomes for global supply chains. *Management & Marketing: Challenges for the Knowledge Society*, 15, pp. 424–438.

Jaiyeoba, H. B. (2021). The spillover effects of COVID-19 on Halal industry: an overview and way forward. *Halalsphere*, 1(1), pp. 72–82.

Kanapathipillai, K. (2020). The impact of the silent enemy (COVID-19 pandemic) on the marketing efforts undertaken by the automotive industries in Malaysia. *European Journal of Management and Marketing Studies*, 5(4), pp. 1–21.

Khairuddin, M. M. and Rahman, N. A. A. (2020). Successful halal compliance factors for air cargo warehouse: warehouse operator perspective. In N. A. A. Rahman, A. Hassan and M. F. Mohammad (Eds.), *Halal Logistics and Supply Chain in South East Asia: Development and Challenges*. Singapore: Routledge, pp. 187–203.

Khairuddin, M. M., Rahman, N. A. A., Mohammad, M. F., Majid, Z. A. and Ahmad, M. F. (2018). Regulator perspective on Halal air cargo warehouse compliance. *International Journal of Supply Chain Management*, 7(3), pp. 202–207.

Kim, K. (2021). Impacts of COVID-19 on transportation: summary and synthesis of interdisciplinary research. *Transportation Research Interdisciplinary Perspective*. doi: 10.1016/j.trip.2021.100305

Laila, N., Rusydiana, A. S., and Assalafiyah, A. (2017). The impact of COVID-19 on the Halal, economy: a bibliometric approach. *Library Philosophy and Practice*, Summer, 5417.

Miani, P., Kille, T., Lee, S-Y., Zhang, Y. and Bates, P. R. (2021). The impact of the COVID-19 pandemic on current tertiary aviation education and future careers: students' perspective. *Journal of Air Transport Management*, 94, 102081.

Musson, A. and Rousselière, D. (2019). Identifying the impact of crisis on cooperative capital constraint: a short note on French craftsmen cooperatives. *Finance Research Letters*, 35, 101290.

NST (2018). *Fostering a True Halal Economy: Global Integration and Ethical Practice*. Retrieved from: www.nst.com.my/opinion/columnists/2018/04/353789/fostering-true-halal-economy-global-integration-and-ethical (accessed 24 November 2021).

Ozili, P. and Arun, T. (2020). Spillover of COVID-19: impact on the global economy. *SSRN Electronic Journal*, https://doi.org/10.2139/ssrn.3562570

Rahman, N. A. A., Mohammad, M. F., Rahim, S. A. and Noh, H. M. (2018). Implementing air cargo halal warehouse: insight from Malaysia. *Journal of Islamic Marketing*, 9(3), pp. 462–483.

Rahman, N. A. A., Majid, Z. A., Mohammad, M. F., Ahmad, M. F., Rahim, S. A. and Mokhtar, A. Z. (2020a). The development of Halal logistics standards in South-East Asia: Halal supply chain standards (MS2400) as a principal reference in Halal logistics and supply chain management in Southeast Asia. In N. A. A. Rahman, A. Hassan and M. F. Mohammad (Eds.). *Halal Logistics and Supply Chain in South East Asia: Development and Challenges*. Singapore: Routledge, pp. 149–160.

Rahman, N. A. A., Rahim, S. A., Ahmad, M. F. and Hafizuddin-Syah, B. A. M. (2020b). Exploring COVID-19 Pandemic: its impact to global aviation industry and the key strategy. *International Journal of Advanced Science and Technology*, 29(6), pp. 1829–1836.

Schild, L., Ling, C., Blackburn, J., Stringhini, G., Zhang, Y. and Zannettou, S. (2020). *Go Eat a Bat, Chang! An Early Look on the Emergence of Sinophobic Behavior on Web Communities in the Face of COVID-19*. Retrieved from: https://arxiv.org/abs/2004.04046 (accessed 24 November 2021).

Siche, R. (2020). What is the impact of COVID-19 disease on agriculture? *Scientia Agropecuaria*, 11(1), pp. 3–6.

Uğur, N. G. and Akbiyik, A. (2020). Impacts of COVID-19 on global tourism industry: a cross-regional comparison. *Tourism Management Perspectives*, 36, 100744.

Index

Note: Page numbers in *italics* indicate figures and in **bold** indicate tables on the corresponding pages.

ACM International Conference Proceeding Series 49
Adaptive Structuration Theory (AST) **57**, 57–58
Agency Theory **57–58**
agrifood sector, Halal 213–214
Aigbogun, O. 57
Akhlaq 116–118
Aksoy, H. 125
Alam, S. S. 53
Al-Ansi, A. 126
Al-Qaradawi, Y. 74, 175–176
Altunişik, R. 222–223
Ambali, A. R. 122
Antonio, M. S. 47
Arienzo, A. 69
Arif, S. 100
Arun, T. 232
Asaari, M. H. A. H. 9, 53
Asian Social Science 49
Azam, A. 74
Azevedo, A. 231
Azmi, F. 56, 57

Bahrudin, S. S. M. 69
Bakar, A. N. 122
barcodes 71, 80–81, 103, 145–146
blockchain 73, 103, 104, 145
Bonne, K. 90
British Food Journal 49
Buddhism 17

certification, Halal 83–84, 90; bodies for, in the Middle East 226–228, *227*; certification bodies roles and history in Malaysia 224–226, *225–226*; in Japan 200–204; logistics sustainability and 101–102; need for 222–223; in South Korea 186–187
Chandra, G. R. 103
Chen, C. J. R. 156
Cluster Theory 40
common method variance (CMV) 156
competitive advantage with tracing and tracking systems 84–85
competitive pressure and transportation 154
compliance 101
containerization 32
contracts 12
cosmetics, Halal 216–218
COVID-19 pandemic 2, 197–199; effects on future development of Halal logistics and supply chain management 230–234; effects on global industry and business 232–233; major effects on markets of **231**, 231–232; supply chain disruption with 233–234
Craighead, D. J. 232
critical success factors (CSFs) in technology and traceability 73–75, *74*; certification 83–84; consistency 83; equipment 82–83; ICT systems 82; legislation 81; punctuality 83; quality of information 82; system validity 83; uniqueness of quality data delivery 83

Daniel, D. R. 73
Darun, M. R. 94

data analysis: Halal logistics *48*, 48–53, *50–51*, **51**–**52**; Halal supply chain 53–58, *54–56*, **57**
Defee, C. C. 32–33, 38, 39–40
Department of Islamic Development Malaysia (JAKIM) 3; Halal certification and 70, 84, 101–102; Halal logistics standards and 26; Halal transportation and 13; meat cartel case and *126*, 126–127, 133–137; meat imports and 114–115; as second stakeholder in Halal integrity 125; standard of procedure and 98, 99–100; *see also* Malaysia
Department of Veterinary Service (DVS), Malaysia 114
Diffusion of Innovation (DOI) 37, 49, **51**, 56–57, **57**
Digman, L. A. 73
Dryden-Palmer, K. D. 152

ecosystem, Halal 20–21, *21*
Ekwall, D. 169
El-Bassiouny, N. 20
electronic data interchange (EDI) 32
employees and Islam 119–120
ethics, Islamic business 116–119

Farag, M. D. E. D. H. 175
Fetzer, T. 232
Fonseca, L. 231
food fraud *see* meat cartel case, Halal
Food Security and Safety Division, Malaysia 114
Franke, G. 157
Fuseini, A. 225

Gefen, D. 156
Ghazali, M. C. 8, 46, 170

Hair, J. F. 155, 157
Halal: definition and principles of *19*, 19–20, 175–176, **176**; ecosystem of 20–21, *21*; integrity of 68–69; Islam encouragement of 89; Toyyiban 9, 19, 67, 89, 94, 122–123
Halal-exclusive retailers 93
Halal logistics and supply chain management (HLCSM) 1–4, 32–33; analysis and discussions of research on 34–40, **35**, *36*; compared to conventional supply chains 178, **178**; COVID-19 effects and future development of 230–234; data analysis and findings on *48*, 48–58, *50–51*, **51–52**, *54–56*, **57**; development of standards for 21–22, *23*; explicit use of theories in 39–40; institutional theory in 38; international studies on **46**, 46–47; international versus local standards on 24–29, **25–29**; introduction to 7–8; literature on 8–9; methods used within theories on 40–42, *41*; new age of standards and guidelines in 27–29, **28–29**; non-LSCM theories in 39; quality assurance/control in 100–101, *181*, 181–183, **182**; Resource-Based View (RBV) in 37–38; review methods for research on 33–34, *34*, 48; supply chain practices in 9–14, *12*, 176–179, *179*; supply chain research 47–48; Technology-Organization-Environment (TOE) Framework in 37, 39; Theory of Planned Behaviour (TPB) in 37, 38–39; traceability technology in (*see* tracing and tracking systems)
Halal logistics service providers (HLSP) 22, *23*
Halal-mixed retailers 93–94
Halal SC 94, *97*, 97–98, 98; logistics sustainability and 96–104
Halal-segregated retailers 93
Haleem, A. 32, 34, 45, 168
Hamid, A. B. A. 37, 40
Haram products 8, 19, 211
Hashim, H. 92
Hew, J. J. 56
Hinduism 17
Hoffman, N. 98
Huang, C. Y. 52
Husny, Z. J. M. 52
Hussein, M. Z. 180

ICT systems 82
IEEE International Conference on Industrial Engineering and Engineering Management 49
Indarti, N. 45, 46
information sharing, Halal supply chain 13–14
Institutional Theory 38, 49, 57–58
integrity, Halal 68–69, 122; accreditation authorities as second

238 Index

stakeholder in 125–126; consumers as first stakeholder in 123–125, *124*; defined 123; impact of Halal meat cartel on 122–126, **124**, *124*; in the supply chain 132–147
International Halal Logistics Standard (IHIAS) 11, 19, 24
International Journal of Islamic Marketing and Branding 33
International Journal of Supply Chain Management 49, 56, 58
International Organization of Standardization (ISO) 69
international versus local Halal logistics and supply chain standards 24–29, **25–29**
Internet of Things (IOT) 47–48, 103, 104, 145
IOP Conference Series Materials Science and Engineering 49
Islamic business ethics 116–119
Islamic employment practices 119–120
Ismail, S. H. S. 53

Jaafar, H. S. 8; Sumitomo Corporation Kyushu in 207, 209
Jaiyeoba, H. B. 231, 232, 233
JAKIM *see* Malaysia
Japan 196–209; Halal certification in 200–204; Halal logistics in 204–207, *206*; introduction to Halal logistics in 196; logistic industry market overview and 197, *201–202*; logistics companies in 199–200; logistics market after COVID-19 crisis in 197–199; Nippon Express Co. Ltd. in 205, 207, *208*; Yusen Logistics in 207
Journal of Critical Reviews 49
Journal of Food Products Marketing 49
Journal of Islamic Marketing 49, 58
Journal of Islamic Marketing (JIMA) 33, 49
Judaism 17–18

Karia, N. 8, 9, 32, 37, 39, 53
Kawabata, T. 203
Ketchen, C. W. 232
Khairuddin, M. M. 20
Khalek, A. A. 53
Khan, M. I. 168
Khan, S. 74
Ko, Y. D. 52
Kock, N. 156
Kosher standards 17–18

Krishnan, S. 122
Kusrini, E. 45–46
Kwag, S. I. 52

Laila, N. 231
Lantz, B. 169
legislation 81
Liow, R. J. 223
logistics, Halal 89–105; and certification opportunities in the Middle East 226–228, *227*; definitions in **180**, 180–181; existing frameworks for 96, *97–98*; framework for sustainability 96–104; issues in 94–95; in Japan *201–202*, 204–207, *206*; in Malaysia (*see* Malaysia); nature of 90–94; packaging in 91–92; retailing in 92–94; in South Korea 189–195; in Spain 218–219; warehousing and transportation in 13, 90–91
logistics and supply chain management (LSCM) 32
logistics studies: data analysis in *48*, 48–53, *50–51*, **51–52**; implications of 58–59; introduction to 45; literature review on 45–48, **46**; research methodology for 95–96
Luco, A. 116

Mahidin, N. 53
Malaysia: development of Halal industry in 18, 20, 49, 67–68; growth of Halal markets in 166–169, *167*; Halal meat supply chain in 111–120, 132–133, *134*; Halal traceability in 70; Halal transportation adoption among SMEs in 151–161; roles and history of certification bodies in 224–226, *225–226*; standard of procedure in 99–100; Trade Descriptions Act (TDA) *126*, 126–128; *see also* Department of Islamic Development Malaysia (JAKIM)
Malaysian Quarantine and Inspection Service (MAQIS) 112, 114
Malaysia Standard (MS) 19, 25–26, **26–27**
Marjudi, S. 74
market, Halal 10–11, 17–19, 78, 89–90, 165–166, 200; growth in Malaysia 166–169, *167*; growth in Spain 211–220; Islamic business ethics and 116–119; need for Halal certification and 222–223

Masayuki, N. 203, 204
Masudin, I. 47
meat cartel case, Halal 122–128; analysis and findings on 127–128; background on Malaysian import meat industry and 132–133, *134*; chronology of 133–137, **135–136**; companies affected by 139–140; conclusions and future research on 128; consumers affected by 138–139; impacts on authorities 140–141, *142*; impacts on Halal integrity 122–126, **124**, *124*; impacts on other countries 141; impacts on stakeholders 137–142; legal process framework for *126*, 126–127; managerial and technological countermeasures after 141–144; news articles about **124**; regulator insight on *126*, 126–127; training in Halal food fraud awareness and risk management after 144–145
meat supply chain, Halal 111–120; authorities and stakeholders involved in import clearance in 112–116, *113*; Department of Islamic Development Malaysia (JAKIM) and 114–115; Department of Veterinary Service (DVS) and 114; employees in 119–120; Food Security and Safety Division and 114; global key Halal manufacturers for 223, *224*; import agents and 115; importers and 115–116; introduction to 111; Islamic business ethics and 116–119; Malaysian Quarantine and Inspection Service (MAQIS) and 112, 114; meat and meat products' import clearance process in 111–112; Royal Malaysian Customs Department (RMCD) and 112; stakeholders in 137–142
Meuwissen, M. P. 69
Middle East standard establishment and reference 27–29, **28–29**
Mohamed, Y. H. 47

Neiburg, O. 223
Ngah, A. H. 37, 38, 53, 91, 152
Ngai, E. W. T. 72
Noorliza, K. 37, 39, 176

Omar, W. M. W. 47
order fulfillment 12–13
organizational readiness 154

Ozili, P. 232
Özsönmez, C. 125

packaging, Halal 91–92
Perdana, F. F. P. 222–223
Pertanika Journal of Social Sciences and Humanities 49
population growth, Muslim 17, 45, 151; in South Korea 186
port development, Halal 165–171; growth of Halal markets in Malaysia and 166–169, *167*; Halal transportation perspective and 169–170; roles of ports and 166
products, Halal 8–9, 11; contracts for 12; determining specifications for 11; orders for 12–13; segregation from non-Halal substances and products 22; supplier selection for 11–12, *12*; transportation of 13; warehousing of 13
punctuality 83
purchasing, Halal 11

QR codes 71, 103, 145–146
quality assurance/control 100–101, *181*, 181–183, **182**
Qurtubi, Q. 45–46

radio frequency identification (RFID) 32, 72, 79–80, 104, 145–146
Radzman, N. W. S. 45
Rahman, N. A. A. 20–22, 37, 39, 228, 231
Raikwar, M. 145
Rasi, R. Z. 179
religious beliefs in food and product selection 17–18
Resource-Based Halal Logistics (RBHL) 39, 53
Resource-Based View (RBV) 37–38, 49, **51–52**, 52
retailing, Halal 92–94
Rigod, B. 125
risk management, Halal food fraud 144–145
Rizk, R. R. 116
Royal Malaysian Customs Department (RMCD) 112
Ruiz-Bejarano, B. 93

Sack, D. 17
Sapry, H. R. M. 227
Sarstedt, M. 157

Sayuti, N. M. 53
segregation between Halal and non-Halal substances and products 22, 69–70
Selim, N. I. I. B. 39
Shahijan, M. K. 37, 38
Shariah law 7–8
Shi, Y.-D. 72
Sidek, S. 100
small and medium-sized enterprises (SMEs): competitive pressure and 154; complexity of 152–153; cost of 153; data analysis on 156–160, 157–160, *158*; discussion and conclusions on 160–161; introduction to 151–152; literature review and hypothesis development on transportation by 152–155, *155*; organizational readiness and 154; research methodology on 155–156; supplier availability and 154–155, *155*
Soong, S. F. V. 92
Sophonthummapharn, K. 154
sourcing, Halal 11
South Korea 186–195; development of Halal industry in 187–189; Halal logistics transportation pilot project in 191–195, *192*; Muslim residents in 186; research on Halal logistics industry in 189; research on Halal product production and distribution status and logistics demand in 189–191, **190**; status of Halal certification in 186–187
Spain 211–220; agrifood sector in 213–214; cosmetics sector in 216–218; Halal logistics in 218–219; introduction to Halal market in 211–212; opportunities for Halal market in 212–218, **213**; tourism sector in 214–216
specifications, Halal product 11
standard of procedure (SOP) 99–100
Standards and Metrology Institute for Islamic Countries (SMIIC) 19, 24–25, **25**
supplier availability and transportation 154–155, *155*; COVID-19 pandemic effects on 233–234
supplier management and food fraud 144–145
supplier selection 11–12, *12*

supply chain analysis 53–58, *54–56*, 57
Surjandari, I. 89, 90, 102
Susanty, A. 89, 94
sustainability, logistics 96–104; certification in 101–102; compliance in 101–104; conceptual framework 98–99, *99*; integrity in the process in 102; quality assurance in 100–101; standard of procedure in 99–100; technology in 103–104
Sustainable Development Goals (SDGs) 111

Talib, M. S. A. 32, 37, 40, 47, 92, 227, 228
Tarmizi, H. A. 52
Technology Acceptance Model (TAM) 49, 52
Technology Adoption Theory 46
Technology-Organization-Environment (TOE) 37, 39, 46, 49, **52**, 53, 152–153
technology tools *see* tracing and tracking systems
Theory of Planned Behaviour (TPB) 37–39, 46, 49, **52**, **57**, 57–58
Theory of Reasoned Action (TRA) 39, 46, 49
Thiesse, F. 156
Tieman, M. 8, 37, 40, 46–47, 89, 93–94, 170, 180
tourism, Halal 214–216
Tovar, P. 125
Toyyiban Halal 9, 19, 67, 89, 94; Halal meat and 122–123
tracing and tracking systems: applied to Halal logistics and supply chain 70–73; barcodes and QR codes 71, 80–81, 103, 145–146; benefits of 79; blockchain 73, 103, 104, 105, 145; competitive advantage with 84–85; critical success factors for 73–75, **74**, 81–85; food traceability in Halal logistics and supply chain 69–70; GPS and 78–79; Halal integrity and 68–69, 145–146; information sharing with 85; introduction to 67–68, 78; radio frequency identification (RFID) 32, 72, 79–80, 104, 145–146
Trade Descriptions Act (TDA) *126*, 126–128
training, Halal food fraud 144

Transaction Cost Theory 39
transparency with tracing and tracking systems 85
transportation, Halal 13, 90–91, 169–170; among SMEs in Malaysia 151–161; competitive pressure and 154; complexity of 152–153; cost of 153; COVID-19 pandemic effects on 233–234; data analysis on 156–160, **157–160**, *158*; discussion and conclusions on 160–161; in Japan 197–199, *198*; literature review and hypothesis development on 152–155, *155*; organizational readiness and 154; in South Korea 191–195, *192*; supplier availability and 154–155, *155*

upstream, Halal 10
Ustadi, M. N. 53, 170

Verbeke, W. 90

Wahyuni, H. C. 47
warehousing, Halal 13, 90–91
Weng, T. F. 53
Wong, L. W. 154

Yousef, D. A. 116
Yunan, Y. S. M. 49
Yusoff, F. A. M. 57

Zailani, S. 10, 37, 39, 227, 228
Zainuddin, A. 176
Zulfakar, M. 7, 38, 40, 47, 94, 96

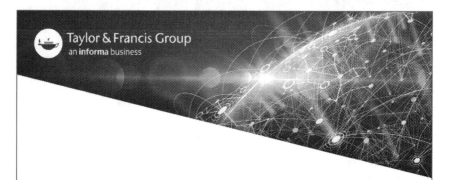

Printed in the United States
by Baker & Taylor Publisher Services